D0906091

Jon Eisenson
CALIFORNIA STATE UNIVERSITY, SAN FRANCISCO

With the Assistance of ARTHUR M. EISENSON

Voice and Diction

A Program for Improvement

Macmillan Publishing Co., Inc.
NEW YORK
Collier Macmillan Publishers
LONDON

PE
1137
.E53
1974
421.5 E36v

Eisenson, Jon

Voice and diction: a
program for
improvement

Dabney Lancaster Library.
Longwood College
Farmville, Virginia.

Copyright © 1974, Macmillan Publishing Co., Inc.

Printed in the United States of America

All rights reserved. No part of this book may be reproduced or
transmitted in any form or by any means, electronic or mechanical,
including photocopying, recording, or any information storage and
retrieval system, without permission in writing from the Publisher.

Earlier editions, entitled *The Improvement of Voice and Diction,*
© 1958 by Macmillan Publishing Co., Inc., and
copyright © 1965 by Jon Eisenson.

Macmillan Publishing Co., Inc.
866 Third Avenue, New York, New York 10022

Collier-Macmillan Canada, Ltd.

Library of Congress Cataloging in Publication Data

Eisenson, Jon, (date)
  Voice and diction—a program for improvement.

  First–2d editions published under title: The improvement of voice
and diction.
  1. English language—Pronunciation. 2. English language—
Phonetics. 3. Voice. 4. English language in the United States—
Pronunciation. I. Eisenson, Arthur M. II. Title.
PE1137.E53   1974   421'.5   73-4050
ISBN 0-02-331940-2

Printing: 1 2 3 4 5 6 7 8   Year: 4 5 6 7 8 9 0

To Jamie and Rosanne

73-04341

Voice and Diction: A Program for Improvement represents an effort to provide a body of knowledge about voice production and diction (articulation, pronunciation, and intonation) for persons interested in knowing what the productive act of speaking is about and applying this knowledge to the improvement of their own speech. The materials include information from the disciplines of speech and hearing science, linguistics, and phonetics. Chapter 10, "Our Changing Speech Patterns," has been expanded to include a discussion of American dialects with some emphasis on the dialect identified as Black English.

A book on voice and diction provided a temptation for the author to be prescriptive, to recommend a standard of what is desirable if not "good." I have avoided this temptation and have tried, especially in the discussions on diction, to be descriptive, to present standards rather than *a standard* of acceptable pronunciation for the major American dialects. So, the decision to employ pronunciations in keeping with one regional dialect or another, to select specific words for conveying meaning, and "how to turn a phrase" become matters of individual choice to be made on the bases of knowledge, motivation, and objectives. Speech is a complex set of habits. Habits can be changed but not readily without strong drive, and not happily nor effectively by imposition.

If this book is used in an academic course, it is likely that the students will fall into one of two groups. The first group will probably include persons who are self-motivated to use their voices effectively and to improve their diction either as a goal worthwhile in itself or as a vocational asset. The first and second editions of this book have, in fact, been used in courses for students preparing for teaching, law, the ministry, and the mass media as well as by persons already in these professions.

A second group is composed of students who may not have been initially self-motivated but were advised, by a teacher, counselor, or friend, to "take a course" in voice and/or diction. Even though the advice may have been accepted reluctantly and the motivation may be "external," the mature student will avail himself of the opportunity for learning somewhat more than he may have known of the mechanism for the human species' specific behavior called speech and learn as well how to use the mechanisms for voice and speech proficiently and effectively. Though speech is a human endowment, how well we speak is an individual achievement. I hope that this edition of *Voice and Diction* will help to make the effort and achievement pleasant if not enjoyable.

J. E.

CONTENTS

Voice

CHAPTER 1

Basic Considerations

Part One of this book has several objectives. The first is to help the reader become aware of what constitutes an effective voice; the second is to indicate how voice can be produced and controlled so that common vocal faults may be overcome or avoided; and the third is to suggest how voice can be used as an effective instrument for communication.

EFFECTIVE VOCALIZATION

Responsiveness

Above all, an effective voice is responsive to the intentions of the speaker. By expressing responsiveness, a speaker's voice helps to communicate his feelings and thoughts so that he is readily able to let his listener know what he thinks and how he feels as well as how he feels about what he thinks.

Appropriateness of Attributes

An effective voice is intimately associated with what the speaker is saying and attracts no attention to itself; it therefore does not distract from what the speaker is trying to communicate. Distraction may result from either the attributes of the voice or the manner in which the voice is produced. If the duration, quality, pitch, loudness, or any combination of these vocal characteristics is faulty or in some way not consonant with the contents of the speech, an element of distraction is introduced. For example, matters of importance are usually spoken slowly rather than hurriedly. Unless secrecy is to be suggested, important content is uttered more loudly than is content of lesser importance. Solemn utterances are usually associated with relatively low pitch and lighter remarks with relatively higher pitch. A reversal of these pitch-contents relationships is likely to be either distracting or misleading. Excessive nasality, huskiness, or any other vocal characteristic that is striking may serve as a distraction. In a somewhat more fortunate way, a very fine voice may also be temporarily distracting if it directs the listener's attention to its unusual qualities. Most listeners, however, soon accept the fine voice and respond to the contents of the speech. On the other hand, a voice that includes a constant element of irritation may continue to distract and thus impair the speaker's ability to communicate.

Manner of Production

A voice may have acceptable characteristics but still be ineffective if the speaker's manner of producing his voice attracts attention. If the speaker is obviously straining to be heard, or if his external throat muscles appear tense or his jaw tight, the listener may be distracted by what he observes. If the listener must force himself to maintain attention, the effort may be unpleasant, and the listener may also become tense as a result of what he sees. On the other hand, the overly relaxed speaker, who seems too tired to vocalize and articulate, may fatigue his listener-observer.

Appropriateness Related to Sex, Age, and Physique

Another area of vocal appropriateness is related to the sex, age, and physical build of the speaker. We expect men's voices to be different from women's. We expect the voice of a mature person to sound different from that of a child, and we expect big persons to have "big" voices. A high-pitched, "thin" voice may be acceptable from a small, delicate girl or a little boy, but it is not likely to be acceptable from either a man, a physically mature-looking woman, or a large boy.

Listener's Criteria of Effectiveness

From the viewpoint of the listener, an effective voice is one that can be heard without conscious effort or strain. It is consonant with the speaker's message and helps make the message readily audible and intelligible. An effective voice is pleasant to hear, but the pleasure should be unconscious and should not dominate the listener's reactions as it might if he were listening to a good singer. To be effective, voice should be as loud as the specific speaking situation demands. If the speaker is talking to a group, his voice should be heard with ease by every listener, but none should be disturbed because of its loudness. In a conversational situation, the listener with normal hearing and normal power of concentration should not have to ask the speaker to repeat because of a failure to hear, nor should he wish to move away to avoid discomfort from overloudness. In summary, the listener, if he were inclined to be analytic, should be able to conclude that the speaker's voice, as well as his actions, suits the words, the over-all situation, and the speaker as an individual.

Objective Self-listening

Although it is not always easy to see ourselves as others see us, the mechanics for hearing ourselves as others hear us are available to most of us. Tape, disc, or cassette recordings of reasonable fidelity can be made at low cost at home, in speech clinics, or agencies specializing in recording equipment. Most academic speech departments have adequate equipment for recording and playing back samples of speech. Although the most useful recording is one made when the speaker is not aware that he is being recorded and so is most himself, "candid" recordings are not always possible. If the recording is staged rather than candid, we recommend that it include conversational speaking as well as material read in a conversational voice and material spoken as if for a small audience. If the speaker frequently makes public addresses, he should also include material spoken as if he were making a public address. The speaker should then play back the recordings on an instrument that has a fidelity at least equal to that of the recording instrument. So set, the speaker should ask himself these questions:

1. Is my voice pleasant to hear?
2. Does my voice have any characteristics that I would consider undesirable in another speaker?
3. Does my voice reflect what I intended to convey in thought and in feeling?
4. Were the changes in pitch, loudness, duration, and quality consonant with the varying contents of my utterances?
5. Would I listen to this voice if I were not the speaker?
6. Does the voice reflect me as a personality?

If the speaker-listener is completely satisfied with all of his answers, then he is one of the fortunate persons who is making the most of the gift of a good, effective voice. If he is not entirely satisfied, he probably recognizes the need for improvement in his voice and is both ready and willing to do whatever is necessary to bring it about.

What an individual hears when he listens to himself is different from what another person hears when listening to him. The speaker who wishes to hear himself as others hear him should make a high-fidelity recording of his voice and listen to the playback at about the same sound level and distance as in a two person speaker-listener situation. The differences between the two listening experiences are at first likely to be striking and possibly even disturbing.

Because we are so close to the source of our voices, we cannot hear how they sound in the same way as can a listener who is at a distance from us. We hear our voices through the tissues of our bodies, especially the bones of the head, as they directly conduct the sounds we produce to our hearing mechanism. We also hear ourselves through the initially external stimulation of the sound waves produced when we talk at the same instant that the sounds are conducted to our hearing mechanism. Some of the differences between these two avenues of auditory stimulation can be appreciated by stopping up your ears while you are talking. You would then be hearing more nearly through bone conduction than you would with your ears "open." Your voice sounds different and somewhat strange. You may contrast this immediately by repeating what you have said with your ears unstopped. If at all possible, you should then contrast this immediately by listening to a high-fidelity recording of your voice. Only then, making allowance for subjective reactions, would you be able to hear yourself as others hear you. Among the important differences resulting from our multiple-conduction feedback system of listening to ourselves is that we may misjudge the pitch, range, loudness, and quality, and possibly the rate of our speech. Because we cannot hear ourselves as others hear us, we must accept the evaluation of others, especially if they are objective and professionally trained voice teachers or therapists. Fortunately, despite the limitations of our self-monitoring system, we have considerable evidence to show that learning to listen to our own voices is helpful in the improvement of both voice and diction.

Listening to Others

Before turning the mirror on ourselves, it might help to do some directed listening to the voices that are part of our everyday living. We may find that some of our acceptances and rejections of individuals are related to their voices. The following are a few projects that should be useful.

EXERCISES FOR LISTENING TO OTHERS

1. Tune in to a daytime television "soap opera" and with your eyes closed listen to the voices of the performers. Can you identify the hero

or heroine through the medium of voice alone? Can you detect the likely role of other characters by their initial utterances? Can you pick out the family friend? What are the specific vocal attributes of each character that influenced your decisions?

2.   Compare the newscaster you habitually listen to with one you seldom hear. Do the vocal characteristics of the newscasters have anything to do with your choice? List for each of them the vocal characteristics you like and dislike. Which of the two has a more favorable balance?

3.   Listen critically to two or three of your friends. Are there any characteristics of their voices you particularly like? Are there any you would like to have modified?

4.   Listen critically to some persons you do not particularly like. Do you hear any vocal characteristics that might account for your reaction to them? Do they remind you of anyone you disliked as a child?

5.   Recall a teacher, present or past, whom you consider especially effective. Is the voice of the teacher an important factor in your judgment? Describe his vocal attributes. Contrast this teacher with one you consider ineffective. Describe the voice of this teacher and determine whether it was a factor in your evaluation.

6.   Tune in to a radio or television round-table discussion on a controversial topic. Do you find yourselves inclined to the point of view of any of the speakers because of the way he sounds? Do you find yourself disinclined to any for the same reason? List as specifically as you can the attributes and their effects on you. How would the following terms suit the individual speakers: *agreeable, irritable, pompous, antagonistic, aggressive, negativistic, soft-spoken, firm, tired, energetic, pedantic, indecisive, weak, complaining, congenial, authoritative, warm, cultured, charming?*

7.   Listen to a radio or television network program in which there is a professional moderator and two or more participants. Compare the vocal tones of the moderator with those of the participants. Observe whether the moderator reveals any partiality or personal prejudices through his voice.

8.   Listen to a group of friends or acquaintances engaged in a conversation or discussion on a controversial topic. Do the participants reveal their personalities as well as their viewpoints through their voices? What terms listed in project (6) or terms of your own choosing would you apply to them?

9. Do you know any public figures who have had voice training? (Many public figures have had such training and some prepare specifically for each important address.) Can you recall any changes resulting from this training? Are there any who might benefit from voice training? What vocal characteristics would you like to have improved?

Physical and Mental Health

For most speakers who are not especially aware of their speech and who are not trained self-listeners, their voices are likely to reflect states and changes in both their physical and mental health. In the absence of any specific, chronic condition affecting either aspect of health, vocal efforts will be adversely affected by such conditions as fatigue, involvements of the respiratory tract, and conditions that produce either hypertense or hypotense musculature.

Perhaps the single cause that most frequently affects our voices is the common cold, which, because it directly involves the nose and throat, impairs normal vocal reinforcement. In addition, if the larynx is involved, the vibrators (vocal bands) may be thickened and so may produce tones that are not adequately reinforced. If there is a significant amount of inflammation, we tend to avoid laryngeal pain by keeping our vocal bands apart, and as a result we produce breathy and husky tones.

Similar to the effects of the common cold are those produced by allergies that involve the respiratory tract. These may include nasal congestion, irritation of the throat and larynx; and coughing. If the coughing is persistent and severe, the vocal bands may become involved. We may begin to appreciate the effects of persistent coughing from the following:

> When you cough you force air through the windpipe at a speed approaching or exceeding that of sound, which is 723 miles an hour at sea level. . . . By the time the air reaches the level of the Adam's apple, its speed has dwindled to hurricane velocity of about 100 miles per hour. When it blows out of the mouth the air is moving at fifteen miles per hour, a mere zephyr.[1]

Most of us may be able to vocalize effectively despite the possible abuse to which our vocal bands are subjected when occasionally air is propelled at up to supersonic speeds. It should be no surprise, however, that many of us cannot be both chronic coughers and effective vocalizers, especially if our coughing is violent and hacking.

Good vocal hygiene calls for either avoiding the conditions that are conducive to poor vocalization or reducing vocal efforts when such conditions cannot be avoided. Persons who must speak often have an obligation to practice good vocal hygiene. This calls for avoiding talking

[1] This note is based on the experimental findings of B. B. Ross, R. Gramiak, and R. Hahn, "Physical Dynamics of the Cough Mechanism," *Journal of Applied Physiology* (1955), 8:264–268. They found that, depending upon various external pressures and the size of the opening of the trachea, the velocity of air during a cough may range from a speed equivalent to a 15-mile per hour wind to that of a 100-mile per hour hurricane. "If . . . the tracheal lumen is compressed to one-sixth its normal cross section area, the linear velocity thus generated is 28,000 cm/sec., nearly 85% of the speed of sound."

under conditions that involve competition with excessive noise or reducing talking to a minimum under such conditions. Otherwise, good vocal hygiene calls for doing whatever is required to keep physically healthy by observing the "rules" for proper rest and exercise and doing whatever else your doctor is likely to tell you if you want to stay in good health.

Personality and Mental Health

A mentally healthy person is one who is aware of what is going on about him and responds, without violence to his own integrity, to the demands of his environment. Mental health and the healthy, well-adjusting personality are attained through continuous effort. Speech and voice are both the tools and the results of the process of adjustment.

The young infant responds to his environment and expresses himself almost entirely through his voice. If a baby cries much of his waking time, he may be colicky. If he whines and is almost always on the verge of crying, he is an unhappy baby. If he coos to amuse himself but does little crying except for evident biological reasons, he is a happy or at least a satisfied baby. If he cries occasionally and coos sufficiently to amuse others as well as himself, he is a normal baby. Whatever his condition, whether it is temporary or chronic, he expresses it through his voice. And at each successive stage of his development, from babyhood to maturity, his voice continues to express—to reveal or to betray—his personality and his mental health.

Earlier in this chapter we suggested that the speaker become an objective self-listener and answer the question of whether the voice he heard reflected him as a personality. Another question to be answered was whether the voice had any characteristic that would be considered undesirable in another speaker. Here are some further questions we hope the listener, if he is a well-adjusted person, can answer in the negative. Does your voice suggest a whine when no whine is intended? Do you sound as if you are complaining about something when you intend only to state a fact? Do you sound defeated? Do you sound aggressive or hostile rather than poised and secure? Do you sound chronically tired, bored, annoyed, or just too, too sophisticated for this mundane world in general and your associates in particular? If the answer is "yes" to any of these questions and there is no intention to suggest the trait that is expressed, insight and recognition should be of help in motivating a change.

Among the more frequent vocal problems associated with maturation is the failure of the voice to drop in pitch during physiological adolescence. Occasionally we meet chronological adolescents and postadolescents who still speak in their childhood pitch range. Sometimes we even find the habitual pitch level raised above that of preadolescence. Although in rare instances this vocal problem may be related to disturbances in motor control or in the glands, more often the cause is emotional. The chronological adolescent, whether boy or girl, who wants to continue to be mother's or daddy's child, or who is apprehensive for other reasons about growing up and assuming grown-up responsibilities, may be announcing the wish or the fear through an infantile voice.

Another adolescent problem frequently associated with vocal disturbance may arise from strong identification with an older person. As a result of this identification, an adolescent girl may imitate the pitch and other vocal characteristics of an idolized adult. Unfortunately, the voice of the adult may be the product of a vocal mechanism unlike that of the imitator. The woman teacher on whom the high school girl possibly has a "crush" may properly be a contralto wtih a pitch range too low for the vocal apparatus of the imitator. The effect may be a strained, husky voice. The problem for the boy in high school may be even more acute if he is intended by nature to be a tenor and his hero-figure is a person with a bass voice.

The author has had several male students who might have had good tenor voices, and possibly even been effective speakers within the upper part of their baritone range, but who wanted very much to speak like bassos. Within the bass range, unfortunately, they were constantly hoarse and could not be heard beyond the first two or three rows of a classroom. Psychological investigation strongly suggested that the young men were overanxious to be recognized as men—and fearful that they might not be so regarded. The author has also had several middle-aged male voice patients with much the same problems of voice and associated psychodynamics. He has also had a number of women voice patients who were referred to him by laryngologists because of thickened vocal bands resulting from habitual vocalization in too low a pitch range. In several instances the women were working in professional areas that until recently had been considered the province of males. The suspicion of "masculine protest" was supported by the psychodiagnostic evaluation.

Sometimes, to the misfortune of the speaker, habits of voice may persist and so reveal the maladjustments, personality, and mental health of a past period. Voice production is a motor act, and motor acts that are repeated tend to become habitual. Thus, the once dependent person may still sound dependent, and the once aggressive "chip-on-the-shoulder" individual may still sound as if he were obviously hostile. With conscious effort, vocal habits can be modified so that we reveal ourselves as we are when we speak rather than as we were during a period of past adjustment difficulties. If, however, adjustment difficulties continue to be present, effective voice is not likely to be achieved unless therapy includes the problems for which the voice is a symptom.

THE EFFECTIVE VOCALIZER

If we examine our reactions to individuals who have effective voices, we are likely to conclude that by and large they are also effective as persons. Voice, or any other attribute of human behavior, is not a free-floating essence or a blithe, disembodied spirit. It is, on the contrary, an essential product and aspect of human behavior. It may sometimes be possible for a mentally or physically sick individual who has had considerable professional training to produce voice effectively for a specific purpose and for a limited time, as actors and some public speakers may be required to do. Even professional performers, however, cannot continue to vocalize effectively, act effectively, or in general pretend effectively for an indefinite period. In our discussion in subsequent chapters we assume that we are addressing ourselves to essentially healthy persons. This assumption permits leeway for the expression of a little bit of neuroticism that is or should be the privilege of all. It also allows for occasional physical ailments—even those that may be classified as psychosomatic because the body does protest what the mind sometimes must accept.

If the reader is at any time in doubt as to whether his lack of effective voice may be associated with either a temporary or a chronic state of subpar physical or mental well-being, proper medical consultation is in order. Certainly no person who has suffered from chronic hoarseness, or who has had any disturbance centered in the larynx, should undertake voice training without examination and clearance from his physician. If possible, the physician should be a specialist in diseases of the throat. Although voice training can improve most person's vocal efforts, such training should not be undertaken when a physician prescribes vocal rest. We would also urge that no person become his own physician or use as a substitute for a physician a friend who has had what may appear to be similar voice symptoms. There is danger in using a friend's prescription. The individual who would be an effective vocalizer should have a personal examination by his own physician.

CHAPTER 2

The Mechanisms for Speech

Early in life, normal human beings develop the ability to produce meaningful wave patterns in light and air that are known as speech symbols. The mechanisms by which the symbols are produced serve the biological functions of breathing and eating. Under voluntary control, however, these mechanisms can be modified in their functioning to serve the purposes of vocalization and articulation and thus the production of symbols used in speaking.

This chapter discusses the mechanisms through which human beings achieve speech, are able to communicate their thoughts and feelings, or, when it suits their needs, are able to conceal rather than reveal their thoughts and feelings. We first consider how speech noise (voice) is produced and then how noise and breath are modified to produce articulated sound in a manner unique to human beings.

The human vocal mechanism deserves understanding and respect for what it is—a sensitive instrument capable of permitting us to produce a type of sound of distinct quality called *voice*. Direct comparisons with mechanical instruments tend to minimize the attributes and potential of the vocal mechanism and its product. There are, however, several parallels between the human vocal mechanism and some musical wind instruments that may help to give us at least an intellectual appreciation of how each functions.

VOICE PRODUCTION

In most wind instruments, sound is produced when air is blown over a reed or through vibrating lips as in the case of a trumpet and a trumpeter. The reed or the reed substitute (lips) is usually near the blowing end of an elongated tube. The quality of the sound produced with a wind instrument is determined partly by the size, shape, and nature of the material, partly by the length, thickness, and type of reed, and partly by the ability of the person doing the blowing. The human voice-producing mechanism permits even the average speaker to be a virtuoso. Without conscious practice, most of us become skilled in making our voice mechanisms respond to our wishes. We play our vocal apparatus through ranges of pitch, loudness, and quality not possible by any known combination of wind instruments. The extreme flexibility of the vocal mechanism is the basis for its superiority over musical wind instruments.

Some Fundamental Definitions

We have used the terms *pitch, loudness,* and *quality* with an assumption that their meanings are understood. Nevertheless, we will define the terms technically, so that their use will be clear throughout our discussions in Part One of this text.

Pitch is the result of the frequency of vibration of the sound source—the vibrating body. Perceptually, pitch is what the auditory system perceives, the auditory correlate, of the vibration of the sound source, which, in phonation (voice production) is the glottis (vocal folds).

Loudness is the sensory response (sensation) related to the amplitude of the sound waves. Moore (1971, p. 2) defines loudness as:

> the sensation related to the amplitude of molecular motion in the sound wave. This movement results from the volume-velocity of the glottal air pulse which is created by the interaction of glottal resistance and the force of the breath. Consequently, . . . loudness is controlled primarily by the vibrator but varies directly with air pressure.

Quality is the sensation, the auditory impression, produced by the complexity of the sound wave.

> This complexity is related to the number and strength of the partials that compose the sound, and these in turn are determined by the combination of the vibratory patterns of the sound source and the selective alterations of the sound in the resonators. (Moore, 1971, p. 2.)

These definitions include both physical and subjective aspects. The physical aspects or properties are those inherent in the sound wave *per se* and can be measured objectively by appropriate instruments. The subjective properties are the sensations or reactions of the listener to the physical phenomena. Our concern is largely with the subjective aspects or properties of the sounds produced by the human phonatory mechanism.

Requisites for Sound Production

In order to produce sound, whether it be music, noise, or voice, three essential conditions must prevail: (1) There must be a body capable of being set into vibration; (2) there must be an available force that may be applied to the body to set it into vibration; and (3) there must be a medium for transmitting the results of the vibration to individuals capable of awareness and response. The first two requisites are found in the normal human mechanisms for breathing and are discussed subsequently. The third requisite is air.

When necessary, a normal person is readily able to modify and control the breathing mechanism to produce voice while sustaining the functions of respiration. We shall be able to understand how voice production is accomplished through a study of the nature and structure of the vocal mechanism. In our discussion an overall view of the voice-producing mechanism rather than a detailed consideration of its component parts is our objective.

The Vocal Bands

The vocal bands or vocal folds (lips) are bodies capable of vibration, thus meeting the first requirement for sound production. Biologically, the potential vibrators function as part of a valve mechanism to prevent foreign matter from entering the windpipe (*trachea*) and involving the lungs. The vocal bands are two small, tough folds of connective or ligamentous tissue situated in the larynx or voice box at the top of the trachea (see Figures 2–1 and 2–2). The bands are continuous with folds of muscle tissue and are connected to cartilages of the larynx.

The *trachea* is a tube or a "pipe" about four inches in length and an inch in diameter that is continuous between the pharynx and the lungs. In construction, the trachea is a series of incomplete rings of cartilage and membranous tissue (see Figures 2–1 and 2–2). This construction provides form and elasticity so that there is no danger of tube constriction or collapse when air is drawn into the lungs. The elastic nature of the trachea also permits movement in swallowing and in speaking. These movements may be felt by finger contact and observed in a mirror. In swallowing, we may note that the top of the trachea moves upward and slightly forward toward the chin. These movements are usually more apparent in men than in women, especially in those men who have a conspicuous Adam's apple.

The trachea subdivides into two tubes known as *bronchi*. Each *bronchus*

Figure 2–1 **Front upright view of the larynx, trachea, and lungs.**
The larynx is a structure of cartilage, muscles, and membranous tissue at the top
of the trachea. The largest cartilage of the larynx is the *thyroid,* consisting of
two fused shieldlike parts. The vocal bands are attached to the inner curved
walls of the thyroid cartilage laterally, and in front to the angle of the two
fused parts of the thyroid. At the back, the vocal bands are attached to the
arytenoid cartilages.
The trachea divides into two *bronchi.* Each *bronchus* divides into tubes of decreasing size known as *bronchioles.*

further divides and subdivides into smaller tubes within the lungs. These
smaller-sized tubes are known as *bronchioles.*

If we could view the vocal bands from above, as in Figure 2–2, they
would appear as flat folds of muscle that have inner edges of connective
tissue. The vocal bands are attached to the inner curved walls of the
thyroid cartilage at either side. At the midline, the bands are attached to
the angle formed by the fusion of the two shields of the thyroid cartilage.
At the back of the larynx, each band is attached to a pyramidal-shaped
cartilage called the *arytenoid.*

Because of their shape and muscular connections, the arytenoid cartilages can move in several directions. In doing so, they directly influence

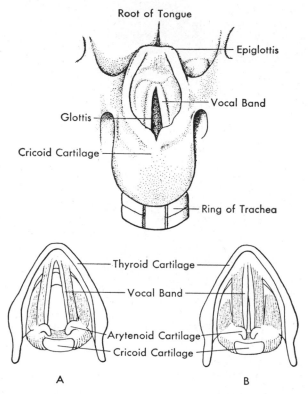

Figure 2–2 **View and diagrammatic representation of the larynx and vocal bands showing attachments to cartilages and larynx.**
Upper Diagram: The larynx viewed from above and behind (posterior aspect).
Lower Diagrams: (A) Vocal bands shown in position for quiet breathing. (B) Vocal bands in position for vocalization.

the position and state of tension of the vocal bands. The arytenoid cartilages can pivot or rotate and tilt backward and sidewise. As a result of these movements, the vocal bands can be brought into a straight line along the midline position so that there is only a narrow opening between them (B in Figure 2–2), or they can be separated for quiet breathing (A of Figure 2–2). If the bands are brought together in a narrow V, as in the upper part of Figure 2–2, noisy whispering or possibly breathy voice would be produced if an effort were made to vocalize.

The small, tough vocal bands, ranging in length from seven-eighths of an inch to one and one-fourth inches in adult males and from less than one-half to seven-eighths of an inch in adult females, are directly responsible for the sound called voice produced by human beings.

The *frequency of vibration* of the vocal bands is determined by their length, thickness, and degree of tension when they begin to vibrate. Pitch, as indicated previously, is our subjective reaction to frequency changes or differences. We think of pitch as being high, medium, or low, or we use such terms as *soprano, alto, tenor, baritone,* or *bass* to designate ranges of vocal pitch.

Although the term *vibration* is used to designate the action of the vocal bands, a more accurate term might be *flutter.* When the column of breath is forced through the narrowed opening between the approximated vocal bands, they are literally blown apart and then come together in a flutter-like manner. If the breath stream is steady and controlled, the result will be a sequence of rhythmical flutters that produce in turn a rhythmical sequence of air puffs. The vocal tone is a product of the number of flutters, or vibrations, per unit of time and the vigor with which the bands are blown apart. The greater the number of flutters or vibrations, the higher is the pitch. The greater the vigor with which the vocal bands are blown apart, the louder is the tone. When the vocal bands flutter or vibrate with evenness and regularity, "smooth" or "pure" tone is produced. Irregularity of vibration, caused either by inadequate control of the breath stream (poor motive control) or from an unfavorable condition of the vocal bands, will result in the production of uneven or "noisy" vocal tones.

Frequency of vibration varies directly (increases) according to the tension and inversely (decreases) according to the mass and length of the vibrating bodies. Because most men have longer and thicker vocal bands than most women, male voices are on the average lower in pitch than female voices. The average fundamental frequency for male voices is 128 cycles (waves) per second; it is between 200–256 cycles [1] per second for adult female voices.[2]

Variation from our fundamental frequencies is, for the most part, a result of the changes in tension of our vocal bands. We have considerable control over their state of tension. Such control becomes evident each time we sing the musical scale or a song or raise or lower the pitch level of a sound or a word when talking. Variation also occurs as a result of involuntary changes in the vocal bands associated with overall states of bodily tension. The tensions of the vocal bands vary as other muscles voluntarily or involuntarily become tense or relaxed. If you are habitually a tense individual, you are likely to vocalize at a higher pitch level than if you are habitually a relaxed person. Immediate responses to situations are productive of overall changes in bodily tension that are likely to be associated with tension changes in the vocal bands and therefore in their frequency of vibration. These changes become apparent in situations conducive to

---

[1] The letters Hz (Hertz) are now commonly used instead of cycles (waves) in referring to frequency. Hz = cycles per second (c.p.s.).

[2] In a recent study Hollien, Dew, and Phillips (1971) found that the mean frequency (pitch) range for adults exceeded three octaves, with individual ranges varying from one and a half to four and a half octaves. "Further, it appears that many normal adults exhibit ranges comparable to those of singers." H. Hollien, D. Dew, and P. Phillips, "Phonational Frequency Range of Adults," *Journal of Speech and Hearing Research,* 14:4 (1971) 755–760.

excitement and elation at one extreme and sadness or depression at the other. (This is considered in some detail in Chapter 7, "Pitch and Effective Vocalization.")

The Motive Force

The second requisite for sound production, the force that vibrates the vocal bands, is the column of air or expired breath stream. In ordinary breathing, the vocal bands are open in a wide-shaped V so that the stream of breath meets no resistance as it is exhaled. For purposes of vocalization, we recall, the vocal bands are brought together so that there is a narrow, relatively straight opening rather than a V-shaped one. The result is that the exhaled air meets resistance. In order for the air to be expired, the air column must be more energetically exhaled than it is in ordinary breathing. The energetic exhalation vibrates the vocal bands and voice is produced.

As indicated, vocalization for speech requires control. Control, which normally takes place without conscious effort on our part, is achieved usually by the action of the muscles of the abdominal wall and the muscles of the chest cavity.

The *chest cavity* (thoracic) consists of a framework of bones and cartilages that include the collarbone, the shoulder blades, the ribs, the breastbone, and the backbone. At the floor of the chest cavity, and separating it from the abdominal cavity immediately below, is the *diaphragm*. We can locate the large, double-dome-shaped muscle called the diaphragm by placing our fingers just below the *sternum* or breastplate and moving them around the front, sides, and back of the thoracic cavity to the spinal column. In breathing, the diaphragm rises toward the chest cavity during exhalation and descends toward the abdominal cavity during inhalation. In breathing for purposes of speech, both the normal respiratory rhythm and the extent of the upward and downward excursions may be modified according to the speaker's immediate needs.

The *lungs*, which function as air reservoirs, contain much elastic tissue and consist of a mass of tiny air sacs supplied by a multiple of air tubes and blood vessels. Because the lungs contain no muscle tissue, they can neither expand nor contract directly. They play a passive role in respiration, expanding or contracting because of differences in pressure brought about by the activity of the abdominal and rib muscles that serve to expand and control the thoracic cavity. Air is drawn into the lungs as a result of outside air pressure when the chest cavity, expanded through muscle action, provides increased space for the air. Air is forced out of the lungs when the chest cavity decreases in size and the pressure of the enclosed air is increased. This is normally accomplished through action in which the diaphragm is passively but importantly involved.

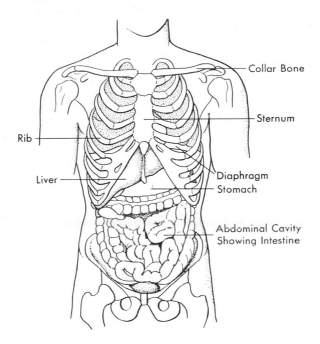

Figure 2–3 **The chest (thoracic) and abdominal cavities.**

Diaphragmatic Action

When the volume of the chest cavity is increased, air is inhaled into the lungs by way of the mouth or nose and the trachea. An increase in the volume of the chest cavity may be effected through a downward, contracting movement of the diaphragm, through an upward, outward movement of the lower ribs, or through a combination of both activities. During inhalation, the diaphragm is active in contracting, thereby lowering the floor of the thoracic cavity. When inhalation is completed, the diaphragm becomes passive and relaxes. The abdominal organs then exert an upward pressure and so the diaphragm is returned to its former position. When it becomes necessary to control exhalation for purposes of vocalization and speech, the muscles of the front and sides of the abdominal wall contract and press inward on the liver, stomach, and intestines. These abdominal organs exert an upward pressure on the undersurface of the diaphragm. This pressure, combined with the downward-inward movement of the ribs, increases the pressure within the thorax, causing the air to be expelled from the lungs. Throughout the breathing cycle, the diaphragm is roughly dome-shaped. The height of the dome is greater after exhalation than after inhalation.

It is important to understand that the diaphragm, though passive in exhalation, does not relax all at once. If it did, breath would be expelled

Figure 2–4 **Diaphragmatic and abdominal activity in breathing.**
A. The thorax or chest cavity.
B. The diaphragm passive and "relaxed" as at the completion of exhalation.
B'. The diaphragm contracted as in deep inhalation.
C. The abdominal cavity. Note the forward movement of the abdominal wall
      that accompanies the downward movement of the diaphragm during in-
      halation.
(The crosshatched portion of the lung represents the additional volume of the
   expanded lung as in deep inhalation.)

suddenly and in a manner that would make sustained vocalization impossible. Fortunately, the diaphragm maintains some degree of muscle
tension at all times. When the diaphragm relaxes because of the pressure
of the abdominal organs, it does so slowly and gradually as the air is
expired. Thus a steady stream rather than a sudden rush of breath is
provided for the purposes of speech.

In regard to thoracic and diaphragmatic action what was just described
is in effect an application of the principle of air motion to breathing. Air,
regardless of its source, flows from areas of relatively high pressure to
areas of relatively low pressure. The pressure of contained air may be decreased by an expansion of the container and increased by compression
of the container. As applied to breathing, air (breath) is moved (breathing takes place) as a result of the muscular changes of the thoracic cavity.
Specifically, when the chest cavity is enlarged (pressure reduced) air

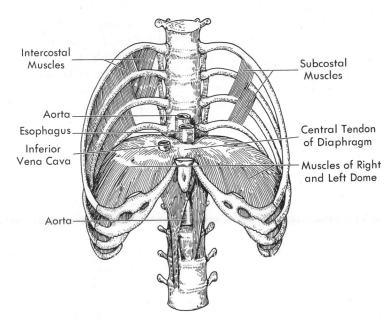

Figure 2–5 The diaphragm, showing upper, or thoracic, surface; dome, or central tendon; and attachments to the lower ribs and the vertebrae. [After V. A. Anderson, *Training the Speaking Voice* (New York, Oxford University Press, 1961), p. 29. By permission.]

flows in; when the chest cavity is reduced in size (pressure is increased), air flows out.

Breathing for Speech

In breathing for ordinary life processes, the periods for inhalation and exhalation are approximately equal. Breathing for speech, however, usually requires that this regular rhythmic respiratory cycle be modified so that the period of exhalation exceeds that of inhalation. Normally, for speech, we inhale quickly between units of utterance and exhale slowly while speaking. This modification necessitates a degree of voluntary control not required for automatic breathing. Such control is usually achieved by abdominal activity.[3] This point is considered in greater detail in our discussion on voice improvement.

In normal nonspeech breathing, an average of about a pint of air (500

---

[3] Stetson demonstrated that in the normal speaking act, short, individual breath pulses that correspond to the successive oral syllables result from the action of the rib-connecting (intercostal) muscles. See R. H. Stetson, *Motor Phonetics*, 2nd ed., Oberlin College, Oberlin, Ohio, 1951, and R. H. Stetson and C. V. Hudgins, "Functions of the Breathing Movements in the Mechanism of Speech," *Archives Neerlandaises de Phonetique Experimentale* (1930) 5:1–30.

cc.) is interchanged in each respiratory cycle. Conversational speech may require little or no more air; vigorous speaking may require more air. Seldom, however, do we use more than 10 to 20 per cent of the total amount of air our lungs are capable of holding. Control of breath and the appropriate use of our resonators for the reinforcement of vocal tones rather than the amount of breath are essential to adequate voice production.

Reinforcement of Sound through Resonance

The requisites of sound production are satisfied when a force is applied to a body capable of vibration and is transmitted or conducted through a medium to a receiver. From a strictly physical point of view, a receiver is not necessary. Psychologically, however, there can be no report or corroboration of the occurrence of a sound unless the sound is received. The receiver must be capable of auditory sensitivity within the pitch range of the vibrating body. Furthermore, the receiver's auditory sensitivity or threshold for hearing must be low enough for the intensity level of the sound. If a receiver is at a distance from the source of a sound (the initiating vibrating body), considerable energy would have to be applied to set the body into vibration with a resultant amplitude to produce a sound of sufficient intensity to be heard. At least, this would be the situation if a body were to be set into vibration in an "open field," by which we mean under conditions in which the sound is not reinforced through resonating bodies. We are assuming, also, that the sound is not amplified through mechanical devices such as an electrical sound system. Fortunately, the human voice does have the immediate benefit of reinforcement through resonating bodies. Later we shall consider how reinforcement through resonance is accomplished in the human voice mechanism. For the present, we shall discuss as briefly and as simply as possible the nature of two kinds of resonance-reinforcement that may take place for any sound.

Forced Resonance. Forced resonance or forced vibration occurs when a body that is set into vibration has a contact with another body that has the capability of the same frequency of vibration. The result of this contact is to set the second body into vibration. In effect, a sound has been directly transmitted from one body to a second, and so the sound is reinforced. This is partly what happens when the sounding body of a piano vibrates and when a vibrating string of a violin transmits sound by way of the bridge to the body of the violin. It is also partly what happens when a tuning fork is set on a box or a board or a table top. The effect is the production of a sound we perceive as louder than would be the case if there were no forced vibration or forced resonance.

Cavity Resonance. A second form of reinforcement that is common for musical instruments, and for sound enhancement in general, takes place as a result of cavity resonance. By a cavity we mean a partially enclosed body. Examples include the shell or conventional stage for an orchestra; the tubular arrangement of a wind instrument; a tumbler or drinking glass; and the "cavities" of the mouth, pharynx, and larynx of the human body. Each cavity, depending upon its size, shape, and opening has a natural frequency range for the sounds it will reinforce with *optimum efficiency*—for the sound range with which *the cavity is in tune*. Even a limited knowledge of musical instruments should lead us to generalize that the larger the cavity body, the lower will be its natural frequency range (the more efficiently the resonating cavity will reinforce low-pitched sounds). Conversely, the smaller the cavity body, the higher will be its natural frequency range. Thus, a bass violin, with its large cavity, is tuned for the reinforcement of low-pitched ranges of sound, and a violin (fiddle), which has a smaller body, is tuned for the reinforcement of high-pitched ranges of sound. These ranges, of course, are relative to the family of string instruments. Comparable correlations between the size and pitch range hold for wind instruments. Thus we can account for the differences in the range of sound for woodwind instruments that are similar in shape but different in size.

Reinforcement and Coloring of Vocal Tones

If we depended only on the energetic use of controlled breathing to make ourselves heard, we would have little "broadcast" ability without the help of mechanical (electrical) amplification. Fortunately, our vocal mechanisms are constructed so that a building up of laryngeal tones takes place through the reinforcement capacities of the resonators of our vocal apparatus. Before considering the contribution of each of our principal resonators—the cavities of the larynx, throat (pharynx), and mouth (oral cavity)—we shall briefly discuss the overall reinforcement of laryngeal tones.

The tones that are initiated in the larynx are modified and reinforced or "built up" in the structures beneath and above the vocal bands. The result of what takes place in these subglottal and supraglottal structures is the production of voice that emphasizes or brings out the potentialities of some vocal characteristics and minimizes or damps out others.

The chest or thoracic structure reinforces and modifies the laryngeal tone through a combination of forced (bone) and cavity resonance. When the vocal bands are set into action, with a resultant vocal tone, the tone is transmitted to the bones of the chest. We can feel this effect by placing a hand on the upper part of the chest while vocalizing an *ah*. We should also be able to note that there is considerably more bone vibration felt with the vocalization of an *ah* than an *ee*. We may then appropriately conclude that our lower laryngeal tones are given considerably more reinforcement through the forced (bone) resonance than are the higher-pitched laryngeal tones. Except to avoid cramped postures, there is nothing we can do to enhance this type of vocal reinforcement. There is, however, much that we can do in regard to cavity reinforcement, which we now consider.

As already indicated, the principal human vocal resonators are the cavities of the larynx, pharynx, mouth, and the nasal passages. To a significant degree, also, the tracheal area just below the larynx as well as the bronchi reinforce laryngeal tones.

Each of the principal resonators by virtue of its size, shape, and tissue texture has special properties that enable it to make a unique contribution to the modification and reinforcement of the initial laryngeal tone and the production of the final or "finished" voice that the listener hears. We should be mindful, however, that at all times the vocal tones that emerge are the products of the contributions resulting from combined characteristics of all the resonators as well as the bony structures of the chest and head. Though some tones may have primary or predominant coloring resulting from the properties of one of the principal resonators, the others contribute to the finished voice. The discussion that follows considers the features of each of the principal resonators and the contribution each makes to our vocal efforts.

The Larynx As a Resonator

Vocal tones, as soon as they are initiated, are reinforced in the larynx. If the larynx is free from organic pathology and not under strain and if the speaker initiates and maintains vocalization without abnormal tension, there is little he can or need consciously do about obtaining good laryngeal resonance. If the speaker has laryngitis, however, normal laryngeal reinforcement is not possible. If you suffer from laryngitis, it is best to reduce your talking to a minimum, and if possible, do no talking. If the condition is recurrent, or persistent, a visit to a physician is in order.

Tension of the extrinsic muscles of the larynx, as indicated, interferes with the reinforcing function of the larynx. Such tension is also likely to interfere with the free action of the vocal bands for good tone production. The extrinsic muscles of the larynx are those that connect it to the jaw and other bones and cartilages so that it will maintain its normal position when at rest and be lifted upward and forward for swallowing. Tension is necessary in the act of swallowing. You can feel the tension of the extrinsic muscles by placing your hand on your throat as you swallow. Such muscular tension should, however, be avoided in most speech efforts. We approximate such tension for the vowels of *see* and *sue* and to a lesser degree for the vowels of *hate* and *hat*.

The Pharynx

The pharynx, or throat cavity, has the necessary attributes for optimum sound reinforcement. How a cavity resonates (reinforces) a given tone or range of tones is determined by several factors. These include the size, shape, and nature (material, tension, and the like) of the cavity walls and the size of its opening as related to the source of sound (vibrating body) and/or other connecting cavities. The pharynx, because of its size and the control we can exercise over it to modify its shape and tension, is much more important as a vocal reinforcer than is the larynx. We modify the length of the cavity each time we swallow or each time the soft palate is raised or relaxed. We change the quality of vocal tones through changes in the tension of the pharyngeal walls. Growths, such as enlarged adenoids or tonsils, may damp vocal tones and modify loudness as well as sound quality. When, because of infection or emotional tension, the pharynx is abnormally tense, the voice quality tends to become strident and metallic. Higher-pitched tones are reinforced at the expense of low tones. The result sometimes is an unpleasant voice that lacks adequate loudness and carrying power. When the pharyngeal tensions are normal, the voice is likely to be rich and mellow—at least as rich and mellow as the individual throat permits.

Our understanding of the action of the pharynx as a resonator can be

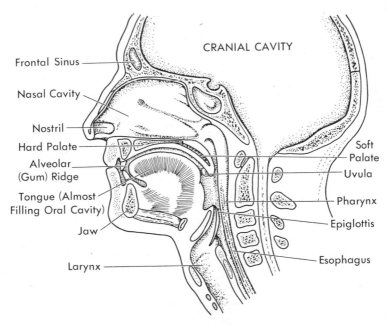

Figure 2–6 Section of head showing principal resonators and organs of articulation.

enhanced by a brief review of its structure. If we examine Figure 2–6 we will note that the pharynx begins just above the larynx and extends up to the entrance to the nasal cavity. The portion near the larynx—the *laryngopharynx*—is capable of considerable modification. The diameter can be changed for the reinforcement of fundamental tones and overtones produced in the larynx. The tones we identify as the vowels of our language are in part produced as a result of action of the laryngopharynx.

The *oropharynx* is the area just above the laryngopharynx. The oropharynx can pair with either the area below (the laryngopharynx), or above (the nasopharynx), or with the oral cavity (mouth), or with all three together coupling to modify vocal tones. As a result, the oropharynx can act subtly or grossly to reinforce tones and to produce sounds of different qualities.

The *nasopharynx* is the uppermost part of the pharyngeal cavity. This area can in effect be separated from the mouth cavity and connected (coupled) with the nasal cavity through the act of elevating the soft palate. When the soft palate is lowered, the nasopharynx can be paired or coupled with the lower part of the pharynx or with the oral cavity. The nasopharynx is directly involved in the reinforcement of the nasal consonants *n, m,* and *ng*.

The Oral Cavity

The mouth, or oral cavity, is the most modifiable of all the resonators of importance for speech. Except for that part of the roof of the mouth that constitutes the hard palate, all the parts that together form or are included in the oral cavity are capable of considerable movement. The lower jaw can move to create an oral cavity limited only by the extent of the jaw's action. The tongue, though attached to the floor of the mouth, can be elevated, flattened, extended out of the mouth, drawn up and curled within the mouth, or can almost fill the closed mouth. The lips can close tight along a straight line, open centrally or laterally to various-sized apertures, or open wide as the lower jaw drops to permit a view of the back of the throat. The soft palate and uvula can be elevated to increase the size of the back of the mouth or relaxed to make the back of the mouth continuous with the throat. Through these many modifications, the oral cavity and the organs within it not only produce the various sounds of our language but reinforce them as well.

The Nasal Cavity

Except when the nasopharynx is coupled with the nasal cavity, we have little direct control over the latter. Unfortunately, the linings of the nasal cavity and the cavity itself are considerably affected not only by physical illnesses involving the upper respiratory tract but by emotional disturbances as well. The condition of the nose, it appears, is often an excellent indicator of what is happening to us physically and emotionally. It fills up when we have a cold, when we are allergic, when we are very happy, and when we are acutely sad. When, for any one of numerous reasons, the nasal cavity is not free, adequate reinforcement of nasal sounds in particular and nonnasal sounds in general is difficult if not impossible.

The Sinuses

The role of the sinuses as resonators has not been clearly established. We have four pairs of sinuses that drain into the nasal cavity. Most of us become aware of our sinuses when they are infected and drain the products of their infection into our respiratory tract. Short of trying to keep well so that we can avoid the unpleasant condition called sinusitis, there is little we can do about the sinuses to influence voice. Unlike most of the other cavities associated with the respiratory tract, we cannot control or modify the size, shape, or surface tension of the sinuses to affect the reinforcement of vocal tones.

Van Riper and Irwin (1958, p. 245), after reviewing the literature on the possible function of the sinuses as nasal resonators come to a conclusion with which we agree "We can pretty well . . . discard the notion that the sinuses play any important part in the production of nasal resonance."

Flexibility of the Vocal Mechanism

Earlier in the chapter we compared the voice mechanism with a wind instrument. In our comparison, the point was made that the vocal mechanism was considerably more flexible and therefore superior to any wind instrument as a producer of sound. The reeds of a wind instrument are fixed in size and degree of tension. Human vocal bands, however, can be changed in length and tension so that a comparatively wide range of pitch is possible. Through muscular contraction our resonating cavities can be modified so that the sound produced by the vocal bands can be variably reinforced. Normally, we can direct our voice through a combination of resonators so that sound emerges either orally or nasally. The manner in which we open and shape our mouths permits us to produce a variety of sounds that are most readily exemplified in the vowels of our language. When the lips, the tongue, and the palate become more actively involved in the modification of sound, articulation, an aspect of sound production peculiar to human beings, becomes possible. This aspect of sound is considered after our discussion of the attributes of voice and some factors that are related to vocal changes.

CHARACTERISTICS OF SOUND—AND VOICE

All sounds, including those that are vocal, have four fundamental characteristics or attributes. These are *loudness, pitch, duration,* and *quality.* When we respond to a given sound, whether it be the barely audible sound of a dropped pin or a clap of thunder, we are responding to a combination of attributes. The results of our experiences enable us to recognize certain sounds as belonging to the things that make them. So, also, we are usually able to associate voices with the persons who produce them. Tom's voice is a complex of his particular vocal attributes, as are the voices of Harry and Dick. If we know Tom, Dick, and Harry well, and have fair sensitivity to voice, we are likely to identify each by his voice. If we lack sensitivity to vocal differences, or if the sum of Tom's vocal attributes is much like Dick's or Harry's, we may occasionally make mistakes in our identification. Usually, however, one attribute of voice is likely to be different enough so that the sum produces a voice that is sufficiently individualized to permit reliable identification.

The human voice as a sound producer is not limited to one given pitch, loudness, duration, or even quality. The human mechanism with its subtle and complex neuromuscular controls is capable of a range of variation for each of the sound attributes. A baritone vocalizer may produce sounds that overlap the upper range of the bass and the lower range of the tenor. A female contralto may be able to overlap the high tenor and much of the soprano ranges. No speaker produces tones at a single loudness level. As we speak, we vary the intensity of our sounds from syllable to syllable, word to word, sentence to sentence, and, of course, from occasion to occasion. We vary the duration or time given to utterance as well as the pitch and loudness. We are able to speak rapidly, slowly, or at a moderate rate according to need as well as habit. Although our vocal qualities are relatively limited by the size and shape of our resonating cavities, these attributes can be modified. Some of us are even able to control vocal quality well enough to imitate other speakers. Most of us who do not habitually speak nasally or harshly can do so at will. All things and sound attributes considered, the normal human being can do considerably more with his sound-making apparatus than expert musicians can do with their musical instruments.

The Individuality of the Human Voice

Although some persons achieve reputations as vocal mimics because of their ability to simulate the vocal production of popular or well-known personages, each of us has a voice with individual features that are almost as distinctive as our fingerprints. Our ability to hear these distinctive features may not be as keen as our ability to see differences in fingerprints, but vocal differences are able to be discerned when they are transformed from audible into visible forms. A device that transforms the vocal features of voice to visible patterns has been developed by the Bell Telephone Laboratories. Voice-prints (such as those in Figures 2–7, 2–8, and 2–9) bring out differences that reveal the individuality of the voice. The recording technique, developed by Lawrence Kersta of Bell Laboratories,

Figure 2–7 **Four spectrograms of the spoken word *science*. The vertical scale represents frequency, the horizontal dimension is time, and darkness represents intensity on a compressed scale. Three of the spectrograms are from three different speakers, and the remaining spectrogram is a repetition of the word by one of the speakers. The spectrograms were made on a Voiceprint Laboratories Sound Spectrograph. [From R. H. Bolt, *et al.*, "Identification of a Speaker by Speech Spectrograms," *Science*, 166 (1969), p. 339.]**

The authors of this article were of the opinion that despite the admitted individuality of the human voice, available results of studies of speech spectrograms are not adequate to establish the reliability of voice identification by this technique. Despite this opinion, several recent court rulings admit voice print identification as legal evidence for identification. For example, United States of America v. Albert Raymond and Roland Addison, United States District Court, Crim. No. 800-71, February 2, 1972. Also, State of Minnesota ex. ref. Constance L. Trimble, Supreme Court of Minnesota, No. 43049, November 26, 1971.

Figure 2–8 (*Left*)   John F. Kennedy's voice-print, made during a talk he gave in the White House, shows Bostonian delivery in compressed dark lines at top. [LIFE Magazine © 1963 Time Inc. All Rights Reserved.]

Figure 2–9 (*Right*)   Elliott Reid uses the same text and intonation as President Kennedy, but the graph his voice makes is radically different. [LIFE Magazine © 1963 Time Inc. All Rights Reserved.]

indicates loudness, resonance, and pitch. In combination, these features are presumably never the same for any two people (see Figures 2–8 and 2–9).

CORRELATES OF VOCAL CHANGES

Unless we consciously try to conceal our feelings as we talk, we are likely to reveal them by the way we sound. Voice, when not intentionally controlled, is a barometer of our affective states, our feelings and our moods. This is so essentially because voice is a product of muscular activity that in turn is intimately related to the emotional state of the organism. In a state of heightened emotion, as in anger or fear, we experience muscular tension. The muscles involved in voice production share in the increased total body tension. Thus when vocalization takes place it is on a higher pitch level than normal. Another involuntary change that accompanies heightened emotion is the addition of sugar to the blood stream. This enables us to engage in energetic activity that is sometimes an aspect of heightened emotion. The effect on a voice is to increase its loudness. The overall effect of heightened feeling on utterance is that the voice becomes high pitched, loud, and rapid.

In contrast, depressed or let-down states are associated with vocal tones that are low in pitch level and relatively weak in loudness. This is so because the muscles of the body as a whole, and the vocal bands in particular, become overrelaxed or hypotonic, and energetic activity is reduced. The overall effect on utterance is to make it relatively low in pitch and volume and slow in rate.

Voice that is dominated by intellect rather than emotion tends to be moderate in pitch as well as in loudness. This does not imply that intellectual efforts are devoid of feeling. It does imply that intellectual efforts accompanied by vocalization are normally not characterized by the exaggerated range and intensity of feeling that is associated with emotional behavior. Under intellectual control, we are able to simulate emotion, to suggest how we would sound if angry, afraid, ecstatically happy, or depressed. When these pretenses are not necessary, we are ourselves. If we are our normal selves, we are usually moderate not only in our behavior in general but in the intensity of our feelings and in the manner in which our voices reveal (or sometimes betray) how we feel and think.

Sometimes our voices express our feelings not about the contents of our utterances but our attitudes toward our listeners or those we think (feel) should be listening. Children may sense this in the notes of impatience and irritation in the voices of their parents and may express their own feelings in their vocal responses to their parents. Our voices, if not controlled, and sometimes when intentionally not "controlled," may reflect our evaluation of the listener or a personality. Occasionally the doubt our voices express is the doubt we anticipate the listener will entertain if, indeed, he has been listening to us.

ARTICULATED SOUND

When breath that is set into vibration by the action of the vocal bands reaches the mouth as part of a speech effort, the breath stream is further modified by the action of the tongue, lips, palate, and/or cheeks to produce voiced articulated sound. If the breath stream is not set into vibration, then voiceless articulated sound may be produced. The organs of articulation serve essentially as interrupters, "filters," or modifiers of the breath stream. Some sounds—vowels and diphthongs—are produced only by an adjustment of the size and shape of oral and adjacent cavities. These adjustments modify but do not impede or interrupt the laryngeal or vocal tone. Other sounds are produced by a stoppage or diversion of the breath or the vocal tone. Thus we have consonants resulting from sudden interruptions, little explosions, or hissings because air is forced through narrow openings. The manner and place of interruption result in the production of articulated speech sounds. Each sound has its own characteristics or phonetic attributes. Oral speech consists of combinations of articulated sounds. When these sounds, produced according to the rules and conventions of our language, are appropriately grouped and readily audible, we speak intelligibly.

The Articulators

Most of the articulated sounds of American-English speech are produced as a result of the activity of the lips and parts of the tongue. These

Figure 2–10 **The oral cavity and its articulators.**
1. Tongue. *1a.* Tongue tip. *1b.* Blade of tongue. *1c.* Front of tongue. *1d.* Back of tongue.
2. Mouth (oral) cavity.
3. Palate. *3a.* Gum, or alveolar, ridge. *3b.* Hard palate. *3c.* Soft palate. *3d.* Uvula.
4. Nasal cavity.

mobile articulators assume positions or make contact with fixed or relatively fixed parts of the upper jaw and the roof of the mouth (see Figure 2-10).

The lips and teeth enclose the oral cavity. The tongue lies within and almost completely fills the oral cavity. From the point of view of articulatory action the tongue may be divided into the following parts: the anterior portion or tongue tip, the blade, the midtongue, and the back. The roof of the mouth may be divided into the gum ridge or alveolar process (directly behind the upper teeth), the hard palate, the soft palate (velum), and the uvula.

The larynx also serves an articulatory function because the presence or absence of vocalization distinguishes many pairs of sounds such as *b* and *p* and *z* and *s*. The sound *h* is produced as a result of a degree of contraction within the larynx sufficient to produce audible friction.

Details as to the manner in which the articulators function to produce the different sounds of our language are considered in Chapter 11. At the present time let us consider briefly the controlling mechanism through which man is enabled to make vocal noises, to modify these noises into distinguishable sounds and intelligible words, to arrange these words into phrases and sentences in order to express his feelings, his wishes, and his needs, and to become a member of a symbol-producing and symbol-responding culture.

The achievement of speech is neurologically related to the development of the cerebrum in man. Except for the cerebrum of the brain, the nervous system of the human being is surprisingly like that of a dog and almost completely like that of an ape. The cerebrum is significantly different in man. It is larger in proportion to the nervous system as a whole than it is in animals including subhuman primates, and it includes a bulgelike frontal area of greater size than that found in animals with otherwise comparable nervous systems. The brain is a coordinator and integrator of activity. In the brain, impulses set up by sounds and movements that are received by the ear, the eye, or other sense organs are translated into images or into words that have significance and meaning.

The Cerebral Cortex

The gray outer covering of the brain is especially involved in the function of speech. The cortex contains ten to twelve billion or more nerve cells. Parts of the cortex have specialized functions that are involved in the peculiarly human ability to produce and understand oral (speech) or written symbols. These areas are indicated in Figure 2-11. The marked areas include those for *hearing, seeing,* and *speech movement.* These areas are significant because of their evident capacity to evaluate specialized experiences *for the brain as a whole.* For example, the auditory area in the lower middle part of the brain evaluates sounds, so that noises may

Figure 2–11 The cerebral cortex and cerebellum and some "specialized" areas related to speech.

be interpreted as *barks, wind in the trees,* or *words.* Similarly, the area in the back part of the brain (the occipital lobe) interprets impulses coming from the eye. Through this area we are able to recognize and identify objects we see and to read, and so to make sense out of markings called letters and words.

Recent evidence (Eisenson, 1971) highlights differences as well as similarities between the left and right cerebral hemispheres. Specifically, there are differences in regard to the nature of auditory events that are processed (perceived and interpreted) by the two temporal lobes. The perception of speech events is normally a function of the left temporal lobe, and the perception of auditory nonspeech events (environmental noises, musical melody, animal noises) is perceived and processed in the right temporal lobe. Figure 2–11 features the specialized areas of the left cerebral cortex that are related to the processing of spoken and written symbols.

THE CENTRAL NERVOUS SYSTEM

Many animals can produce vocal noises, but only man can make sounds that carry and convey specific differential messages. We speak—

phonate and articulate—because we are able to integrate organs that biologically serve the functions of digestion and respiration for the nonbiological purpose of producing oral symbols, an achievement unique to the human species.

Figure 2–12 **The central nervous system in relation to speech.**
The *cerebrum* performs the integrative activity upon which normal, meaningful speech is dependent.
The *cerebellum* "sorts and arranges" muscular impulses that come to it from higher brain centers. Impulses are here correlated so that precise muscular activity such as is needed for speech becomes possible.
The *pons* is a bridge of nerve fibers between the cerebral cortex and the medulla.
The *medulla* contains the respiratory and other vital reflex centers.
The *spinal cord* and its nerves control the respiratory muscles.
The *phrenic nerve* emerges from the spinal cord in the neck region and extends to the diaphragm. It supplies the impulses that cause the diaphragm to contract in breathing.

Other Parts of the Central Nervous System and Their Functions in Speech

In addition to the cerebrum, other parts of the central nervous system are essentially involved in the production of speech. These parts, which are represented in Figure 2–12, serve the following functions in the integrated speech act.

The *cerebellum*, or little brain, receives impulses from higher brain centers. The impulses are sorted, arranged, and correlated so that the coordinated and precise muscular activity needed for speech becomes possible. Damage to the cerebellum may seriously impair the flow and control of coordinated speech activity. Damage of this sort is found in many cases of cerebral palsy.

The *medulla* contains the center essential for respiration, and damage to it may impair normal breathing. Bulbar polio involves such damage, and requires the use of a mechanical respirator.

The *bulb*, the *spinal cord*, and the nerves emanating from them control the muscles involved in the coordinated act of speaking. The *phrenic* nerve, which emerges from the spinal cord in the region of the neck, extends to the diaphragm. The phrenic nerve supplies the impulse that causes the diaphragm to contract and so brings about inhalation in breathing.

Other nerves that initiate movements involved in speech are the trigeminal (face and jaw muscles), the glossopharyngeal (tongue and pharynx), the recurrent laryngeal (larynx), and the glossal (tongue).

In the absence of pathology, the central nervous system, dominated by the cerebral cortex, controls the impulses involved in the act of speaking. Through this system, we are able to be articulate about our impressions, to reveal what we think and how we feel. Sometimes, if it suits our purpose, we conceal rather than reveal either our feelings, our thoughts, or both. The degree of expertness with which we use our speech apparatus varies considerably from person to person. All of us, however, with unimpaired physical mechanisms and with normal personalities should be capable of speaking adequately. How to make the most of our mechanisms so that we fully utilize our capabilities to vocalize and articulate with ease and intelligibility is considered in the chapters that follow.

REFERENCES

Denes, P. B., and E. N. Pinson. *The Speech Chain: The Physics and Biology of Spoken Language*. Bell Telephone Laboratories, 1963. Chapters 4–7.
Eisenson, J. "The Left Brain Is for Talking." *Acta Symbolica* 2 (1971) 1, 33–36.
Moore, P. *Organic Voice Disorders*. Englewood Cliffs, N.J.: Prentice-Hall, Inc., 1971.
Van Riper, C., and J. V. Irwin. *Voice and Articulation*. Englewood Cliffs, N.J.: Prentice-Hall, Inc., 1958.

CHAPTER 3

Breathing for Effective Vocalization

Physicians specializing in the treatment of the throat, and those few who treat vocal disorders as well as diseases of the throat, recognize that most vocal disorders are a result of the use of *inappropriate force, wrong pitch, incorrect breathing, or a combination of these faults.*[1]

Although our experience does not show that most speakers necessarily breath incorrectly, use force inappropriately, or pitch their voices at wrong levels, a knowledge of what can be done to improve voice may be helpful to all of us. Certainly the speaker who wants a better than ordinary voice or who aspires or needs to use voice as an instrument for his vocation or profession has an obligation to himself as well as to his listeners to know what students in the field of voice recommend as to the use of force, pitch, and breathing. We begin with a consideration of breathing.

[1] For a discussion of this viewpoint by a physician, see F. S. Brodnitz, *Keep Your Voice Healthy* (New York: Harper & Row, Publishers, Inc., 1953), Chap. XII.

The basic physiology of respiration is succinctly and clearly considered in T. E. Rogers' *Elementary Human Physiology* (New York: John Wiley & Sons, Inc., 1961), Chap. VIII.

A brief and authoritative discussion on phonation is included in Chap. III of G. Paul Moore's *Organic Voice Disorders* (Englewood Cliffs, N.J.: Prentice-Hall, Inc., 1971).

BREATHING FOR SPEECH (VOICE AND ARTICULATION)

Earlier, in our discussion of the mechanism for speech, we pointed out that breathing for speech calls for a modification of the normal respiratory cycle so that (1) the inspiration-expiration ratio is changed to provide a much longer period of exhalation than of inspiration and (2) a steady stream of air is initiated and controlled by the speaker to ensure good tone. These modifications, we have found, are usually achieved most easily by the type of breathing that emphasizes abdominal activity.

At the outset, we would like to point out that good breathing for speech production is by no means synonymous with deep breathing. Many good speakers use no more breath for vigorous speaking, or public speaking, than they do for conversational speech. Seldom is it necessary for any person to employ more than one fifth of his breath capacity for any ordinary vocal effort.

Breathing for speech should meet the following objectives:

1. It should afford the speaker an adequate and comfortable supply of breath with the least awareness and expenditure of effort.

2. The respiratory cycle—inhalation and exhalation—should be accomplished easily, quickly, and without interference with the flow of utterance.

3. The second objective implies ease of control over the outgoing breath so that breathing and phrasing—the grouping of ideas—can be correlated functions.

If these are not established and are not habitual accomplishments, they can be most readily achieved through establishing abdominal control of breathing.

Abdominal Breathing

If we observe the breathing of a person or an animal who is sleeping on his back or side, we should be able to note that during inhalation the abdominal area moves upward or forward, whereas during exhalation the abdominal area recedes. Figure 2–4 visualizes what we can see in the way of abdominal activity as well as what we cannot see in the way of diaphragmatic activity for breathing that emphasizes abdominal control. (See page 21.)

The essential point for us to appreciate is that in breathing that is characterized by the action of the abdominal muscles, the muscles of the abdomen relax in inhalation and contract in exhalation. When we learn how to contract or pull in the abdominal walls consciously, and how much and how fast to control such contraction, breathing for speech becomes *voluntary if needed*. If the reader is now exercising such control unconsciously, the suggested exercises that follow are not particularly important for him. If he is not, or if he finds that he cannot easily sustain a hum or a gentle whisper for from twenty to thirty seconds, then the exercises should be followed. These exercises are designed to create awareness and conscious control of abdominal action in breathing.

EXERCISES FOR CONTROL OF ABDOMINAL ACTION IN BREATHING

1. Lie on a couch or bed with a firm mattress. Spread your hands on the abdominal area immediately below the ribs so that the thumbs point to the rear and the fingers point forward. Inhale for normal, nonspeech breathing. Your hands should rise during inhalation and fall with the abdomen during exhalation. If the action is reversed, then the breathing is incorrect and should be changed to bring about the suggested activity. Repeat until the suggested action is accomplished easily. Be sure that you are not wearing a tight belt or a confining article of clothing while doing this and the following exercises.

2. Sit in a relaxed position in a comfortable chair with a firm seat. Your feet should be flat on the floor. Place your hands as in exercise (1). Now the abdominal walls should push forward during inhalation and pull in during exhalation.

3. Repeat as in exercise (2). Then inhale gently for about five seconds and exhale slowly, sustaining the exhalation for ten seconds. If you find yourself out of breath before the end of the ten-second period, then you have probably exhaled too quickly. Try the exercise again, intentionally slowing down the exhalation.

4. Inhale fully and then breathe out slowly and completely. Your hands should still be following the movement of the abdominal walls. Repeat, but this time press gently but firmly with your hands to force the expulsion of air from your lungs. Repeat, counting to yourself while exhaling. At this point you should be able to count for about thirty seconds before becoming uncomfortable.

5. Repeat, but this time vocalize a clear *ah* while exhaling. *Start your vocalization the moment you begin to exhale.* Stop before becoming uncomfortable. Repeat, vocalizing a sustained *hum* while exhaling. The *ah* and *hum* should be sustained longer than a nonvocalized exhalation.

6. Inhale deeply and then count out evenly and slowly until you feel the need for a second breath. Maintain even pitch and loudness levels. Repeat, but this time keep your hands at your sides and concentrate on a gradual pulling in of the abdominal wall during the counting. You should be able to count to at least twenty on a sustained exhalation. In any event, continue to practice until a count of at least fifteen is attained. With continued practice, a count of twenty to thirty (at the rate of two numbers per second) should become possible after a normal inhalation and a full thirty-second count after a deep inhalation.

7. With hands at your sides, repeat this exercise on two successive

breaths. Be certain that you do not exhale to a point of discomfort. Nor should you inhale so deeply that some air has to be exhaled for the sake of comfort.

8. Repeat, reciting the alphabet instead of counting. Avoid wasting breath between utterance of the letters. Note how far you are able to go on a single normal breath and on a single deep breath.

9. Repeat, whispering the alphabet. Note the letter you reached before requiring a second breath. Depending upon the degree of whisper, this might be only a third or a half of the number of letters of your vocalized effort. This is normal. A whisper is wasteful of breath.

10. Count, with vocalization, in groups of three. Avoid exhalation during pauses. Did you come close to the number you reached in counting without grouping? If you did not, then you probably exhaled between groups of numbers. Try it again until the two counts are about even.

11. Repeat exercise (10), using the alphabet instead of counting.

12. Recite the months of the year with pauses after March, June, and September. You should have no difficulty reciting all twelve months even with "seasonal" pauses.

13. Try to say each of the following sentences on a single breath.

    a. Let all who enter here beware!
    b. The road is long that has no turning.
    c. Alone, alone, all, all alone.
    d. The day was warmed by a gentle breeze.
    e. All aboard who are going aboard.

14. If you had no difficulty with the single sentences, then try uttering these longer sentences and complete each on a single, sustained breath. Do not, however, force the expulsion of air beyond a point of comfort.

    a. He's a fool that makes his doctor his heir.
         —BENJAMIN FRANKLIN
    b. Plato held that rhetoric was the art of ruling the minds of men.
    c. Her blue eyes sought the west afar,
       For lovers love the western star.
         —SIR WALTER SCOTT, *The Lay of the Last Minstrel*
    d. For he who fights and runs away
       May live to fight another day;
         —OLIVER GOLDSMITH, *The Art of Poetry*
    e. Upon what meat doth this our Caesar feed,
       That he is grown so great?
         —WILLIAM SHAKESPEARE, *Julius Caesar*
    f. The day is cold, and dark, and dreary;
       It rains, and the wind is never weary;
         —HENRY WADSWORTH LONGFELLOW, *The Rainy Day*

g. Party is the madness of the many for the gain of the few.
   —ALEXANDER POPE, *Thoughts on Various Subjects*

h. In their religion they are so uneven,
   That each man goes his own By-way to heaven.
   —DANIEL DEFOE, *The True-Born Englishman*

The following exercises involve the use of speech sounds that have an aspirate quality. They are normally more wasteful of breath than most of the previous exercises. They are, however, important in establishing breath control because much of what we say includes nonvocalized (voiceless) sounds as well as those that have a definite whispered or fricative quality.

EXERCISES FOR ESTABLISHING BREATH CONTROL

1. Inhale normally and then release the breath while producing the sound *s*. Be sure the sound is evenly maintained. Try to sustain the *s* for ten seconds. Repeat with the sound *sh*, then *th* as in *think*, and *f* as in *fall*.

2. Inhale deeply, but avoid discomfort. Repeat exercise (1). Compare these efforts with the length of time for a sustained *m* or *ah*. You are not likely to sustain any of these breathy sounds as long as *m* or *ah*, but you should come fairly close.

3. Try saying each of the following sentences on a single breath. If you do not succeed the first time, try a deeper inhalation on successive trials. Do not intentionally whisper.

   a. Whenever he thought about it, Harry pictured himself as a hero.
   b. His faithful dog Fido shared Harry's self-image.
   c. Heaven is said to help those who help themselves.
   d. The sun sank slowly and was followed by darkness and a foggy chill.
   e. What is held as truth by most of us is not essential truth for all of us.
   f. When I was five, I thought my father was the smartest person alive.
   g. The crisp and crackly leaves fell from the tree.
   h. If you listen in respectful silence, you may appear to be very wise.
   i. The rushing stream washed the soil along with it.
   j. Some critics hold that several of the plays attributed to Shakespeare were written by Marlowe.
   k. Other cynical critics hold that many of Shakespeare's plays were written by another author with the same name.

4. If you have been successful with all of the sentences, then try these couplets, each on a single breath. If you pause at the end of the line, try not to exhale at the pause.

a. My life is like a stroll upon the beach,
   As near the ocean's edge as I can go.
   —HENRY DAVID THOREAU, *The Fisher's Boy*

b. Words are like leaves; and where they most abound,
   Much fruit of sense beneath is rarely found.
   —ALEXANDER POPE, *An Essay on Criticism*

c. The drying up a single tear has more
   Of honest fame than shedding seas of gore.
   —GEORGE GORDON, LORD BYRON, *Don Juan*

d. Those who in quarrels interpose
   Must often wipe a bloody nose.
   —JOHN GAY, *The Mastiffs*

e. The naked every day he clad
   When he put on his clothes.
   —OLIVER GOLDSMITH, *Elegy on the Death of a Mad Dog*

f. Of all the tyrannies on human kind
   The worst is that which persecutes the mind.
   —JOHN DRYDEN, *The Hind and the Panther*

5. Try uttering the following longer sentences and triplets, if possible, on a single breath. However, if you do not succeed, be sure you pause for breath between phrases (breath groups).

a. He who would distinguish the true from the false must have
   an adequate idea of what is true and false.
   —BENEDICT SPINOZA, *Ethics*

b. The soft complaining flute,
   In dying notes, discovers
   The woes of hopeless lovers.
   —JOHN DRYDEN, *A Song for St. Cecelia's Day*

c. Music resembles poetry; in each
   Are nameless graces which no methods teach,
   And which a master-hand alone can reach.
   —ALEXANDER POPE, *Essay on Criticism*

d. Life is surely given us for higher purposes than to gather what
   our ancestors have wisely thrown away.
   —SAMUEL JOHNSON, *The Rambler*

Clavicular Breathing

Older readers, or readers who have had older teachers, may have been exposed to a type of breathing that emphasized movement of the upper part of the rib cage and the clavicles. It is difficult now to understand the rationale of this type of breathing for speech. If there was a rationale, it was somehow based on the belief that by expanding the least expandable part of the thoracic cavity, more space for air and, with deep breathing, more air could be brought into the lungs. With the additional hard-to-get quantity of air, better physical hygiene in general and better voice in particular were then supposed to be readily achieved. Now, with our understanding that it is not the amount of breath but the control of the breath stream that is important, any technique that emphasizes quantity of air is not held in high regard. Even if quantity of air were important, it could be more easily increased through deep breathing with abdominal and lower rib-cage activity than with clavicular breathing, which, at best, merely elevates the chest as a whole. In fact, clavicular breathing tends to be shallow rather than deep and requires more frequent inhalation than does abdominal breathing. Beyond this, clavicular breathing has definite disadvantages in that it has been found to be associated with a marked tendency of the muscles of the larynx and throat to become too tense for proper vocalization and reinforcement of tone.

To check on any tendency toward clavicular breathing, stand before a full-length mirror and breathe in deeply. Relax, then exhale fully. Repeat twice. Note, and correct, any tendency of the shoulders to be appreciably elevated or of the chest as a whole to be raised. Abdominal breathing, which we recommend, would call for little or no movement of the shoulders or upper chest. Movement, if it is to be discerned, would be of the lower chest and abdominal areas. Usually this will require a profile rather than a full-front view.

An added check, as well as an exercise to correct the tendency toward clavicular breathing, is the following: Place your hands on your chest with your fingers spread and the thumbs pointing toward the collarbone. Take a deep breath, then say the days of the week. Observe, and, if necessary, use the pressure of your hands to prevent any appreciable upward movement of the upper chest and shoulders. For variety, the exercise might be done with counting from one through ten or reciting the alphabet in sequences from *a* through *l* and *m* through *z*. If upper chest movement is inhibited, the normal compensatory action will bring about the desired movement of the abdominal and the lower chest muscles. Be certain that the movement is forward during inhalation and inward during exhalation.

Breathing and Phrasing

In the exercises to establish abdominal breathing and the awareness of breath control, our emphasis was on sustaining a sound, a series of words, or a sentence on a single breath. For ordinary conversational speech, and for most public speaking purposes, length of uninterrupted utterance is not as important as the interruption of a unit of thought because of the need for additional breath. The occasions are infrequent when a speaker will need to utter more than twelve to fifteen syllables on a single breath. The speaker must learn to anticipate inhalation and to stop at an appropriate point to inhale. If he learns this, he will avoid having to stop at an inappropriate point because he cannot continue speaking without another breath. The appropriate or natural stopping places are at the ends of units of thought, *between phrases or sentences.* Unless the speaker is reading or reciting verse with regular meter, the units of thought are likely to be of varying lengths. Breathing must therefore be adjusted to anticipated needs. For example, if the speaker cannot comfortably quote Emerson on a single breath to the effect that "His heart was as great as the world, but there was no room in it to hold the memory of a wrong," he has a choice of at least two stopping places. He may, without doing violence to the thought, stop at the places indicated by the vertical lines: "His heart was as great as the world || but there was no room in it || to hold the memory of a wrong." We might note, incidentally, that some but not all units of thought are marked off for us by punctuation. Some units of thought have no punctuation marks. The reader must, on the basis of meaning, decide where and whether to phrase. The good vocal phraser uses punctuation as a guide but is not a slave to it.

A speaker with a fair breath capacity and good breath control might easily go as far as the second vertical line before stopping for a breath. Unless he feels that he is equal to the entire sentence, however, he should not try to go beyond the second vertical line because to do so would mean interrupting a unit of thought in order to inhale.

In exercises (1)–(5) that immediately follow, possible stops for inhalation are indicated by vertical lines. In terms of your own breath capacity, mark off the places at which you plan to inhale. Inhale briefly at these places so that there is no suggestion of awkward pausing. Try to inhale as infrequently as possible so that the reading does not become jerky. Maintain abdominal control of breathing. If necessary, place your hands on the abdominal wall to feel the pushing away at the inhalations and the pulling in at the exhalations while reading aloud.

EXERCISES FOR ABDOMINAL BREATHING AND PHRASING

1.   Breathe in as you would for inhalation during casual conversation, then count at the rate of two numbers per second, pausing, and if necessary inhaling, at the marked places.

    1-2-3-4-5-6-7-8-9-10-11 || 12-13-14-15-16-17-18-19-20-21

The first grouping should have been produced easily on a single breath; the second would be somewhat more difficult because of the additional syllables.

2. Repeat as directed, but this time pause and renew your breath supply after fourteen; then count from fifteen through twenty-one.

3. Count as long as you can on a single deep breath, but avoid becoming uncomfortable either because of too deep an inhalation or too exhaustive an exhalation. Note the point at which you pause for breath. Then count again, but this time intentionally pause and inhale two numbers earlier in the sequence than you needed to pause the first time. Count again to the same number.

4. Recite the alphabet, pausing, and inhaling if necessary, only at the marked places. Be sure to pause if you do not need to inhale.

a-b-c-d-e-f-g-h || i-j-k-l-m-n-o-p-q || r-s-t-u-v-w-x-y-z

Were you able to go beyond the first group? With practice, the entire alphabet should be recited easily after a single, moderate inhalation.

5. Read the following sentences aloud, pausing, and breathing if necessary, at the marked places. In addition to the initial breath, it should not be necessary to inhale more than once for each sentence.

a. Sheridan advised that conscience || has no more to do with gallantry || than it has with politics.

b. A classic is something that everybody wants to have read || and nobody wants to read.
   —MARK TWAIN, *The Disappearance of Literature*

c. The more things a man is ashamed of || the more respectable he is.
   —GEORGE BERNARD SHAW, *Man and Superman*

d. Fear cannot be without hope || nor hope without fear.
   —BENEDICT SPINOZA, *Ethics*

6. In the following exercises, read the material aloud to determine where you need to stop for breath. Pause to indicate phrasing, but inhale only when you cannot go on comfortably to the next phrase on the remaining breath.

a. Lord Chesterfield recommended: "Never hold any one by the button or the hand in order to be heard out; for if people are unwilling to hear you, you had better hold your tongue than them."

b. "What a blessed thing it is," said Holmes, "that nature, when she invented, manufactured and patented her authors, contrived to make critics out of the chips that were left."

c. Oscar Wilde, who helped to make cynicism an English fashion, held that though education was an admirable thing it was well to remember from time to time that nothing that was worth knowing could really be taught. Perhaps what Wilde really meant was that what is worth knowing is what is left after the specifics we have been taught have been forgotten.

d.   Adam was but human—this explains it all. He did not want the apple for the apple's sake, he wanted it only because it was forbidden.

—MARK TWAIN, *Pudd'nhead Wilson*

e.   One will rarely err if extreme actions be ascribed to vanity, ordinary actions to habit, and mean actions to fear.

—FRIEDRICH NIETZSCHE, *Human, All Too Human*

f.   I am in the habit of looking not so much to the nature of a gift as to the spirit in which it is offered.

—ROBERT LOUIS STEVENSON, *New Arabian Nights*

Avoiding Waste of Breath

If while executing the exercises earlier in the chapter the reader had difficulty in counting up to fifteen on a single breath, it may have been that too much breath was wasted in the vocal effort. The most likely cause of wasted breath is a failure to bring the vocal bands close enough together to prevent leakage of air during vocalized speech efforts. Whispered or semiwhispered speech is necessarily wasteful of breath because then the vocal bands are kept fully or partially open. This may be noted in an examination of Figure 3–1, which shows the positions of the voice bands in quiet breathing, whispering, and vocalized speaking. In order to overcome breathiness, it will help first to become aware of a speech effort, which, by nature of the sounds employed, is necessarily breathy. The following sentences contain a number of voiceless fricative and plosive sounds that are normally and appropriately characterized by a breathy quality. Hold your palm turned inward, about six inches in front of your mouth, as you say:

1.   The humid air made the day sultry and uncomfortable.
2.   Peter and Paul enjoyed playing outside.
3.   The gray mist settled over the city and rested for the night.
4.   Sharon and Pam liked to window shop.

In contrast with these sentences, those that follow contain only voiced sounds and few that have a plosive quality. Say the following, again holding your hand in front of your mouth to feel the difference in breathiness.

1.   Dan will do all a man may do.
2.   Will was never ill.
3.   The boys ran around the bend.
4.   None knew the old man.

The following sentences contain a few sounds that are normally breathy. Try to say them with as little waste of breath as possible. Shorten

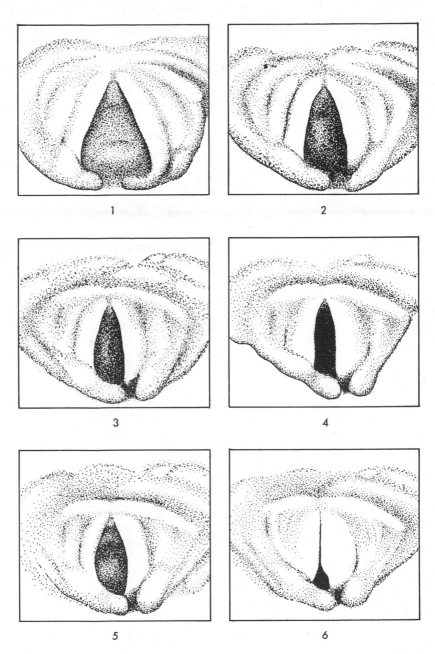

Figure 3–1 Diagrams based on high-speed photos showing changes in positions of vocal bands from quiet breathing (*1, 2*) to whispering (*3, 4, 5*) to vocalization (*6*).

all *f, v, th, s, z,* and *sh* sounds to reduce the length of these fricative-breath consonants. With good breath control, each sentence should require only a single inhalation.

1. Joseph Conrad observed that a fool should be made serviceable according to his folly.
2. Sometimes the spin-offs of inventions are worth more than the initially invented products.
3. The siren warned that a house was on fire.
4. The ship set out to sea despite the storm.
5. Goethe thought the man happy and wise who is able to appreciate the difference between his wishes and his powers.

Excessive breathiness may be a result of carrying over the aspirate quality of a sound to the succeeding vowel. This effect may be avoided, or reduced, by taking care not to prolong the aspirate sounds and to emphasize the full vocalization of the vowels and diphthongs. Special caution is necessary when the initial sound is an *h* as it is a particularly breath-consuming sound. With these thoughts in mind, try to say the following pairs of words so that there is no more aspiration on the vowel or diphthong of the second word of the pair than there is on the first. There should, of course, be no aspirate quality in the first word of each pair.

I	sigh	arm	farm
ale	pale	own	shown
oar	core	arc	park
air	fair	eel	wheel
ear	tear	mold	hold
add	fad	end	send
am	ham	will	fill
awe	saw	aid	shade

In each of the following sentences, emphasize the production of the vowel or diphthong sounds. Despite the temptation provided by initial aspirate sounds, avoid excessive carry-over of breathiness to the succeeding sounds.

1. Harry wished his friends health and happiness.
2. Hoping against hope is hoping still.
3. Paul hiked four miles through the forest.
4. People need not be poets to be impressed with the coming of spring.
5. George Eliot wrote that because a woman's hopes are woven of sunbeams, a shadow can quickly disperse them.
6. Goldsmith pointed out that people seldom improve when they simulate themselves.

7. Schlegel considers the historian to be a prophet who looks backwards.

8. Cicero held that it is fortune, not wisdom, that controls man's life.

9. Chesterfield wrote that style is the dress of thought.

10. Ben Franklin observed that pride that dines on vanity sups on contempt.

Affected or Imitative Breathiness

Many persons vocalize with a breathy quality out of choice. The choice is not always a conscious one. Frequently it has its beginning in imitation born of admiration of a popular figure. Often for adolescents and young adults the figure is a performer, a star of radio, screen, and television. So called "sultry-voiced" singers influence the vocal efforts of many high school and college adolescents who want to be sultry-voiced whether or not they can sing. Many young children have husky and breathy voices because of unconscious imitation of their mothers, and a few, perhaps, of their fathers. Unfortunately, excessive breathiness frequently has an adverse effect on the laryngeal mechanism as well as on the ability of the speaker to maintain as long a series of phrases or sentences as the nonbreathy speaker. The overall result is a vocal habit that loses its attractiveness in the postadolescent period. The breathy vocalizer then finds himself a fatigued speaker, and occasionally one with thickened vocal bands. If this becomes the case, then considerable vocal reeducation is in order. Good voice production is achieved with good breath control. With such control, clear rather than breathy quality should be established throughout the normal pitch range. Clear tones are produced with a minimum use of air for a maximum vocal effort. Clear vocal tones are economical for spent energy.

The following exercises are intended as a general review opportunity for the practice of breath control. In doing them, make certain (1) that there is no evidence of clavicular breathing; (2) that abdominal activity and lower chest activity characterize the breathing for vocalizations; (3) that inhalations are correlated with units of meaning; and (4) that there is no waste of breath at pauses for phrasing when there is no need for inhalation, or because of excessive aspiration on specific speech sounds, or as a characteristic of the vocal effort as a whole.

EXERCISES FOR PRACTICE OF BREATH CONTROL

1. If men and women are to understand each other, to enter into each other's nature with mutual sympathy, and to become capable of genuine comradeship, the foundation must be laid in youth.

—HAVELOCK ELLIS, *The Task of Social Hygiene*

2.   Training is everything. The peach was once a bitter almond; cauliflower is nothing but cabbage with a college education.

—MARK TWAIN, *Pudd'nhead Wilson*

3.   Laughter is not at all a bad beginning for a friendship, and it is far the best ending for one.

—OSCAR WILDE, *The Picture of Dorian Gray*

4.   A man's real life is that accorded to him in the thoughts of other men by reason of respect or natural love.

—JOSEPH CONRAD, *Under Western Eyes*

5.   Horace Mann considered that the telling of truth was a serious responsibility. He advised, "You need not tell all the truth, unless to those who have a right to know it all. But let all you tell be truth."

6.   Were we deprived of the power to choose,
We should in fact our very being lose;
Machines we would be by the Almighty wrought,
Curious automatons endowed with thought.

—VOLTAIRE, *On Liberty*

CHAPTER 4

Production of Clear Tones

Voice, we now realize, is a product of integrated muscular activity. The combination of tendinous tissue and muscles that constitute the vocal bands is set into vibration as a result of integrated activity of the muscles of respiration and those controlling laryngeal action. When the integration is right and the approximated vocal bands are brought together closely enough so that there is sufficient resistance to the column of air being forced up from the lungs, voice is produced. When the vocal bands are not approximated so that there is adequate resistance to the column of air, then the result is either a semivocalized effort or unvocalized breathing, depending upon the degree of approximation (see Figure 3–1). Our immediate concern is to establish the concept and technique for the initiation of good, clear tones.[1]

Good tones are free from the effects of tension or strain. Good tones are initiated with ease, appropriately reinforced by the resonating cavities, and sustained with ease. Tonal (vocal) impurities result most frequently from tensions of the muscles of the throat and neck that interfere with the free action of the muscles of the larynx, and so of the vocal bands. Tonal impurities may arise indirectly from incorrect breathing habits, which, we recall, may be associated with laryngeal tension. Tonal impurities may also be caused by inappropriate resonance.

---

[1] Tone as used in this chapter refers to *vocal tone*—the vocal product considered with reference to its attributes of quality, pitch, and loudness.

51

In the absence of any structural defect of the voice-producing mechanism, a defect of hearing that makes vocal monitoring difficult, or any emotional disturbance associated with either excessive or inadequate muscular tonicity, reasonably good vocal tones should be possible for all speakers. Some speakers, we realize, will have mechanisms whose parts are so well combined that they have excellent voices without effort or training. Others may not be so fortunate in the structure of their vocal mechanisms. For them, effort and training are necessary to make the most of their vocal instruments. Our concern is to suggest how we can use what we have so that, without too much effort, most of us will be able to initiate and sustain good vocal tones.

INITIATION OF TONE

To initiate and maintain good tone, the vocal mechanism must be *ready for vocalization*. Readiness implies anticipation and preparation. For voice production, this means that the vocal bands must be aligned (approximated) a moment before the column of air is forced up from the lungs to set them into action. If the column of air precedes the approximation of the vocal bands, then the vocal product will begin with a whisper or an unvocalized breath. The vocal bands must be tense enough to set up resistance to the column of air, but not so tense as to be fully successful in their resistance. With excessive tension (hypertension), the vocal bands may not be able to vibrate. With a lack of sufficient tension (hypotension), vibration may take place, but with an accompanying air leakage or breathiness.[2] What is needed is sufficient tension to require a forceful, sustained column of air to set and maintain the vocal bands in action. In brief, the tension should be just enough to permit the sustained column of air to produce an even fluttering of the vocal bands (see discussion in Chapter 2). Although voice can be produced even though the laryngeal tensions become excessive, the vocal tones become strained and generally unpleasant.

The exercises that follow will help to establish awareness of *proper laryngeal tension* as well as *readiness for vocalization*.

EXERCISES FOR DEVELOPING READINESS TO VOCALIZE

1. Contract the throat muscles as you would to swallow some food or water. Note the sensation of the contracted muscles. Now open your mouth as if to produce a gentle *ah* sound. Do your throat muscles feel more or less tense than they did when you pretended to swallow? Unless they are more relaxed than for swallowing, they are likely to be too tense

---

[2] Review the discussion on breathing for avoidance of breathiness (pages 46–49).

for the initiation of a good tone. Note the sensation of the contracted muscles so that you will know what to avoid. Be sure that your *ah* production is gentle and sustained.

2. *Yawn gently* with your mouth half open. Breathe in and out through your mouth. Note the feeling of air in the back of the throat. Now swallow, and contrast the easy breathing sensations with those in swallowing. If the yawning is gentle and the breathing easy, your throat muscles should be relaxed. This is the state of muscle tonus needed for vocalization.

3. Sit comfortably in a chair with your feet flat on the floor. Permit your head to drop to your chest as if your head were a dead weight. Yawn gently and then breathe in and out three or four times through your mouth. Note the sensation. Now swallow, and again contrast the tonus of the throat muscles in swallowing with that in gentle yawning. Repeat the gentle yawning and easy mouth breathing until the sensation of relaxed throat muscles is fixed in your mind.

4. Stand erect but at ease. Repeat exercise (3) in a standing position.

5. In a standing position, with the throat muscles relaxed, say the *vowels* only of the following words, each to a slow count of from one to three: *alms, all, Alps, ooze, eel.* Now vocalize from one vowel to the next without interruption. You should be able to note somewhat increased throat and laryngeal tension for the vowels of *ooze* and *eel* compared with those of *alms, all,* and *Alps.* This is proper if the different vowel values are to be produced. Try, however, to avoid excessive tension.

6. Get ready to say *all* but do not produce any sound until your mouth is open and shaped for the vowel of *all.* Then produce the word. Now, by contrast, intentionally begin vocalizing *before your mouth is open* and you are set to articulate the word *all.* Did you hear or feel a difference? Unless your vocal habits are so good that you could not follow a direction to do the wrong thing, the first effort should have been clearer and easier than the second. The second effort might have been characterized by initial tension and possibly by a "click" in the larynx.

7. Repeat the first half of exercise (1) with three to four successive utterances of the words *one, my, ah,* and *eel.* For each word, produce the successive utterance without intervening pauses. Check for initial tension or laryngeal click at the initiation of the effort. If your timing is right and you are prepared to vocalize before you set your vocal folds into vibration, the tone should be clear.

8. Open your mouth as though for a gentle yawn, but instead of yawning say *ha, how, ho, ha, haw, ho.* Next, try the sentence *Who am I?* These efforts should begin with some breathiness for the words that begin with an *h* sound, but the breath should not be noticeably carried over to the vowel that follows. Be sure that you maintain a relaxed throat throughout the exercise.

9. With a relaxed throat, count from one to ten, emphasizing the

activity of the lips and tongue. Try to become aware of oral activity in the *front of your mouth*. Now, count from one to twenty. Do not force your exhalation beyond a point of comfort. If you note any tendency to tighten the throat muscles, it may be because you are attempting too much speech on a single exhalation. Pause to inhale before excessive tension sets in.

10. Say the alphabet while emphasizing activity in the front of the mouth. Do not attempt to go beyond the letter *k* on your first attempt. On successive attempts go as far as you can in the alphabet up to the point of laryngeal or throat tension. You may note a feeling of lip fatigue. If so, it is likely that you do not habitually articulate with sufficient activity at the front of the mouth. With practice, the feeling of fatigue should disappear.

11.   Read the following materials aloud, always maintaining a relaxed throat. Make certain that you are *set for vocalization* before you begin to speak. If at any time your throat muscles become tense, or you become aware of laryngeal tension, return to exercises (1)–(8).

    a.   Only in men's imagination does every truth find an effective and undeniable existence.

                —JOSEPH CONRAD, *A Personal Record*

    b.   To travel hopefully is a better thing than to arrive.

                —ROBERT LOUIS STEVENSON, *El Dorado*

    c.   Liberty, like charity, must begin at home.

                —JAMES BRYANT CONANT, *Our Unique Heritage*

    d.   The snow fell softly in the quiet air.

    e.   Andrew was unfortunately not inclined to let facts get in the way of his opinions.

    f.   But what am I?
        An infant crying in the night:
        An infant crying for the light:
    And with no language but a cry.

                —ALFRED, LORD TENNYSON, *In Memoriam*

    g.   Although I enter not,
       Yet round about the spot
          Oftimes I hover:
       And near the sacred gate,
       With longing eyes I wait,
          Expectant of her.

         —WILLIAM MAKEPEACE THACKERAY, *At the Church Gate*

    h.   I have had playmates, I have had companions,
       In my days of childhood, in my joyful schooldays,
       All, all are gone, the old familiar faces.

             —CHARLES LAMB, *The Old Familiar Faces*

    i.   It is true, I never assisted the sun materially in his rising; but doubt not, it was of the last importance only to be present at it.

—HENRY DAVID THOREAU, *Walden*

j. Biographies are but the clothes and buttons of the man—the biography of the man himself cannot be written.

—MARK TWAIN, *Autobiography*

k. What cannot be removed, becomes lighter through patience.

—HORACE, *Odes*

AVOIDANCE OF GLOTTAL INITIATION

The chapter opened with the statement that voice is a product of integrated muscular activity. Integration, of course, implies synchronization—timing necessary to produce the desired vocal result. The "glottal attack" or "glottal catch," unless intentionally produced, is a manifestation and product of poor synchronization. Basically, phonation characterized by "glottal catch" results from excessive tension of the laryngeal muscles that in turn requires more than the normal amount of energy to provide the breath pressure to set the vocal bands into motion. The result of this combination of factors is that the vocal bands are violently blown apart, producing the "catch" or "click" instead of the even phonation that is associated with "flutter" action. Van Riper and Irwin describe glottal initiation as follows:

> In this, the "glottal" catch (glottal stroke, coupe de glotte), the vocal folds (and often the ventricular folds) are brought together and strongly tightened *prior* to the starting of the chest pulse of air pressure. The normal synchrony of timing is thus disturbed . . . , and the vocal cords are very suddenly blown widely apart. Phonation occurs more abruptly than ever . . . and strident voices may result.[3]

From this description it should be clear that unless the vocal bands are somewhat relaxed, or at least not excessively tense, and phonation is initiated in time to set the bands into flutter activity, vocal efforts may start with a click or coughlike blast. Except when glottalization is an accepted characteristic of the speech of a national or cultural group—as it is among the Scots voice accompanied by glottal clicks strongly suggests that the speaker's throat and larynx are hypertense and under strain. Added evidence of this condition is the presence of a high, narrow pitch range.

[3] C. Van Riper and J. V. Irwin, *Voice and Articulation* (Englewood Cliffs, N.J.: Prentice-Hall, Inc., 1958), p. 303.

Glottal attacks are most likely to occur at the beginning of sentences or phrases with initial vowels. Some speakers, however, glottalize on almost all initial voiced sounds. The overall result tends to be detrimental to the speaker and unpleasant to listeners for whom glottalization is not an accepted speech characteristic.

For readers who are still uncertain about their tendency to initiate vocalization with a glottal attack, the following added explanation should illustrate what should generally be avoided. A glottal stop noise is normally and appropriately produced when you clear your throat with a light, unvocalized cough. You can feel this stroke, click, or flapping of the vocal bands by gently placing your thumb and index finger just below the Adam's apple as you cough. If voice is added to the light cough, the result is likely to be the production of an *ugh* sound.

Vocal Fry

Another type of "glottal voice," one characterized by a low pitch, and glottal clicking has been designated by voice scientists as *vocal fry*. Moore presents a succinct description of vocal fry.

> This voice quality is distinctive for its repetitive popping or ticking sound. The vocal pitch is always extremely low and the frequency of the pulses that produce the popping characteristic may become slow enough to be heard as separate vocal pops or ticks. Breath noises are weak or absent with this type of voice, and it usually cannot be produced loudly or with the normal phonatory breath flow. The characteristic low frequency range of vocal fry sound and its presence in most voices at the extended low portion of the total vocal range has caused it to be considered by some as a vocal register. If an individual uses this type of voice frequently, it can be classified as functionally deviant in the same sense that persistent use of the falsetto is so classified.[4]

The exercises to establish proper laryngeal tension, readiness for vocalization, and easy initiation of tones should be reviewed by readers who have a tendency to initiate voice with a glottal attack. In addition, the following exercises should be of help.

EXERCISES FOR OVERCOMING GLOTTAL PHONATION

1. Produce the sound *aw* as in *awful* with intentional breathiness (semiwhisper). Repeat, prolonging the *aw* for the equivalent of a count of six. Decrease the breathiness so that on the final two counts the *aw* is

---

[4] G. Paul Moore, *Organic Voice Disorders* (Englewood Cliffs, N.J.: Prentice-Hall, Inc., 1971), pp. 8–9.

fully vocalized. Maintain a relaxed throat so that there is neither glottal initiation nor tension as vocalization increases.

2.   Repeat exercise (1), using the vowels of *alms, ooze, ohms, any* and *ease*. Be especially careful that on the last vowel there is no excessive strain or glottal "explosion."

3.   Try to say each of the following words without initial glottalization. If you note a glottal attack, prefix a lengthened *h* before each of the words, and move from the *h* to the word without increasing the laryngeal tension and without glottalization.

inch	arm	ohm	ale	eat	easy
instant	asp	own	at	am	east
only	all	ill	ace	and	aster

4.   Repeat exercise (3), prefixing the sound *m* if there is any tendency to a glottal attack. Repeat with an initial *n*.

5.   Try each of the following sentences, being especially careful to avoid glottalization on the initial vowels. Words that begin with vowels *within a phrase* should be pronounced as though they were actually linked or blended to the last sound of the preceding word. The sounds that are most likely to be glottalized are in italics.

   a.   Andrew *enjoyed all active* sports.
   b.   *Every* man must *at* one time *inhabit* his *own island*.
   c.   Edward *enjoyed* cakes *and ale*.
   d.   *An ohm is a unit of electrical* resistance.
   e.   *It is easy* to grow *asters in* the *east*.

6.   The following phrases may be somewhat more difficult because they contain many normally tense vowels in initial positions and so provide opportunities for glottal initiation. If you initiate the vocalization with just enough tension for the proper articulation of the vowel, but with no more than that much tension, the glottal shock should be avoided.

easy access	apt and alert
up and over	apprehensive attitudes
every opportunity	insistent inclination
each event	esoteric antics
in every instance	anxious acts
any avenue	alien enemy

7.   The following selections offer opportunity for additional practice.

   a.   There is a feeling of Eternity in youth, which makes us amends for everything. To be young is to be as one of the Immortal Gods.
       —WILLIAM HAZLITT, *The Feeling of Eternity in Youth*

   b.   Inconsistencies of opinion, arising from changes of circum-
       stances, are often justifiable.
                                  —DANIEL WEBSTER, Speech, July 25, 1846
   c.   History is the essence of innumerable biographies.
                                  —THOMAS CARLYLE, *On History*
   d.   I am in earnest. I will not equivocate; I will not excuse; I will
       not retreat a single inch; and I will be heard.
                         —WILLIAM LLOYD GARRISON, Speech, January 1831
   e.   A hen is only an egg's way of making another egg.
                              —SAMUEL BUTLER, *The Way of All Flesh*

The Glottal Stop As an Articulatory Fault

Although many persons initiate voice without a glottal attack, they
may have a glottal quality in their speech because of an articulatory habit.
The habit or fault is one of substituting a glottal grunt or click for a *t* or
a *d* in words in which either of these sounds is followed by an *l* or an *n*.
This sound substitution is considered in somewhat greater detail in our
discussion of specific sound improvement. For the present, the reader
should test himself on the list of words and the verse that follow. If he
can feel or hear himself produce a glottal explosive for the *t* or *d* on more
than one or two of the words, he should make a special effort to articulate
a clear but light and not exaggerated *t* or *d* to avoid giving his speech
an overall glottal quality.

bottle	fettle	button	ladle
kettle	rattle	mutton	paddle
settle	written	patent	saddle
metal	bitten	mountain	hidden
little	subtle	kitten	nettle

Tender-handed stroke a nettle,
   And it stings you for your pains:
Grasp it like a man of mettle,
   And it soft as silk remains.
           —AARON HILL, *Verses Written on a Window in Scotland*

CHAPTER 5

Making Yourself Heard

Adequate loudness, as was previously pointed out, is an essential attribute of an effective voice. For most of us, adequate loudness usually means being easily heard in conversational situations. Sometimes it means competing with environmental noises, both human and mechanical. Occasionally, however, we must speak to a group in a physical setting that demands louder than normal conversational voice. Sometimes we must speak under conditions that demand more loudness than is ordinarily needed. We may, for example, have to yell a warning, issue a command, or address a large group without the assistance of an electronic amplifier.

CONTROL OF LOUDNESS

Loudness is best regulated through breathing control. One way to speak loudly is to increase the energy with which the breath sets the vocal bands into vibration. The greater the amplitude (the more extensive the swing of the vocal bands) the louder is the vocal tone. In addition, loudness is also related to the way our resonating cavities reinforce our vocal tones. It usually requires less energy than we think to vocalize loudly enough to be readily heard.

If we recognize that the vocal attribute we think of as loudness is a result of the amplitude or swing of the vocal bands and the amount of reinforcement afforded the initiated tone by the resonating cavities acting as reinforcers, we will not overstress the amount of force or energy it takes to speak as loudly as the occasion requires. The danger in using added energetic action to produce loud tones is that it may result in pharyngeal and laryngeal strain. The effect of such strain is to reduce the efficiency of the cavities of the pharynx and larynx as reinforcing cavities. As a result, the vocal tones are less loud than they might otherwise be. In carrying out the suggestions for increasing loudness, the reader should avoid increasing tensions of the larynx or of the throat. In addition to the physical feeling of strain, listen for elevation of pitch. If your vocal tones are higher in pitch than normal, the muscles (walls) of your resonating cavities are probably excessively tense.

To understand the change in action of the abdominal wall for loud vocalization, place your hands on the abdomen and shout aloud, "All out!" You will (or should be able to) note that there is a sudden pulling in of the abdominal muscles and that the pulling in is greater than for normal conversation. If this does not occur, and you are not readily able to speak as loudly as you would like to and should reasonably expect to, then the following exercises should be of help in establishing adequate loudness.

EXERCISES FOR DEVELOPING ADEQUATE LOUDNESS

1. Review the exercises for proper breath control (see Chapter 3). This should create an awareness of abdominal action established for conversational voice needs.

2. Place your hands on the abdomen and say *ah* as you might for a throat examination. Then take a moderately deep but comfortable breath and again begin to say *ah*. This time apply pressure suddenly with your hands. The tone should increase in loudness. If you have not caught yourself by surprise, and exhaled without vocalization, the *ah* should have become appreciably louder. Whether or not you have caught yourself by surprise, repeat the exercise and produce a loud *ah*.

3. Repeat exercise (2), producing three loud *ah*'s without straining. Breathe in if necessary after each *ah*. Lould voice production requires more breath than normal conversation, so that more frequently inhalation becomes necessary to maintain a loud voice without strain. Try again, this time with *aw*.

4. Repeat, except this time exert direct control over the abdominal muscles as you produce your loud *ah*'s and *aw*'s.

5. Say the following short commands, each on a single breath, without strain and without an elevation of pitch level toward the end of the phrase.

    a. We're ready!
    b. Time out!

    c. You go!
    d. Stop him!
    e. Look lively!
    f. Give him a hand.
    g. Lower away!
    h. Let him go!
    i. Turn around.
    j. Silence, please!

6. Try the following sentences on a single breath if possible. Speak as if there were a need to use a loud voice to assert yourself.

    a. No, this will not do.
    b. Let's waste no more time.
    c. Certainly, I meant what I said.
    d. Old fellow, just pack up and go.
    e. We'll talk about this matter later.

The following exercises are intended to help in the building up and control of degrees of loudness rather than in the sudden production of loud voice. Such practice is closer to the normal use of loudness for emphasis and vocal variety in speaking.

EXERCISES FOR CONTROLLING LOUDNESS

1. Initiate an *ah* in a tone that is barely audible; gradually increase the loudness of the *ah* until it is louder than your usually conversational voice, and then reduce the loudness until the tone is again barely audible. Do not change the pitch or force the length of exhalation beyond a point of comfort.

2. Count from one to five increasing the loudness on each number. Begin with a barely audible *one* and end with a *five* that can easily be heard across a forty-foot room.

3. Count to seven, increasing the loudness up to *four* and then decreasing loudness from *five* through *seven*. Maintain the same pitch level throughout the count.

4. Say each of the following phrases or sentences three times, increasing loudness from a normal conversational level to one that can easily be heard across a forty-foot room.

    a. I'll go!
    b. Come back!
    c. Please!
    d. No!
    e. I won't!
    f. Enough!
    g. Who's there?

5. Lengthen the vowel in each of the following words and maintain uniform loudness throughout the lengthened production of the vowel. Do not, however, distort the vowel by excessive lengthening.

alms	gnaw
bomb	thaw
father	walk
pause	tall
awe	mall

6. Lengthen and maintain the force for the vowels or diphthongs of the stressed syllables in the following phrases. Again, avoid distorting the vowel or diphthong to a point where a listener would not be certain of the words you are saying.

go away	stark madness
loud laughter	hearty applause
come on time	honest and true
almost always	large house
bounce the ball	ardent author
worthy cause	gone yonder

7. Read each of the following sentences, first in an ordinary conversational tone and then as if you were trying to address a person in the tenth row of a crowded room.

    a. Are you there, Tom?
    b. I'll go in a few minutes.
    c. The hour is now.
    d. I'll say this for the last time.
    e. Listen if you wish to understand.
    f. Are you John Jones?
    g. Who is that man?

Strengthening the Voice

Our discussion of loudness has thus far been based on the assumption that the speaker could make himself heard under normal conditions but might be in need of help to make himself readily heard under difficult conditions. Occasionally, however, we find persons whose habitual loudness levels are too weak for easy hearing even under relatively good speaking conditions. Such speakers need help to be heard even in quiet conversation.

In some instances, the cause of a weak voice is physical and may be attributed to a structural disturbance or anomaly of the vocal mechanism. Such instances are comparatively rare and require specialized treatment rather than self-help to improve the voice as much as possible. Sometimes a weak voice is a carry-over from a physical state during sickness or the subsequent period of convalescence. A sick person may not have the energy to make himself heard, and in the early stages of recovery he may not care whether or not he can be heard. When the patient is finally well enough to care, he may somehow decide that perhaps making others strain to hear him is not without advantage. So a habit of weak vocalization may persist. There is also a possibility that as a child the speaker was brought up in a home with an ill relative, or a crotchety one who believed that children should be seen, if necessary, but were not ordinarily worthy of being heard. The barely audible voice may then have become the safer one, the one that did not bring isolation or a scolding.

Occasionally, the weak or barely audible voice characterizes the individual who feels that what he has to say is unworthy of a listener or that as a speaker he lacks value. His weak sounds may be interpreted as apologetic noises or noises that are produced because he feels a social need to say something but at the same time fears that if he is heard he may be held responsible for what he says.

Such physical and mental conditions, however, are not the usual causes of weak voice. Much more frequently, a weak voice is the result of poor vocal habits such as poor breath control, habitual breathiness, excessive tension of the vocal mechanism, inappropriate pitch, or improper use of the resonating cavities to reinforce vocal tones. If the reader has no reason to believe that there is anything physically wrong with his vocal apparatus, if he is not longing for the advantages and immunities of the sickbed or the attentions associated with his convalescence, if he is a reasonably well-adjusted person, audible voice should be his for the trying.

The earlier discussion on how to control loudness through breath control obviously holds for the person with a weak voice. In addition, the following exercises should be of help.

EXERCISES FOR STRENGTHENING A WEAK VOICE

1. Drop your jaw for a gentle but open-mouthed yawn. Inhale with your mouth open, and then pull in slowly but firmly on the abdominal muscles. Now permit a yawn to escape as you exhale as a "by-product" of the position of mouth and the controlled breathing.

2. Repeat exercise (1) five times, making the yawn louder each time but maintaining the same pitch.

3. Now, instead of yawning, prepare to say *aw* as in *awful*. Maintain an even pitch. Repeat five times.

4. Repeat exercise (3), but this time with the sound *oh*.

5. Say *oh* as follows: (*a*) as if surprised, (*b*) as if horrified, (*c*) as if pleased, and (*d*) as if you are shouting a warning.

6. Pretend you are imitating a siren on a fire truck, increasing and decreasing the loudness of your voice on the sound *oh*. Repeat, using the

sound *aw*. Avoid any feeling of tension of the throat or larynx, and do not extend the length of vocalization to a point of discomfort.

7. Imagine yourself a drill sergeant and give your platoon the following orders.

    a.   Forward, *march!*
    b.   Platoon, *halt!*
    c.   About *face!*
    d.   At *ease!*
    e.   To the rear, *march!*
    f.   Fall *out!*

8. Count from one through five, increasing the loudness on each count but maintaining the same pitch level. Repeat three times.

9. Practice each of the following in a voice loud enough to be readily heard across the length of your living room.

    a.   Blow, blow, thou winter wind,
        Thou art not so unkind
          As man's ingratitude:
        Thy tooth is not so keen,
        Because thou art not seen,
          Although thy breath is rude.
                —WILLIAM SHAKESPEARE, *As You Like It*

    b.   Out of the night that covers me,
          Black as the Pit from pole to pole,
        I thank whatever gods may be
          For my unconquerable soul.
                —WILLIAM E. HENLEY, *Invictus*

    c.   Give me your tired, your poor,
        Your huddled masses yearning to breathe free,
        The wretched refuse of your teeming shore,
        Send these, the homeless, tempest-tossed, to me:
        I lift my lamp beside the golden door.
                —EMMA LAZARUS, *The New Colossus*

    d.   Give a man a horse he can ride,
          Give a man a boat he can sail;
        And his rank and wealth, his strength and health
          On sea nor shore shall fail.
                —JAMES THOMSON, *Gifts*

    e.   And we are here as on a darkling plain
        Swept with confused alarms of struggle and flight,
          Where ignorant armies clash by night.
                —MATTHEW ARNOLD, *Dover Beach*

    f.   Roll on, thou deep and dark blue Ocean—roll!
        Ten thousand fleets sweep over thee in vain;

Man marks the earth with ruin—his control
Stops with the shore;
> —GEORGE GORDON, LORD BYRON, *Childe Harold's Pilgrimage*

g. If a word
Our orators let fall, save what pertains
To peace, I'll raise a storm of words, and rain
A very tempest of abuse upon them!
> —ARISTOPHANES, *The Acharnians*

h. Let the great world spin forever down the ringing
grooves of change.
> —ALFRED, LORD TENNYSON, *Locksley Hall*

i. He flung himself from the room, flung himself upon his
horse and rode madly off in all directions.
> —STEPHEN LEACOCK, *Gertrude the Governess*

j. Shrill and high, newsboys cry
The worst of the city's infamy
> —WILLIAM VAUGHN MOODY, *In New York*

k. Lay on, Macduff
And damn'd be him, that first cries,
"Hold, enough!"
> —WILLIAM SHAKESPEARE, *Macbeth*

l. Pour the sweet milk of concord into hell,
Uproar the universal peace, confound
All unity on earth.
> —WILLIAM SHAKESPEARE, *Macbeth*

m. "My name is Ozymandias, King of Kings.
Look on my works, ye Mighty, and despair!"
> —PERCY BYSSHE SHELLEY, *Ozymandias*

n. The cataract strong
Then plunges along,
Striking and raging
As if a war waging
Its caverns and rocks among—
> —ROBERT SOUTHEY, *The Cataract of Lodore*

10. If you have no difficulty making yourself heard across your living room, try the same selections again but this time pretend that your room is forty feet long and as many feet wide. If you are successful in this exercise, then repeat the selections as if you were addressing an audience from the stage of a moderate-sized theater.

11. Read the following as if you were addressing four hundred persons waiting for your announcements in an auditorium that has no public address system.

a. The meeting is adjourned. Return in two hours.
b. Tomorrow's meeting will begin at 9 A.M.

    c.   Refreshments will be served in the recreation hall.
    d.   John Smith is the winner.
    e.   There will be no school tomorrow.
    f.   Please leave by the nearest exit.

FORCE

In our earlier discussion of loudness and force (breath-energy), we emphasized the production of voice so that it would be readily audible in varying speaking situations. At this time we assume that the speaker has no problem in generating and controlling the necessary force to produce vocal tones at appropriate loudness levels. The speaker is able to make adjustments in force for situations that include intimate small group conversations as well as meeting the demands of a public audience. The speaker is now concerned with more subtle matters relative to controlling force so that appropriate changes in vocal levels will provide color and meaning to what he wishes to say.

Syllable Stress

Differential syllable stress is a feature of English speech. We use differential stress or accent in the pronunciation of polysyllabic words so that "normally" a word such as *rainy* or *beautiful* would be uttered with primary stress or accent on the first syllable. In the word *beautiful* a secondary stress may be heard on the final syllable. In a word such as *unkind,* the "normal" syllable stress is on the second syllable. In some contexts, however, a speaker may intentionally stress the first syllable of the word *unkind* to communicate his meaning; for example, "Yes, he certainly is an *unkind* man." Syllable stress for polysyllabic words is characterized by increased force or loudness associated with relatively longer duration and higher pitch than for the unstressed syllables of the words.

Some words differ in parts of speech, and so in meaning, according to their syllable stress. What are the differences in meaning for the following words when the accent or syllable stress is shifted from the first to the second syllable?

*con*duct	con*duct*
*con*vert	con*vert*
*con*vict	con*vict*
*di*gest	di*gest*
*dis*charge	dis*charge*
*ex*tract	ex*tract*
*fre*quent	fre*quent*
*ob*ject	ob*ject*

*per*mit	per*mit*
*pro*duce	pro*duce*
*re*bel	re*bel*
*sur*vey	sur*vey*

Stress in Compound Words

In general, compound words differ from polysyllabic words in stress.[1] For compounds, the stress is "normally" equal or almost so for each of the components. Compounds are similarly distinguished in stress from the components of the compound by relatively equal stress for the two parts of the former. Thus we may distinguish the meaning of "Jack is in the white house" from "Jack is in the Whitehouse," or "After a half hour of fishing, I hauled in a weak fish" from "After a half hour of fishing, I hauled in a weakfish."

Indicate the differences in meaning for the following comopunds and the paired words by incorporating them into sentences—e.g., "Joe made the doorstop" and "Joe made the door stop." Besides differences in stress, what other vocal feature do you detect in the utterances of the compound words as distinguished from the sequence of words that comprise the compound?

birthday	birth day
blowout	blow out
bluebell	blue bell
breakthrough	break through
campground	camp ground
greenhouse	green house
hideout	hide out
Irishman	Irish man
lightmeter	light meter
middleman	middle man
paperback	paper back
sometime	some time

How do you determine the meaning of the following pairs of sentences?

---

[1] Although many compound words suggest a single concept formed by the "wedding" of the two component words of the compound so that a distinction may be made between a *blackfish* and a *black fish*, this semantic feature is by no means consistent. For reasons other than semantic, some unfortunate persons may have *kidney stones* while others have *gallstones*.

Also, for reasons that are not readily apparent, the morpheme *still* has several contextual variations. It is a separate word in *still hunt* (a noun, meaning a hunt for game carried on stealthily) but is hyphenated in the verb *still-hunt* (to pursue by a still hunt). However, in the noun form *still life*, there is no hyphen. *The American College Dictionary* (New York: Random House, Inc., 1958).

Hilary was a lighthouse keeper.
Hilary was a light housekeeper.

Sue spent considerable time in the greenhouse.
Sue spent considerable time in the green house.

Tom enjoyed being a middleman.
Tom enjoyed being a middle man.

Variety

Except for public speaking situations in which the speaker does not
have the help of amplification, large differences in force are rarely necessary. Change in the use of loudness rather than in the amount of degree
of loudness is the factor of variety which permits the speaker to give
importance to one idea and to subordinate other related ideas. A desired
effect in giving special meaning is sometimes better achieved when the
significant words are spoken with reduced rather than increased loudness,
as in the sentence, "Please, my love, be still." If the words *be still* are
spoken so that they are barely audible, they are given more complete
meaning than might otherwise be possible.

Change in loudness may be used to achieve dramatic as well as subtle,
intellectual effects. A deliberate, degree-by-degree increase in loudness
from a low to a high level helps to produce a dramatic effect. A reduction from a moderately high to a low level may also be dramatic as well
as sophisticated providing *the content is worthy of the technique.*

EXERCISES FOR CHANGE IN LOUDNESS

1. Read the following sentences, changing the stress from the first
word of the sentence to each succeeding word. Do not, however, stress
articles, conjunctions, or prepositions. How do the meanings of the sentences change with the differences in word stress?

    a.   John said that he and I will go.
    b.   Ted was poor but honest.
    c.   One or the other must leave.
    d.   Mary is quite fond of Bill.
    e.   Is he the man you said you like?
    f.   What is your answer now?
    g.   This at last is your reward.
    h.   Joe is indeed a brilliant fellow.
    i.   We thought he had returned.
    j.   He will not be long for this world.
    k.   Thursday was the day of reckoning.
    l.   She and she alone can do anything.
    m.   Fred was almost run down.

2. Read sentences (*a*), (*b*), and (*c*) of exercise (1) stressing the conjunction. What are the changes in meaning?

3. Use controlled and moderate changes in stress to bring out the flavor and meaning of the wit and wisdom of the following items from Benjamin Franklin's *Poor Richard's Almanac*.

    a. The worst wheel of the cart makes the most noise.

    b. Genius without education is like silver in the mine.

    c. He that would live in peace and at ease, must not speak all he knows, nor judge all he sees.

    d. A man in a passion rides a mad horse.

    e. None but the well-bred man knows how to confess a fault, or acknowledge himself in an error.

    f. Seven wealthy towns contend for Homer dead,
Thro' which the living Homer beg'd his bread.

4. The same approach—the use of controlled and moderate changes in stress—should be used in bringing out the essential meanings of the following passages.

    a. What I must do is all that concerns me, not what the people think. This rule, equally arduous in actual and intellectual life, may serve for the whole distinction between greatness and meanness. It is the harder because you will always find those who think they know what is your duty better than you know it. It is easy in the world to live after the world's opinion; it is easy in solitude to live after our own; but the great man is he who in the midst of the crowd keeps with perfect sweetness the independence of solitude.
            —RALPH WALDO EMERSON, *Self-Reliance*

    b. He may as well concern himself with his shadow on the wall. Speak what you think now in hard words and tomorrow speak what tomorrow thinks in hard words again, though it contradict everything you said today—"Ah, so you shall be sure to be misunderstood."—Is it so bad, then, to be misunderstood? Pythagoras was misunderstood, and Socrates, and Jesus, and Luther, and Copernicus, and Galileo, and Newton, and every pure and wise spirit that ever took flesh. To be great is to be misunderstood . . .
            —RALPH WALDO EMERSON, *Essays*

    c. More important than winning the election, is governing the nation. That is the test of a political party—the acid, final test.
            —ADLAI STEVENSON, *Speech accepting nomination,*
            July 20, 1952.

    d. If a man has a talent and cannot use it, he has failed. If he has a talent and uses only half of it, he has partly failed. If he has a talent and learns somehow to use the whole of it, he has gloriously succeeded, and won a satisfaction and a triumph few men ever know.

—THOMAS WOLFE, *The Web and the Rock*

5. Use more marked changes in stress to communicate the meanings of the following passages:

a. Four freedoms: The first is freedom of speech and expression —everywhere in the world. The second is freedom of every person to worship God in his own way—everywhere in the world. The third is freedom from want—everywhere in the world. The fourth is freedom from fear—anywhere in the world.

—FRANKLIN D. ROOSEVELT, *Message to Congress*, January 1941.

b. We, too, born to freedom, and believing in freedom, are willing to fight to maintain freedom. We, and all others who believe as deeply as we do, would rather die on our feet than live on our knees.

—FRANKLIN D. ROOSEVELT, *Speech, Harvard University*, 1941.

c. The fact that man knows right from wrong proves his *intellectual* superiority to the other creatures; but the fact that he can *do* wrong proves his *moral* inferiority to any creature that *cannot*.

—MARK TWAIN, *What is Man?*

d. John Milton asked, "What is strength without a double share of wisdom? Vast, unwieldy, burdensome, proudly secure, yet liable to fall by weakest subtleties; strength's not made to rule, but to subserve, where wisdom bears command."

e. Read the following stanza with increased but controlled force up to the next to the last line; try reading the last line with a marked reduction in force to achieve dramatic contrast.

O masters, lords and rulers in all lands,
How will the future reckon with this man?
How answer his brute question in that hour
When whirlwinds of rebellion shake the world?
How will it be with kingdoms and with kings—
With those who shaped him to the thing he is—
When this dumb terror shall reply to god,
After the silence of the centuries?

—EDWIN MARKHAM, *The Man with the Hoe*

CHAPTER 6

Reinforcement of Vocal Tones Through Resonance

The materials and exercises in the preceding chapter emphasized the application of appropriate breathing and, when necessary, the energetic and controlled use of breath (force) in situations when more than a conversational level of loudness is required. In Chapter 2, in our discussion of the resonating cavities the point was made that cavity reinforcement—resonance—"builds up" vocal tones and makes it possible for us to be heard with a minimal use of force. Because of this effortless and energy-conserving phenomenon of cavity resonance, most of us are able to speak at length without experiencing fatigue even under less than optimal conditions. The use of electronic devices for amplifying speech further reduces the need for speaking at a greater than conversational level.

The chief resonators, it will be recalled, are the cavities of the larynx, pharynx (throat), mouth, and nose. If these cavities are not temporarily irritated or inflamed by a respiratory ailment or obstructed by organic growth such as enlarged tonsils or adenoids, good reinforcement of tone should be possible. Muscular tension may also impair the effective production of vocal tones, but unless such tension is chronic or regularly associated with some speech efforts, the effect of tension is likely to be transitory.

IMPROVEMENT OF RESONANCE

The manner in which the combination of our resonators reinforces our vocal tones produces that attribute by which the quality or timbre of our voices is identified. Unless we make a conscious attempt to disguise our voice, and frequently despite such an attempt, we are revealed by our vocal tones. Some of us are fortunate and have voices that are naturally pleasant to hear. A few of us, by misuse, do harm to our vocal apparatus. A very few may not have been generously endowed by nature and have mechanisms that at best are only fair. In this small number may be persons whose combination of laryngeal, pharyngeal, oral, and nasal cavities do not optimally or even adequately reinforce the basic tones to produce acceptable vocal qualities. Fortunately, most of us, including the members of the last group, can learn to treat our mechanisms with respect. By doing so we can make the most effective use of what we have. The discussion that follows should be helpful.

In our earlier discussion of the initiation of tones, we considered the relationship of physical and emotional tension to voice production. Specific suggestions and exercises were presented to establish proper initial vocalization. Our present concern is to create an awareness of resonance as one of the objectives for effective voice. As we continue our discussion of resonance, we must bear in mind that none of our resonating cavities acts independently of the others. Changes of the oral cavity are likely to affect the pharynx, and changes in the pharynx are likely to affect the oral cavity, larynx, and/or the nasal cavity. Despite this interdependence, specific modifications in one of the resonating cavities can result in vocal qualities that may be described by such terms as oral, guttural, and nasal.

Pharyngeal Resonance

Earlier we described the pharynx and its characteristics as a cavity resonator (see pages 25–26). We pointed out that this large resonating structure may enable the voice to sound full and rich if it is open and relaxed, or strident and metallic when the walls of the pharynx are tense. The implications of abnormal tissue growth or of infection relative to the damping of tone were also suggested. We now expand on this discussion.

Because the pharynx is a large resonator, it is best suited to the reinforcement of vocal tones in the lower pitch range. Normally, also, the relatively "soft" or relaxed tissue of the pharynx damps out the higher-pitched tones and reinforces the lower or fundamental vocal tones. If, therefore, the pharynx is relaxed and "open," the full potentialities of the pharynx are exercised for the reinforcement and coloring of the low vocal tones. If, however, as a result of tension or pathology the pharyngeal walls are tense, the potentialities of the pharynx as a resonator are not realized.

The tense or "hardened" surface reinforces the higher pitches, and the vocal overtones.

If a physical pathological condition accounts for abnormal pharyngeal tension, then medical treatment is in order. If, however, the pharyngeal tension is a product of habit, or of temporary mental tension, or of the residual effects of mental tension that once influenced the behavior and control of the pharynx, then a change may take place as a result of our own efforts. We may accept as a basic truism that a throat that is constricted, that is associated with a sensation of tightness, will produce a tense and strident voice. An open, relaxed throat is more likely to produce a full, rich, and mellow voice.

Because of the relationship between the continuous and coupled oral and pharyngeal cavities, suggestions and exercises for optimal pharyngeal resonance are presented following the discussion of oral resonance.

Oral Resonance

Oral resonance is likely to be improved if the speaker makes a conscious effort to emphasize lip and tongue activity while speaking. Such activity helps to accomplish the objective of the singing teacher who directs his student to "place his tones forward in the mouth." In our attempt to achieve oral resonance, however, we must not so exaggerate articulatory activity as to make it obvious to our listener-observer, and so make us self-conscious. Nor should we create a condition of excessive articulatory tension that will carry over to the muscles of the throat.

Optimum oral resonance can be obtained only when the back of the oral cavity is open and relaxed so that we are able to initiate and maintain vocalization with an open throat. The following exercises should be of help for this purpose.

EXERCISES FOR ORAL AND PHARYNGEAL RESONANCE

1.   The optimal use of the pharynx as a resonator presupposes proper breath control and the avoidance of any tension that might result from forced breathing or vocalization with residual air. The first step, therefore, is a review of the exposition and the exercises for breathing for effective vocalization (see pages 37–50).

2.   Establish a feeling of overall bodily relaxation, as follows: (*a*) Slowly clench your hands to make tight fists. Note the related tension in the arms as well as the fingers. Note also the associated tension of the jaw as your fingers are clenched into fists. (*b*) Relax slowly and gently until your fingers are extended. Do not, however, extend your fingers so that they become tense. Now note the associated relaxation of your arms and the muscles that control the jaw. Note also the easing of the muscles of the throat.

3.   Breathe in gently and then exhale with a "soft" sigh. Note the relaxed feeling in your throat. If your throat is not relaxed, it is likely that either your inhalation or your exhalation was not sufficiently gentle. Try again until you achieve a gentle, sustained, vocalized sigh. Your tongue should lie almost completely flat at the bottom of the mouth, with a minimum of back of the tongue elevation.

4.   Inhale deeply, but not to a point of discomfort, and then yawn as if you were sleepy. Open your mouth wide, but avoid any feeling of tension of the muscles of the face or jaw. Your throat should feel relaxed if the yawn was convincingly but not energetically produced.

5.   Optimum pharyngeal resonance is inconsistent with excessive back-of-the-tongue tension. Were you aware of any inclination toward such tension in any of the preceding exercises? Recall that the mouth and throat are continuous, coupled resonating cavities. If the back of the tongue is buckled or humped, the result is a narrowing of the coupling passage. The effect is a narrowed resonator, constriction, and a loss of reinforcement of the low-pitched tones. So, produce a free, open, and sustained *ah*. Note the state and feeling of the back of the tongue. The back of the tongue should be elevated slightly, but not enough to block the view of the pharynx. Use a mirror, preferably a hand mirror, so that you can see the position of the back of the tongue and the throat. Associate the tongue position and the feeling of an almost flattened tongue and an open, easy-to-view throat.

6.   Drop your head to the chest, and vocalize an easy, sustained *aw*. Now roll your head gently and smoothly from shoulder to shoulder while sustaining the *aw*. Repeat with a long *ah*.

7.   Begin as in exercise (5), but this time add an *m* to the *ah* so that the result is *ahm*. Repeat five times.

8.   With an open throat and relaxed lower jaw, say each of the following three times. Say each slowly, and stop for a breath between vocalizations.

mah, bah, dah, nah, hah, pah, fah, thah, shah, yah

In the immediately succeeding exercises, it will not be possible to keep your throat as relaxed as for exercises (1)–(5). Make certain, however, that your throat and mouth muscles are as relaxed as they can be while producing the indicated sounds. The exercises will emphasize oral activity and articulation in the front of the mouth.

9.   Observe your mouth in a mirror as you say the following words in pairs. Note the change in lip and jaw positions.

he	who	elf	off
it	hook	am	ought
ate	oat	alp	alm

10. Observe lip and tongue activity as you say each of the following:

lilting lyric	drippy prospect
temper tantrum	calm and balm
do or die	petty person
tense times	polished pewter
twice told tales	pretty polly
tip to toe	winsome wiles

11. Say the following, with proper regard for tongue and lip activity.

   a. Tic, tac, toe, away we go.
   b. Hip, hip, hop; take ten steps and stop.
   c. Who are you and who am I?
   d. Jeanie tiptoed up the hill.
   e. The wind whistled a tune in the trees.
   f. The silvery moon shed its light on the lake.
   g. A wag once defined an American college as a football stadium with a few associated academic buildings.
   h. Is basketball replacing baseball as the most popular American sport?
   i. Poets are fond of picking on December as a dreary time of the year.
   j. A university must be both a place and a state of mind for ideals and ideas and opportunities to put them into practice.

12. The following selections should be read with emphasis on articulatory action in the front of the mouth.

   a. Two barrels of tears do not heal a bruise.
      —Chinese Proverb
   b. In *The Magic Mountain* Thomas Mann observes: "Order and simplification are the first steps toward the mastery of a subject—the actual enemy is the unknown."
   c. The grey-ey'd morn smiles on the frowning night,
      Chequ'ring the eastern clouds with streaks of light.
      —WILLIAM SHAKESPEARE, *Romeo and Juliet*
   d. And, after all, what is a lie?
      'Tis but
      The truth in masquerade.
      —GEORGE GORDON, LORD BYRON, *Don Juan*
   e. Man passes away; his name perishes from record and recollection; his history is as a tale that is told, and his very monument becomes a ruin.
      —WASHINGTON IRVING, *The Sketch Book*
   f. Admirers of cats insist that all kittens and cats, whether they

be of low estate or of Royal Persian blood, resent, reject, and
ignore human patronage.

g. I speak severely to my boy,
I beat him when he sneezes,
For he can thoroughly enjoy
The pepper when he pleases.
—LEWIS CARROLL, *Alice's Adventures in Wonderland*

Nasal Resonance

We have already suggested that the importance of the nasal cavities
for vocal reinforcement can be appreciated when we are suffering from a
head cold. This condition not only deprives us of the ability to produce
proper nasal sounds but generally and adversely affects all our vocal
efforts. We become especially aware of the need for nasal reinforcement
when we try to produce the nasal sounds *n*, *m*, and *ng* /ŋ/. These nasal
consonants are articulated orally, but they are reinforced in the nasal
cavities and emitted through the nose. In order for the sound to enter the
nasal cavities, the soft palate must be relaxed and lowered. Lowering the
soft palate produces a large opening at the posterior entrance of the nasal
cavities (the nares) and a narrow avenue through the nares for the sound
to be resonated as it emerges from the nostrils. The characteristic differences in the three nasal consonants result from modification in the oral
cavity. For the sound *m*, the entire cavity is used because the tongue lies
comparatively flat at the floor of the mouth; for *n*, the tongue is raised so
that a smaller part of the mouth is used; for the *ng*, only a narrow area
at the back of the mouth behind the raised tongue is used as a supple-
mental reinforcer.

Although there are only three English sounds that are characteristically (predominantly) nasal, there is little doubt that, in connected
speech, sounds in close proximity to the nasals are also partly reinforced
nasally. It is virtually impossible to avoid some degree of nasality on the
vowels of words such as *nine, mine,* and *ring*. How to avoid inappropriate
and excessive nasalization of vowels is considered later. At the present
time we prefer to make a case for proper nasal reinforcement, rather than
to create anxiety about excessive nasality as a defect of vocal production.

Appropriate nasal reinforcement provides both roundness and carrying
power to the voice. It permits us to be heard with relatively little expenditure of energy. We can become aware of these effects by sustained, easy
humming. To hum easily, make certain that the throat muscles, the
tongue, and the soft palate are relaxed. The jaws should be almost but
not quite together. The lips should barely touch so that a slight tickling
sensation is experienced when humming. An easy, properly produced hum
should be felt as well as heard. You should be able to feel it not only on

the lips but at the sides of the nostrils if your thumb and index finger are placed gently at these areas.

The fullness of tone and vibrating effects associated with proper nasal reinforcement can be appreciated by contrasting a phrase or sentence with many nasal sounds with another containing no nasals, such as the following:

1. Norma enjoys candy. Betty likes fruit.
2. Mary may marry. Bob is likely to tarry.
3. Amanda murmured in the moonlight. Rod was discreetly quiet.
4. Norman, enough of complaining. Erase those surly looks.
5. MacDonald was the canniest member of his clan. Trusdale was the brightest of his relatives.

The following exercises should help to create awareness of nasal resonance as well as to afford an appreciation of the fullness of tone and carrying power that may be obtained with the careful production of nasal sounds. At first, exaggerate the length of each nasal sound, but avoid any intentional increase of effort in vocalization. Also be certain that each exercise is performed with a relaxed throat and jaw. Sustain your tones evenly through controlled, gradual abdominal contraction on exhalation.

EXERCISES FOR AWARENESS AND IMPROVEMENT OF NASAL RESONANCE

1. Hum up and down the musical scale. Then sing the musical scale with the conventional *do—re—mi*. . . . Compare the two vocal efforts. Request a friend to do the same while you listen to his vocal efforts. Which sounds fuller? Was humming easier than the conventional singing? If your humming was done with lips barely touching, the result should have been the production of a series of full or relatively full, easy-to-produce tones.
2. Occlude your nostrils and count from one through ten. Which numbers were not normally produced? Why?
3. Hum gently for the equivalent of a count of four on a sustained breath. Repeat five times.
4. Drop your jaw and bring the tip of the tongue in position for *n*. Produce *n* for the equivalent of a count of four. Repeat five times. Repeat with the sound *m*.
5. Blend a hum with the sound *ah* (*mah*). Make certain that the soft palate is raised for the *ah*. Repeat five times.
6. Blend a lengthened *n* with *ah*, then do the same for *n* and *aw*. Repeat each five times.
7. Blend a lengthened *m* with *ah* and follow by another *m* (*mahm*). Do the same for *m* and *aw* (*mawm*). Repeat each five times.
8. Repeat exercise (5) with *n* before and after the sounds *ah* and *aw* (*nahn* and *nawn*). Repeat each five times.

9. Exaggerate the length but *not the loudness* of the nasal sounds for the materials that follow:

a. | meandering movements | mined for minerals |
    |---|---|
    | meaningful motions | monumental mansions |
    | lament for mankind | mournful numbers |
    | means to an end | memories of man |
    | man's inclinations | nameless unto eternity |
    | mundane miscellany | nocturnal animals |

b. —Many Canadians speak both English and French.
    —In the Northern Hemisphere, November is an autumn month.
    —Mason was known for his mathematical acumen.
    —Norton was fond of mountain climbing.
    —A monody is a poem or a song in which one person laments the demise of another.
    —Amanda was fond of meandering through winding lanes.
    —The Ming dynasty is considered by some historians to be the last one of true Chinese origin.
    —Manganese is a chemical element employed in the making of steel to give it hardness and toughness.
    —Melvin wanted to be known as a man about town.
    —Nicaragua is a Central American nation.

c. For the common man, the best memorial is some beneficent thing or function that shall bear his name.
                                        —CHARLES T. COPELAND, *Speech, 1906*

d. In his actions, however various,
    He was consistently nefarious.
                                        —J. E., *The Variable Man*

e. Of manners gentle, of affections mild.
    In wit a man; simplicity a child.
                                        —ALEXANDER POPE, *Epitaph on Gay*

f. It is the very error of the moon;
    She comes more near the earth than she was wont,
    And makes men mad.
                                        —WILLIAM SHAKESPEARE, *Othello*

g. We all have strength enough to endure the misfortunes of others.
                                        —DUC FRANÇOIS DE LA ROCHEFOUCAULD, *Maxim 19*

h. I bring fresh showers for the thirsting flowers,
        From the seas and the streams;
    I bear light shade for the leaves when laid
        In their noonday dreams.
    From my wings are shaken the dews that waken
        The sweet buds every one,

When rocked to rest on their mother's breast,
    As she dances about the sun.
I wield the flail of the lashing hail,
    And whiten the green plains under,
And then again I dissolve it in rain,
    And laugh as I pass in thunder.
                —PERCY BYSSHE SHELLEY, *The Cloud*

i.   The end crowns all,
And that old common arbitrator, Time,
Will one day end it.
            —WILLIAM SHAKESPEARE, *Troilus and Cressida*

NASALITY

Our orientation in this book has been to emphasize the positive. We preferred, for example, to explain how vocal tones could be produced clearly, with adequate loudness and proper breath control, rather than to discuss how to overcome hoarseness, breathiness, or any other vocal inadequacy or defect. This was also our approach in considering resonance and the reinforcement of tone by the nasal cavities. As a precautionary measure, however, we believe it advisable at this point to discuss separately the prevalent fault of *excessive nasality*. Fortunately, when we have learned either to avoid or to overcome excessive nasality, we shall also have attained the positive objective of establishing appropriate nasal reinforcement.

Causes of Excessive Nasality

The most common cause of excessive nasality is failure of the soft palate to rise when necessary to block off the stream of breath (sound) as it enters the oral pharynx. If the soft palate is elevated, the sound is directed forward and emitted orally. A relaxed soft palate permits the sound to enter the nasal cavities where it is reinforced to become qualitatively nasal.

If failure to elevate the soft palate has a physical basis, medical attention is in order. If the failure is caused by a general indifference to speech efforts, to listener reactions, and superficially at least to the world in general, psychotherapy may be indicated. Excessive nasality is frequently associated with articulatory sluggishness. Often the jaw, lips, and tongue as well as the soft palate move without precision and alertness. The overall result is speech that sounds slovenly and voice that sounds tired, monotonous, and nasal.[1]

For the most part, excessive nasality is a manner of speech that has been learned unconsciously. Even if this manner of speaking reflected at one time an attitude of thinking or of behavior, change for the better can take place if the will to change is present.

The following exercises are based on the assumption that there is no organic basis for the excessive (inappropriate) nasality and no psychological need for its persistence.

EXERCISES FOR AWARENESS OF PALATAL ACTION

1. Stand before a mirror and yawn with a wide-open mouth. Note the upward movement of the soft palate and uvula while the yawn is maintained. Stop the yawn and relax. Repeat and note the feeling as well as the action of the elevated palate.

2. Hum gently, then think but do not vocalize a lengthy *ah*. Be certain that your mouth is open and the tongue almost flat. Observe the action of the soft palate as it is elevated and maintained for the *ah*. Now, by way of contrast, permit the soft palate to relax and produce a nasalized *ah*. Again, raise the soft palate for an appropriately vocalized *nonnasal ah*. Capture the feeling of the elevated soft palate when the *ah* is properly vocalized and orally reinforced. Repeat for the vowels of *all* and *ooze*.

3. Close your nostrils by pinching them. Say *ah*. Repeat with open nostrils. Whether the nostrils are pinched or free there should be no identifiable nasality for the sound. Repeat for the vowels of *whose, hull, home, haw, hog, harm.*

4. Say *n* while noting (feeling) the action and position of a relaxed soft palate. Then say *ah* and again note the action and position of the elevated palate. Alternate between the two sounds until you have an immediate awareness of the difference in palatal position.

5. Place a clean, cold hand mirror under your nostrils and produce a lengthy *ah*. If the soft palate is elevated, there should be no clouding of the mirror. Practice until there is no clouding, then repeat for all the vowels of exercise (3).

6. Repeat exercise (5) with the vowels of *eel, if, ail, elf, at, ask.* Check with a mirror for nasalization. Be especially careful about the vowels of *elf* and *ask.*

7. Pinch your nostrils closed as you say each of the following sentences. (If you note a feeling of stuffiness in your nose, or a feeling of

---

[1] Van Riper and Irwin in *Voice and Articulation* (Englewood Cliffs, N.J.: Prentice-Hall, Inc., 1958), p. 246 indicate that listeners are inclined to perceive nasality, although it may not be objectively present, when the speaker's utterance is characterized by poor articulation, inappropriate pitch range, or generally by any feature that has a negative value in speech production.

pressure in your ears, then you are being excessively nasal. Lift your soft palate to block off the entrance of air to the nasal cavity.)

    a.   The beagle chased the fox up the tree.
    b.   The boy walked the dog through the field.
    c.   The fog rested at the top of the hill.
    d.   What is it you wish to see?
    e.   Peter helped Pat pick the flowers.
    f.   For Shakespeare brevity was the soul of wit.
    g.   Paula preferred tea to coffee for supper.
    h.   Ted liked to tell droll stories.
    i.   All causes have effects; all effects have causes.

    8.   Say the following pairs of words with your attention focused on the avoidance of nasality in the second member of each pair. Make certain that your palate is elevated immediately after the nasal consonant is produced in the first member of each pair and through the production of the second member. It may also help to lessen any tendency toward nasality if you exaggerate the articulatory activity of the lips and the front part of the tongue.

me	be	new	do	nest	lest
knit	lit	nook	book	knife	life
nail	dale	note	dote	meat	beat
met	wet	nought	bought	more	bore
mat	bat	not	dot	may	bay
mask	bask	man	ban	my	bye
need	bead	mare	bare	mean	bean
mud	bud	near	dear	male	bale
mile	bile	maze	daze	mike	bike
nice	dice	new	due	mob	bob

Associated or Assimilated Nasality

    Earlier we learned that three sounds in American and English speech appropriately require nasal reinforcement for their production. These sounds are *m, n,* and *ng* /ŋ/. In connected speech, unless there is almost anxious care to avoid the effect, sounds in close proximity to nasal consonants are likely to be slightly nasalized. The nasalization is a "contamination by association" resulting from the manner of the articulation of the nasal sounds. Specifically, one of the following may happen.

    1.   The lowered soft palate may not be raised in time to prevent the following sound from being somewhat nasalized. Delay in raising the soft palate after the production of a nasal consonant probably accounts for the nasalization of the vowels that succeed the nasals in words such as *my, may, mate, new,* and *note.*

2. The soft palate may be lowered while the sound preceding the nasal is articulated as in words such as *aim, and, whom, only, sing,* and *young.* Here the nasalization is in anticipation of required articulatory movement (the lowering of the soft palate for appropriate reinforcement of a succeeding nasal sound).

3. The soft palate may not be sufficiently elevated because of the influence of preceding as well as succeeding nasal consonants as in *name, man, among, number, singing, ringing,* and *longing.*

There is no reasonable objection to some traces of nasalization resulting from the assimilative influence of nasal consonants. *What needs to be avoided is an overall effect of dominant nasality* merely because some nasal sounds are present.

The exercises recommended earlier for gaining awareness and control of the soft palate are, of course, applicable for overcoming the effects of excessive nasalization resulting from the influence of nasal consonants. Here also emphasis on front of the mouth (tongue and lip) activity is important. The following additional exercises should also be helpful.

**EXERCISES FOR AVOIDANCE OR REDUCTION
OF ASSIMILATIVE NASALITY**

1. When the nasal consonant precedes the vowel, lengthen the nasal consonant. Lengthening the consonant will afford you the extra moment of time needed to elevate the soft palate. This should reduce the "contaminating" assimilative effect of associated nasality and permit you to give appropriate reinforcement to the nasal sound in the given context.

    a. Practice on the following sound combinations. At the outset, exaggerate the length of the nasals to a marked degree. Then reduce the degree of exaggeration, but maintain the actual duration of the nasal sound for a time you consider about twice as long as normal. Finally, reduce the length of the nasals so that they are of normal duration, or as close to normal as possible, without nasalizing the succeeding sounds.

m	ee	n	ee
m	oo	n	oo
m	ay	n	ay
m	ah	n	ah
m	aw	n	aw

    b. Practice saying the following words, at first exaggerating the length of the nasal sounds. Then practice with the same words, this time with as little exaggeration as possible consistent with the avoidance of assimilated nasality.

meek	mock	need	nick
meal	mood	neat	noose
mill	mull	nill	nook
mell	mode	nail	note
mate	maul	never	nought
mat	mob	nack	not
mask	moth	nap	nock
mud	mirth	nut	nerve

c.   Practice with the following phrases, being careful at first to lengthen the nasal sounds and to avoid excessive nasality on the sounds that follow. Go over the same phrases, this time lengthening the nasals only as much as necessary to avoid assimilated nasality.

a man of moods	not my meat
more and more	now or never
new to me	native of Norway
no news	many a moon
move the map	next-door neighbor

d.   Practice with the following sentences, observing the same precautions as in the preceding exercise.

—Matt enjoyed his work as a mailman.

—Noah Webster believed that language as well as speech were immediate gifts of God.

—Ben Franklin observed that laws which are too gentle are seldom obeyed and those which are too severe are seldom enforced.

—Seneca advised that men learn best when they teach.

—In *Don Juan,* Byron remarked that the night shows stars and women in a better light.

—According to a Chinese proverb, it may be easier to rule and control a nation than a son.

2.   Emphasize oral activity for the sounds that precede the nasal consonants in the following exercises.

am	rant	lounge	turned
aim	town	lunch	joined
end	any	round	found
own	only	yearn	haunt
on	anger	hunger	penny

3.   Incorporate the words of the preceding exercise into short sentences such as the following:

a.   There is nothing without an end.

b.   Big Jim owned the town.

    c.   Courage is not only for the strong.

    d.   We joined the group in song.

4.   The following exercises emphasize combinations in which the nasal consonants both precede and follow vowels or diphthongs. They therefore provide an opportunity for careful control to avoid temptation and inclination to excessive assimilative nasality. Nasality of the nonnasal sounds can be minimized if you lengthen the first nasal consonant and emphasize oral activity for the succeeding vowel or diphthong. Your objective should be only as much lengthening of the nasals as is necessary to avoid assimilated nasality.

    a.   Practice on words such as the following:

mine	noon	innumerable	murmuring
mean	nine	rumbling	Neanderthal
nimble	meander	underneath	known
main	numerous	crowning	mentor
meant	numb	ambition	mince
moan	mournful	grinding	minnow
moon	meaningful	reminding	muttering

    b.   In sentence contexts, the tendency for assimilative nasality is increased. Practice careful enunciation of the following:

—Living language undergoes constant change.

—Martin, in common with most men, was more mindful of his own misfortunes than those of his next-door neighbor.

—The winter snows were followed by spring rains.

—If Benson had any inclination toward genius, it was in his ability to ignore any suggestion that he might resist temptation.

—Anthony was against any position initially taken by another. This inclination earned him the nickname of Contrary Tony.

—Samuel Johnson's famous *Dictionary* included a number of personalized definitions. One example is for the term *pension*, which Johnson defined as "An allowance made to anyone without an equivalent. In England it is generally understood to mean pay given to a state hireling for treason to his country."

—"And all the days of Methuselah were nine hundred sixty and nine years," says Genesis IV:27.

—"One precedent creates another. They soon accumulate and constitute law" is a principle in *The Letters of Junius*.

5.   The following provide additional combinations in which the nasal consonants both precede and follow vowels or diphthongs.

    a.   American football teams consist of eleven men.

    b.   Dreams furnish opportunities for persons who are meek to become strong and to crown their unconscious ambitions and

strivings with neither qualms nor anxieties about consequences.

c. Mournful sounds are often made by nonmournful gainfully
employed minstrels.

d. According to a Persian maxim, a person endowed with a long
tongue may have a shortened life.

e. Morton's farm background did not prepare him for employ-
ment on Madison Avenue.

f. Anne preferred a short plane trip to a long one by train.

g. Man is a subject of thought, of scorn, of controversy, and of
near divinity. Poets and thinkers through ancient times to the
present have expressed their views. Here are two of them.
—Carlyle maintained that man was the miracle beyond all
miracles, "the great inscrutable mystery of God."
—Mark Twain, not entirely in humor, once proclaimed: "There
are times when one would like to hang the whole human race,
and finish the farce."

6. As a test of your ability to resist the temptation of assimilated
nasality, use the materials of exercises (1), (2), and (4), intentionally
exaggerating the overall nasality of your speech. Then, to demonstrate
your control, go over the exercise materials without yielding to the temptation to commit assimilated nasality. By way of variety, try the same
techniques for the following:

a. The strongest is never strong enough to be always the master,
unless he transforms strength into right, and obedience into
duty.
—JEAN JACQUES ROUSSEAU, *The Social Contract*

b. So long as a man imagines that he cannot do this or that, so
long is he determined not to do it; and consequently, so long
it is impossible to him that he should do it.
—BENEDICT SPINOZA, *Explanation*

c. What man has assurance enough to pretend to know thoroughly the riddle of a woman's mind, and who could ever
hope to fix her mutable nature?
—CERVANTES, *Don Quixote*

d. There is no man so good, who, were he to submit all his
thoughts and action to the laws, would not deserve hanging
ten times in his life.
—MICHEL DE MONTAIGNE, *Of Vanity*

e. Hereby, too, I shall indulge the inclination so natural in old
men, to be talking of themselves and their own past actions;
and I shall indulge it without being tiresome to others, who,
through respect to age, might conceive themselves obliged to
give me a hearing, since this may be read or not as any one

pleases. And, lastly (I may as well confess it, since my denial of it will be believed by nobody), perhaps I shall a good deal gratify my own vanity. Indeed, I scarce ever heard or saw the the introductory words, "Without vanity I may say," etc., but some vain thing immediately followed.

—BENJAMIN FRANKLIN, *Autobiography*

f.   No nightingale did ever chaunt
More welcome notes to weary bands
Of travelers in some shady haunt,
Among Arabian sands.

—WILLIAM WORDSWORTH, *The Solitary Reaper*

g.   When, musing on companions gone,
We doubly feel ourselves alone.

—SIR WALTER SCOTT, *Marmion*

h.   Voltaire maintained that doctors are men who prescribe medicine of which they know little, to cure diseases of which they know less, in human beings of whom they know nothing.

i.   If the mountain won't come to Mohammed,
Mohammed must go to the mountain.

—English proverb

j.   In a wonderland they lie,
Dreaming as the day goes by,
Dreaming as the summers die.

—LEWIS CARROLL, *Through the Looking-Glass*

k.   In *Pudd'nhead Wilson's New Calendar* Mark Twain observed: "Man is the only animal that blushes. Or needs to."

l.   He who meanly admires mean things is a snob.

—WILLIAM MAKEPEACE THACKERAY, *The Book of Snobs*

m.   Of all the tyrannies on human kind
The worst is that which persecutes the mind.

—JOHN DRYDEN, *The Hind and the Panther*

CHAPTER 7

Pitch and Effective Vocalization

In our discussion of the mechanism for voice production the point was made that vocal pitch should be related to properties inherent in the individual's vocal mechanism. We are not free to choose a habitual pitch level or pitch range according to our attitudes, tastes, or whims or to change the pitch level and range according to mood or fashion. An essential task for a speaker who wants to be certain that he is making the best use of his vocal instrument is to determine the pitch level and pitch range most appropriate for him. Fortunately, most speakers normally vocalize at pitch levels and within pitch ranges that are appropriate for them. Under abnormal conditions, with or without a conscious awareness of the pitch level and range that we consider optimum, vocalization may suffer because control is impaired. A teacher may vocalize quite well, except when annoyed by her pupils, at which time her pitch may rise beyond the range of easy vocalization. If the occasions for annoyance are frequent, so are the opportunities for inappropriate vocalization. A salesman may have no cause for thinking about his voice until he becomes anxiously concerned while talking to a sales prospect. On such occasions he may phonate within an elevated pitch range, with accompanying strain and excessive effort. The resultant effects may be both displeasing and potentially harmful to his laryngeal mechanism. A few persons, however, may habitually vocalize at pitches that are not natural or optimum, and so their voices are less effective, less pleasant, and frequently much less comfortable than they could be. Before discussing how to determine the optimum pitch level and the most suitable pitch range, a few working definitions are presented.

Optimum or *natural pitch* is the level within a speaker's pitch range at which he can initiate vocalization with ease and effectiveness in a *given set of* circumstances. This pitch level is basically determined by the specific physical characteristics of each person's vocal mechanism. However, optimum pitch level is not fixed. It may vary, but probably not more than a level or two according to the speaker's state of fatigue, the amount of speaking the speaker has done during a time period, the speaker's physical environment (the size and acoustic features of the place of speaking), the number of listeners, the presence of mechanical amplification, and the degree of affect (emotion) associated with the speech content and the overall situation. Optimum pitch will also vary with the amount of air flow, which is in turn associated with the loudness of the vocalization. With all of the factors and circumstances considered, optimum pitch is still the level at which the individual's vocal mechanism functions with greatest ease and efficiency. Because optimum pitch is related to the structure of the vocal apparatus, it is sometimes referred to as *structural pitch*. Moreover, because optimum pitch is usually the product of "doing what comes naturally," providing there are no negating physical, emotional, or cultural pressures, the term *natural pitch* is also used. However, nothing we have said about optimum pitch should suggest that it would be natural or desirable for a speaker to maintain a monotone vocalization even at his optimum level. This level is the desirable one, "other things being equal" to initiate vocalization, and so determines the base for the optimum range for effective voice production.

Habitual pitch is the pitch level at which an individual most often initiates vocalization. Habitual range refers to the pitch levels that are most frequently employed in speaking. Range itself refers to the pitch levels that a speaker is capable of producing below and above his habitual pitch level. It is obviously desirable that the speaker's optimum pitch and optimum range be the ones that he habitually uses. If this is not the case, then changes need to be directed toward (1) becoming aware of optimum pitch and learning to produce this pitch level at will, (2) establishing the optimum pitch as a habit, and (3) developing a pitch range with optimum pitch as the basic level for initiating vocalization.

DETERMINATION OF OPTIMUM PITCH

For most speakers, optimum pitch is likely to be the level one-fourth to one-third above the lowest level within the entire pitch range.[1] If, for

[1] Pitch range may be defined as the "distance" between the lowest pitch, including falsetto (vocal fry) to the highest pitch, including upper falsetto or vocal fry.

example, the speaker has a twelve-level pitch range (musical tones and half tones according to the scale), his optimum pitch would probably be the third or fourth level above his lowest. If his pitch range were wider and were to include fifteen levels, his optimum pitch would most likely be about level five. For a speaker with a twenty-one–level pitch range, optimum pitch would be about level six.

Several approaches and techniques may be used to arrive at optimum pitch. Ultimately, the best technique is the one that works successfully for the individual; it should not be limited by any voice or speech teacher's personal prejudices. We consider the techniques we personally have found useful and easily demonstrable without any pretense of having a monopoly on all the workable ones.[2] For most cases, the first of these techniques is usually sufficient to establish awareness of optimum pitch.

TECHNIQUES FOR ACHIEVING OPTIMUM PITCH

1. Relax the throat muscles. Take a moderately deep breath and vocalize an evenly sustained *ah* at whatever pitch comes out naturally. Do not think of the pitch until after you hear yourself produce it. Do not attempt to modify the tone once it has been initiated.

2. Relax, and vocalize, but this time intentionally do so at a level lower than in exercise (1).

3. Continue, going down the scale, until you have produced the lowest-pitched tone you are capable of vocalizing. It may help to think of a descending musical scale in going from your initial pitch level to your lowest. Do not strain for an abnormally low pitch. Stop at the level at which your voice becomes a low-pitched whisper.

4. Return to the initial pitch you produced in step (1). Now produce tones on an upward scale until you reach the highest-pitched falsetto. If you started vocalization at your natural pitch, you should be able to go up in pitch above twice the number of tones you were able to descend below your initial level. If this is the situation, then you are probably initiating vocalization at or very close to your optimum or natural pitch.

Perkins, after reviewing the literature on optimum pitch, concludes: "Most authorities agree . . . that the optimal modal point in the range, particularly for males, is somewhere near one-fourth up from the lowest pitch that can be phonated." W. H. Perkins, in L. E. Travis, ed., *Handbook of Speech Pathology and Audiology* (New York: Appleton-Century-Crofts, 1971), p. 508.

Zemlin makes essentially the same observation. He says: "There is good reason to believe that there is a particularly suitable pitch level for each individual. This level, which is sometimes called the 'natural level' is largely determined by the individual characteristics of the individual vocal mechanism. . . . The natural pitch is located about one-fourth up the total singing range (including falsetto), when the range is expressed in musical notes." W. R. Zemlin, *Speech and Hearing Science* (Englewood Cliffs, N.J.: Prentice-Hall, 1968), pp. 182–183.

[2] Other approaches for arriving at *optimum pitch* are presented by G. Fairbanks, *Voice and Articulation Drillbook*, 2nd ed. (New York: Harper & Row, Publishers, Inc., 1960), pp. 123–129.

An alternate technique for determining optimum pitch is through the matching of vocal and piano tones throughout the pitch range including the first low and first high falsetto tones.

1. Sing or chant from your lowest to your highest tone, matching each tone with a corresponding one on a well-tuned piano. If your own sense of pitch discrimination is not reliable, obtain the help of a friend with a reliable ear to establish your vocal range.
2. Repeat the singing or chanting several times so that you are certain that you have established your entire range. Your optimum or natural pitch is likely to be between one-fourth and one-third above the lowest tone you can produce.
3. Reproduce this tone until it is firmly fixed in your mind and you can initiate it without the help of the piano.

This approach should be repeated at different times during a day and on several different days. Pitch range may vary somewhat under conditions of fatigue or tension, but unless the variation is great, the optimum pitch level should not deviate by more than a single level.[3]

HABITUAL PITCH

In order to know whether there is any need to make a conscious effort to initiate voice at the optimum pitch level it is necessary to compare your habitual pitch with your optimum pitch. If the two are the same, or no more than a single pitch level (a half or a full tone) apart, then there is no need to think about your initial pitch. For most persons who have had no physical ailment or emotional trauma, the likelihood is that habitual pitch and optimum pitch are close enough so that no special concern is necessary. Just to be certain, however, all who are interested in producing

[3] Another approach for arriving at optimum pitch is through a technique of vocalizing while chewing. Froeschels, who is largely responsible for the discovery and popularization of the chewing technique for vocal therapy and vocal improvement, recommends the following as an approach: ". . . the patient is asked to chew as usual with closed lips, but without anything in his mouth, and to observe his tongue, which moves continually during the chewing. Immediately afterward he is asked to chew like a savage, that is, by opening the mouth, and with extensive movements of the lips and tongue. . . . If the chewing is done correctly, that is with vigorous movements of the lips and the tongue, a great variety of sounds escape the mouth. If uniform sounds, like *ham-ham-ham* are heard, the movements of the lips and tongue do not vary sufficiently." E. Froeschels, "Hygiene of the Voice," *Archives of Otolaryngology* (August, 1943), 38:122–130.

Our experience has been that persons who chew and vocalize in the manner described by Froeschels reflexively produce vocal tones at or close to their optimum pitch. For persons who have a poor sense of pitch discrimination and who are not excessively self-conscious, chewing may be used successfully as a technique for arriving at optimum pitch. It is not, however, a cure-all for all vocal ills.

voice according to their maximum capabilities might observe the suggestions that follow for determining habitual pitch and comparing it with optimum pitch.

Look over several easy prose passages and select one containing material that is neutral in affective (emotional) content and not particularly challenging in intellectual content. (Three such selections are provided under "Reading Selections to Determine Habitual Pitch," following.) Make sure also that the selected passage includes no words that cause you uncertainty as to pronunciation. First read the selection aloud in as natural and conversational a manner as you can. On the second and third readings, when the thought content has been reduced to insignificance because of repetition, level off toward a monotone in pitch. You can accomplish this by intentionally avoiding inflectional changes. The final reading—fourth or fifth—will begin to sound like a chant. When this happens, you have probably arrived at a single level, or at least a narrow pitch range, at or close to your habitual pitch. At the conclusion of your chanted passage, vocalize a sustained *ah* at the same pitch level.

Locate the last level on a piano. Then say a series of *ah*'s, matching your voice with the piano note. Count from one to ten on this level. Then say the alphabet on this level. If possible, have a companion listen to you to help you locate the level.

Compare your optimum pitch with your habitual pitch. Are the two nearly the same or no more than a tone or two apart? If they are, then you need not be further concerned about the matter of initial pitch. If not, then work to bring your habitual pitch closer to your optimum pitch. This accomplishment will pay large dividends if you are interested in good voice production. The most generous permissible margin of error between habitual and optimum pitch should not exceed two levels for persons with a narrow pitch range. This may be extended to one third of an octave for individuals with a wide (two or more octaves) pitch range. In general, the closer habitual pitch is to optimum pitch, the better the voice is likely to be.

READING SELECTIONS TO DETERMINE HABITUAL PITCH

1. The term and the concept of classical conditioning is historically associated with the Russian physiologist Ivan Pavlov. Pavlov, who lived from 1849 to 1936, was one of the first to observe that some responses are the result of a preceding presentation of a stimulus. He demonstrated that a stimulus, which by itself did not have the power to evoke a particular response, could gain that power by association with another stimulus that had such power. In psychological terms, a stimulus that does not elicit a response can be given this potential if it is paired with a stimulus that is effective in eliciting a particular response. The historic Pavlovian example of this phenomenon is the use of food power with dogs to elicit, as it

reliably does, the response of the secretion of saliva. If a stimulus that does not elicit the salivary response, e.g., the ringing of a bell, is paired (associated) with the administration of the food power, the bell ring after a number of pairings will be able to elicit salivation. The stimulus that initially elicits the response is called the unconditioned stimulus; the paired stimulus is the conditional one.

2.   An index is a listing, almost always in alphabetical order, of the topics treated in a book or periodical. In most books the index is in the back. The purpose of a book index is to help the reader to locate the pages of subjects and names about which information is provided. The subject and the number or numbers of the pages on which the information is found is called the entry. A good indexer is able to anticipate where, in the listing of topics, a reader is likely to look for an item of information or a subject treated in the book. Some books have one index for proper names and another for other entries.

3.   The French consider a sauce the foundation of good cooking. Sauces may be made with butter, with oil and vinegar, with wine, and with bones and vegetables as basic ingredients. Although French chefs accept the need to spend hours in the preparation of a sauce, most American cooks are less patient. For example, a French housewife may spend half a day selecting, preparing, and cooking a combination of vegetables and bones to make a brown sauce. The American housewife is much more inclined to use canned beef gravy for the same purpose.

WIDENING THE PITCH RANGE

How wide a pitch range should we have? Practically, the answer is *wide enough to be effective as a speaker,* but not at the expense of strain or discomfort. Some persons with a demonstrably wide pitch range tend to speak habitually only at the lower end of their range. Others, especially when they are under emotional stress, may confine their vocalizations to the higher end of their range. The result for both types of speakers may be inefficient vocalization. For the listeners the result may be unpleasant exposure to monotonous or strained vocal efforts. Although experimental evidence is not consistent, some studies have shown that effective speakers and male speakers considered to have good voices tend to use both greater variability and a wider range of pitch than do less effective speakers.[4] Better speakers, by and large, make greater use of the upper part of their

[4] See J. W. Black and W. E. Moore, *Speech* (New York: McGraw-Hill Book Company, 1955), p. 56. Fairbanks, says: "A good speaker usually distributes his pitches over a *pitch range* of about two octaves while reading a short (75–100 words) sample of factual prose." G. Fairbanks, *Voice and Articulation Drillbook,* 2nd ed. (New York: Harper & Row, Publishers, Inc., 1960), p. 122.

pitch ranges, and their pitch ranges generally cover at least an octave and a half. Poor speakers, in contrast, tend to have pitch ranges limited to about half an octave.

Extending Pitch Range Upward

Since optimum pitch is at the lower end of the pitch range, it follows that the direction for extending pitch range for most persons is likely to be up rather than down. With this in mind, the following exercises should be undertaken.

EXERCISES FOR EXTENDING PITCH RANGE UPWARD

1. Review the discussion of optimum pitch. Check your optimum pitch and your total pitch range.

2. Count from one through ten at your optimum pitch level. Now count to ten in a monotone three tones above your optimum pitch. Raise the pitch level three more tones, and repeat the count. Finally, count to ten at the very top of your normal pitch range.

3. Say the sentence "We're going for a walk" at your optimum pitch. Practice the same sentence, initiating the first word on successively lower levels until you reach the lowest comfortable pitch level. Start again from your optimum pitch and now initiate the first word of the sentence at successively higher pitch levels until you have reached the top of your range.

4. Read the following sentences and paragraphs first in a manner that is natural or habitual for you and then intentionally extending the pitch range upward.

> a. Heraclitus the Greek cast a long shadow before him. He contended that one cannot step in the same river twice.
>
> The Greek was going beyond the assertion that no two things are exactly alike to the assertion that no one thing is ever twice the same, that reality is to be regarded as a process. And we might enlarge his contention by pointing out that one may not step in the same river twice, not only because the river flows and changes, but also because the one who steps into it changes too, and is never at any two moments identical.
> —WENDELL JOHNSON, *People in Quandaries*
>
> b. Blessed are the forgetful; for they get the better even of their blunders.
> —FREDERICH NEITZSCHE, *Beyond Good and Evil*
>
> c. He flattered himself on being a man without any prejudices, and this pretension itself is a very great prejudice.
> —ANATOLE FRANCE, *The Crime of Sylvestre Bonnard*

d. At moments she discovered she was grotesquely wrong, and then she treated herself to a week of passionate humility.

—HENRY JAMES, *The Portrait of a Lady*

e. Good breeding consists in concealing how much we think of ourselves and how little we think of the other person.

—MARK TWAIN, *Notebooks*

f. Benjamin Franklin held that "There are two ways of being happy: we may either diminish our wants or augment our means. Either will do, the result is the same. And it is for each man to decide for himself and do that which happens to be the easiest. . . ."

g. Young men are fitter to invent than to judge; fitter for execution than for counsel; and fitter for new projects than for settled business.

—FRANCIS BACON, *Of Youth and Age*

h. There is no season such delight can bring,
As summer, autumn, winter, and the spring.

—WILLIAM BROWNE, *Variety*

Extending Pitch Range Downward

Except for persons with a very narrow pitch range, all of us have more levels from the optimum range toward the top of the pitch range than for the bottom. However, there is "room" (pitch range) toward the bottom level that can be used effectively for expressing feeling and communicating meaning through vocal variety that is appropriate to the speech content. Thus, if after determining your optimum pitch and your habitual pitch range, it becomes apparent that you are making little use of your lower pitch levels, some practice is in order. Do not, however, go so low in your range that your voice becomes throaty, excessively breathy, or barely audible. Avoid strain or any low tone that seems to be lacking in substance or is difficult to sustain or results in the production of a low-pitched falsetto. In general, try to incorporate tones into your pitch range that are one or two levels above your lowest tone within your pitch range. The following exercises, which present material on sober matters, should provide you with opportunity to emphasize tones at the lower end of your pitch range.

EXERCISES FOR EXTENDING PITCH RANGE DOWNWARD

1. Sadness is a wall between two gardens.

—KAHLIL GIBRAN, *The Prophet*

2. We must anticipate that some days of our lives, like the weather, must be dark and dreary.

3. The deeper the sorrow, the less tongue it hath.

—*The Talmud*

  4.   The nurse of full-grown souls is solitude.
—JAMES RUSSELL LOWELL, Columbus

  5.   The history of the world is but the biography of great men.
—THOMAS CARLYLE, Sartor Resartus

  6.   Man is his own star; and that soul that can
      Be honest is the only perfect man.
—JOHN FLETCHER, Upon an "Honest Man's Fortune"

  7.   People who make no noise are dangerous.
—JEAN DE LA FONTAINE, Fables

  8.   Time does not become sacred to us until we have lived it.
—JOHN BURROUGHS, The Spell of the Past

  9.   A man in armor is his armor's slave.
—ROBERT BROWNING, Herakles

10.   Many of us have learned in sadness, if not in sorrow, that when we return to a place of youthful joy we seldom relive even one moment of that joy.

11.   Here, where the world is quiet,
      Here, where all trouble seems
      Dead winds' and spent waves' riot
      In doubtful dreams of dreams,
      I watch the green field growing
      For reaping folk and sowing,
      For harvest time and mowing,
      A sleepy world of streams.

      I am tired of tears and laughter,
      And men that laugh and weep,
      Of what may come hereafter
      For men that sow to reap.
      I am weary of days and hours,
      Blown buds of barren flowers,
      Desires and dreams and powers,
      And everything but sleep.
—ALGERNON CHARLES SWINBURNE, The Garden of Proserpine

12.   And the earth was without form, and void;
      and darkness was upon the face of the deep.
—Genesis

SPEECH MELODY (INTONATION)

Speaking and Singing

All of us, including those who are resigned to being classed among the nonsingers because of the violence we do to the melody of a song, use melody in our speech. The music of speech, however, is usually subtle, and the changes in pitch may not be as wide or as distinct as they are in singing. When speaking, our voices glide from sound to sound with an almost continuous change in pitch. In singing, changes in pitch are usually more clear-cut and usually take place in discrete steps equivalent to musical tones.[5] Some of us, without intention, somehow manage to sing between the tones and our voices fall "flat" into the cracks between the piano keys. A few singers have earned a reputation by doing intentionally and under control what seems to have come naturally, accidentally, and inconsistently for others.

Intonation

Intonation, or patterned vocal variation, is an inherent feature of spoken utterance. Interestingly, despite phonological and morphemic variations in natural languages, intonation contours, especially for declarative sentences, are essentially alike. Lieberman makes the general observation based on both eastern and western languages that "short declarative sentences usually end with a falling fundamental frequency contour." [6]

In some languages, the changes in vocal tones are relatively slight, whereas in others, such as Chinese, the changes are marked. Languages, such as Norwegian, Swedish, and Lithuanian, have relatively fixed patterns of pitch changes. English pitch variation is relatively free. The melody of English speech is determined in part by conventions of sentence formation and in part by the mood and subjective responses of the speaker to the content of his speech and the overall speech situation. Despite this highly individual determinant of American-English speech melody, there are several features that characterize the direction of inflectional changes (pitch changes that occur without interruption of phonation) for sounds of words. There are also characteristic pitch changes within word groups that constitute recognizable intonation patterns in our language.[7]

Figures 7–1 and 7–2 (adapted from Lieberman, *Intonation, Perception, and Language*, pp. 69–70) present physiological and acoustic data for a

[5] Some singers depart from the musical score and do produce glides and vibrato effects as individual expressions in their renditions of a song. This, however, is the exception rather than the rule in singing.

[6] P. Lieberman, *Intonation, Perception, and Language*, M.I.T. Research Monograph No. 38 (Cambridge: M.I.T. Press, 1968, p. 39). Lieberman also points out (p. 39) that normal breath-group (phrase utterance) "is a synchronized standard pattern of activity wherein the respiratory and laryngeal muscles act to produce phonation on the flow of expiratory air. The normal breath-group of all languages are similar in that they end with a falling fundamental frequency contour."

[7] See R-M. S. Heffner, *General Phonetics* (Madison: University of Wisconsin Press, 1949), pp. 216–223, for a review of basic tendencies relative to intonation patterns and alternate systems for their representations.

Figure 7–1 Acoustic and physiologic data for speaker 1 reading the declarative
sentence "*Joe* ate his soup."
The speaker used a normal breath-group, but he placed prominence on the word
Joe by means of a momentary increase in the subglottal air pressure. The fundamental frequency, subglottal air pressure, and the volume of air in the speaker's
lungs are plotted as functions of time. A quantized wide-band spectrogram is also
presented.

short declarative sentence. The variations in contour according to the word
stressed should be noted.

Figure 7–3 shows several other "representative" simplified and generalized intonation contour patterns of American English. These patterns
illustrate the basic downward inflection for the simple declarative sentence
and the pitch elevation for the stressed work within the sentence or within
the breath-group (phrase) for multiple phrase sentences. In contrast, note
the difference in contours for the question-sentence. So-called wh-questions
end with falling inflections whereas questions that ordinarily may be
answered by a "Yes" or "No" end with rising inflections.

Figure 7–4 is a graphic representation for a somewhat more complex
sentence than most of the others.

Figure 7–2 **Acoustic and physiologic data for speaker 1 reading the declarative sentence "Joe ate his *soup*."**
The speaker used a normal breath-group, but he placed prominence on the word *soup* by means of a momentary increase in the subglottal air pressure. Note that the subglottal air pressure and fundamental frequency both fall at the end of the sentence.

Types of Pitch Changes

Two categories of pitch changes together constitute the overall pitch variation or *intonation* of American-English speech. These are inflections and shifts or steps. Inflections are modulations of pitch that occur during phonation. *Shifts* are changes of pitch that occur between phonations. Inflections may be subclassified according to contour or "direction" of change as downward, upward, and circumflex. For any but very short uninterrupted phonatory efforts or flows of utterance we are likely to have several inflectional changes. Because shifts properly occur only between subunits of utterances when the speaker takes a moment to pause to indicate a unit of thought or a "phrase," inflectional changes will almost always outnumber shifts. The uses and implication of pitch changes are considered in the discussions that follow.

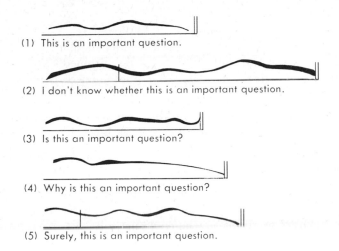

(1) This is an important question.

(2) I don't know whether this is an important question.

(3) Is this an important question?

(4) Why is this an important question?

(5) Surely, this is an important question.

Figure 7–3

Not one but many men will suffer the results of this action.

Figure 7–4

Shifts

Shifts, or steps in pitch, indicate the importance we give to a unit of thought within an utterance or phonatory effort. If we regard a phonatory effort as a sentence, even a two-word sentence may have two related subunits of thought, each appropriately uttered at a different pitch level. Thus, sentences such as "Go now" or "Come here" may be uttered for effect with a momentary pause at the end of the first word and a shift in level of pitch from the first to the second word. In both of the examples given, the "normal" shift in level of pitch would be upward, so that we might represent the sentences as:

$$\overrightarrow{\text{Go}} \parallel \overrightarrow{\text{now}}$$

$$\overrightarrow{\text{Come}} \parallel \overrightarrow{\text{here}}$$

EXERCISES FOR CHANGE IN PITCH LEVEL

1.   Practice the following short sentences using a higher initial pitch level on the second word than on the first. However, end the second word with a downward inflection.

Please come	Go home
Don't run	Come soon

That's enough	We're late
You're out	Mary shouted
They left	Bob listened
Jack fell	Bill hurried
We're ready	Jane winced

2.   What would be the effect on the meaning of the statement if the second words were produced on a lower pitch level than the first?

3.   Practice these longer sentences changing the level of pitch as indicated by the direction of the arrow:

    a.   Winter came— |↑| wind, freeze, and snow.
    b.   He stopped suddenly, |↑| then turned to the right.
    c.   Why Tom did it, |↓| he could not tell.
    d.   Our team lost, |↓| but the game was close.
    e.   Will you |↓| or won't you?
    f.   It can't be done, |↑| no matter how you beg.
    g.   Come now, |↓| that's enough.
    h.   We're tired, |↑| much too tired.

4.   How would you be inclined to shift the pitch for the following sentences after the indicated places for pause? What changes in meaning would you imply by reversing the direction of the pitch change? By using the same general level on the second part of the sentence as the first?

    a.   It's late, || perhaps too late.
    b.   Come early, || come often.
    c.   Did you care || or just pretend?
    d.   It can be done || if you really try.
    e.   Waste not, || want not.
    f.   He spoke quietly || but with certainty.
    g.   He stopped || just in time.
    h.   Don't write, || phone him.
    i.   He sped away || out of sight.
    j.   Look out, || look out!

Downward or *falling inflections* (↘) are generally used to indicate the completion of a thought, and to give emphasis to an idea. The sample sentences that follow would end with falling inflections. The second sentence would probably have falling inflections on both italicized words.[8]

1.   This is your *pen*.
2.   *Certainly*, this is your *pen*.

Command statements also end with falling inflections.

3.   Stop *now!*

---

[8] In the examples presented the italicized words are those on which inflectional changes might be anticipated.

A question that begins with an interrogative word—*when, where, who, why, how, whom*—for which an answer other than the single word "Yes" or "No" is anticipated, also ends with a falling inflection.

4. Why did Bill *go?*
5. Why did you read this *book?*

Upward or *rising inflections* (↗) are generally used to suggest doubt, uncertainty, or incompleteness. It is also used for questions that call for a simple "Yes" or "No" answer. And we are likely to use rising inflections in statements that enumerate a series of items until the last item is stated. The last item would be spoken with a falling inflection.

6. It apparently didn't occur to *us* that this was your *book.*
7. Is this your *book?*
8. We bought *groceries, meat* and *fruit* at the supermarket.

Circumflex Inflections

We would get into great difficulty if we attempted to illustrate how irony, innuendo, sarcasm, cynicism, skepticism, or surprise combined with disbelief or incredulity are expressed in pitch. These intellectual states and attitudes all have marked degrees of feeling. Most native Americans would probably employ some form of circumflex (down-up, up-down, or down-up-and-down) inflection to express them. If, for example, surprise and "I can't believe it" were to be expressed at the choice of a candidate through the use of the single word *Him!*, the inflection might be:

Him! ↘↗

A longer statement such as "Of all persons, to choose—him!" in which a related sentiment might be expressed relative to the same person might employ a series of circumflex inflections. The specific form of inflection is likely to be even more individualized than in the illustrations previously presented.

Generalizations Relative to Intonation and Inflectional Changes

The examples presented and the generalizations we are about to make might serve as guides for a speaker who has somehow not been able to get the tune of American-English speech. Once the basic tune is learned, the speaker should feel free to indulge in variations from the fundamental melodic theme or pattern.

1. Pitch change to some degree is almost continuous in normal conversational speech.
2. Major pitch changes occur at the end of phrases and sentences and on the most significant words within the phrase or sentence.
3. Falling or downward inflections are used when we make definite

or positive assertions and when we wish to indicate the completion of a thought (examples 1, 2, and 3 on page 100). A falling inflection is also used on the final word of a question that begins with an interrogative word (examples 4 and 5, page 101).

4. A rising inflection is used to suggest incomplete or dependent thoughts and to express doubt or uncertainty. The rising inflection is also used in questions that may logically be answered by the words "Yes" or "No" (examples 6, 7, and 8, page 101).

5. The pitch level of the most important word within a phrase or unit of thought is likely to be at a different level from the other words of the unit. Most frequently, it will be higher in level, but occasionally the emphasized word may be uttered at a distinctively lower level than the other words of the unit.

6. The stressed syllable of a word is usually spoken on a higher pitch level than the unstressed syllable or syllables of the word.

The exercises that follow afford opportunity for the application of the generalizations relative to inflectional changes and intonation patterns of American-English speech.

The first group of sentences would ordinarily end with falling inflections unless special meanings are read into them. For the present, avoid special meanings and read the sentences "straight" to indicate assertions and completed thoughts.

EXERCISES FOR FALLING INFLECTIONS

1. Tom starts today.
2. This tastes good.
3. I like to skate.
4. This is enough.
5. Bill enjoys hiking.
6. Sue likes to sew.
7. Spring comes in March.
8. It's good to be through.
9. Good lawns require care.
10. Not all roses are red.
11. Joe is always hungry.
12. Ned is a good golfer.
13. Ted is a fast reader.
14. Come when you're ready.
15. This is the path.
16. That's not so!
17. It's time for tea.
18. Now we're done.
19. Take your time.
20. Dan found the book.

Many of the items in the next group, if read straight, would normally employ falling inflections on the last words. If read to suggest doubt or uncertainty or to express an incomplete thought, rising inflections are employed. The questions ordinarily answered by a "Yes" or "No" also end with rising inflections.

EXERCISES FOR RISING INFLECTIONS

1. I'm just not sure.
2. Well, perhaps.
3. You're going to ski?
4. I guess that's right.
5. Well, we'll see.
6. Is Tom going?
7. Do you like pie?
8. Shall we dance?
9. Do you like fishing?
10. Is this Ben's?
11. Can you wait?
12. Is Bill late?

All questions, we recall, do not end with rising inflections. Those that begin with interrogative words usually end with falling inflections when the questions are intended to elicit information. When a rising inflection is used for questions beginning with interrogative words, some special implication or meaning is intended other than the asking of information. Read the following sentences first with the expected falling inflection and then with a final rising inflection and note the change in meaning.

1. What is today's date?
2. What's your name?
3. Who came late?
4. Where are we going?
5. When shall we leave?
6. Why should we go?
7. Who knows his lines?
8. What does this cost?
9. How long is the road?
10. What time is it?
11. How did you know?
12. What makes this right?

As indicated in some of our earlier sample sentences, inflectional changes may take place within a sentence, normally on the last word of a phrase as well as at the end of the sentence. By and large, the nature of the inflectional change will be determined by the intended meaning and will be consistent with the generalizations previously listed relative to inflectional changes and intonation patterns.

Read the following sentences according to the indicated inflectional changes. What are the differences in implied meanings? [9]

1. Give me liberty,↗or give me death.↘
2. Give me liberty,↘or give me death.↗
3. Give me liberty,↘or give me death.↘
4. While there is life↗there is hope.↘
5. While there is life↘there is hope.↘
6. Please give me the bread,↗butter,↗and jam.↘
7. Please give me the bread,↘butter,↘and jam.↘
8. Please give me the bread,↗butter,↗and jam.↗
9. She came,↗he saw,↗she conquered.↘
10. She came,↘he saw,↘she conquered.↗
11. She came,↘he saw,↘she conquered.↘

EXERCISES FOR PRACTICE OF INFLECTIONAL CHANGES

1. Say the word *yes* to indicate (*a*) certainty, (*b*) doubt, (*c*) indecision, (*d*) sarcasm.

2. Say the word *no* and, by changes of inflection, indicate the following:

   a. "Definitely not."
   b. "Well, maybe."
   c. "I'm surprised to learn that."
   d. "I'm annoyed to learn that."
   e. "I'm pleased and surprised to learn that."

3. Say the sentence *I shall come* so that the following attitudes are implied:

   a. Determination.
   b. Pleasant agreement.
   c. Surprise.
   d. Annoyance.

4. Say the sentence *He's really somebody* to bring out the following meanings:

   a. You admire the person about whom you're talking.
   b. You dislike the person.

[9] See G. Fairbanks, *Voice and Articulation Drillbook*, 2nd ed. (New York: Harper & Row, Publishers, Inc., 1960), Chap. 14, for additional exercise materials on inflectional changes.

    c.   You are surprised at the newly discovered qualities of the person.

5.   Speak the sentence *I like Bill* to bring out the following:

    a.   A direct statement of fact. (You mean literally what the words say.)

    b.   A contradiction of the literal meaning of the words. (You definitely do not like Bill.)

    c.   Irritation and surprise that anyone could conceivably accuse you of liking Bill.

    d.   Indecision as to your feelings about Bill.

    e.   Specific indication that your liking is for Bill and not for anyone else who may be present.

    f.   Your answer to the question "Who likes Bill?"

    g.   An aggressive, emphatic answer to the question "Who could possibly care for a fellow like Bill?"

Avoidance of Monotony

In discussing the differences in pitch variation between singing and speaking, we pointed out that most pitch changes in song melody are discrete and take place in distinct steps. Each song syllable is likely to be maintained on a recognizable pitch level (note) longer than is likely to be the case in either conversational or public speech. Variation in speaking is almost continuous. Distinctive changes, however, should be noted when pitch is used for purposes of emphasis. For emphasis, pitch change is likely to be on a higher rather than on a lower level than the preceding or following words. When the pitch change is to a lower level, the speaker must maintain or increase the volume of his voice to give the word or phrase the desired emphasis.

Repetition of pattern in singing constitutes melody. This is considered a desirable characteristic of classical song. In speaking, where verbal content rather than pitch pattern is usually important, the repetition of pitch pattern should be avoided. In American and English speech, subtleties of ideational content are expressed through pitch change. If pitch changes become patterned and repeated, shades of meaning cannot readily be communicated. Beyond this, pitch changes, if they can be anticipated, no longer command attention and tend to work against rather than for the maintenance of interest. For these reasons the effective speaker not only uses as wide a range of pitch as he can within his normal pitch range but is careful to avoid pitch patterning and its consequent monotony.

Pitch Variation in Content Characterized by Strong Feelings

Speech content that is characterized by strong feelings, which is more significant for its emotional than for its intellectual content, tends to use less pitch variation than most conversational speech. When we wish to establish a dominant mood, or to share a strong feeling with a listener, we begin to approximate the melody of song or the relatively sustained pitch of lyrical poetry. A passage from the Bible should not be read as one reads an item from the day's news. Neither should it be read with an unvarying cadence and stereotyped intonations. It follows also, despite the tendency of some news commentators, that a news item should not be spoken as one should read a passage from the Bible.

In general, the pitch changes for an effective reading of poetry or emotional prose are individually more extensive but collectively less varied and longer sustained than for an effective reading of intellectual material. The exception is content of heightened feeling when lightness rather than loftiness is to be expressed. Then the changes in pitch are likely to be more sweeping and to occur as often as or more often than for predominantly intellectual material. Anger is also likely to be expressed wtih relatively wide pitch changes and in the upper pitch range. With these points in mind, the following passages should be read. Use pitch variation to emphasize changes in thought and feeling. Sober and solemn moods are probably best expressed through the use of relatively low, sustained pitch levels.

EXERCISES FOR PRACTICE OF PITCH VARIATION

1. Modesty and unselfishness—these are virtues which men praise —and pass by.

    —ANDRÉ MAUROIS, *Ariel*

2. The perversion of the mind is only possible when those who should be heard in its defense are silent.

    —ARCHIBALD MACLEISH, *The Irresponsibles*

3. In a real dark night of the soul it is always three o'clock in the morning.

    —F. SCOTT FITZGERALD, *The Crack-up*

4. There is a certain blend of courage, integrity, character, and principle which has no satisfactory dictionary name but has been called different things at different times in different countries. Our American name for it is "guts."

    —LOUIS ADAMIC, *A Study in Courage*

5. Fame has also this great drawback, that if we pursue it we must direct our lives in such a way as to please the fancy of men, avoiding what they dislike and seeking what is pleasing to them.

    —BENEDICT SPINOZA, *Ethics*

6. The happiness of life is made up of minute fractions—the little soon forgotten charities of a kiss or smile, a kind look, a heartfelt compliment, and the countless infinitesimals of pleasurable and genial feeling.

    —SAMUEL TAYLOR COLERIDGE, *The Friend*

7. But they that wait upon the Lord shall renew their strength; they shall mount up with wings as eagles; they shall run, and not be weary; and they shall walk, and not faint.

—*Isaiah* 40:31

8. In your reading of Psalm 23, level, sustained tones will help to establish the solemnity and reverence of your thought. Do not, however, fall into a patterned, unchanging reading.

   The Lord is my shepherd, I shall not want. He maketh me to lie down in green pastures; he leadeth me beside the still waters. He restoreth my soul; he leadeth me in the paths of righteousness for his name's sake. Yea, though I walk through the valley of the shadow of death, I will fear no evil: for thou art with me; thy rod and thy staff they comfort me.

—*Psalm 23*

9. Golden lads and girls all must
   As chimney sweepers, come to dust.

—WILLIAM SHAKESPEARE, *Cymbeline*

10. I was angry with my friend:
    I told my wrath, my wrath did end.
    I was angry with my foe:
    I told it not, my wrath did grow.

—WILLIAM BLAKE, *A Poison Tree*

11. Say, wouldst thou guard thy son,
    That sorrow he may shun?
    Begin at the beginning
    And let him keep from sinning.

    Wouldst guard thy house? One door
    Make to it, and no more.
    Wouldst guard thine orchard wall?
    Be free of fruit to all.

—FRANCESCO DA BABERINO, *Of Caution*
(Translated by Dante Gabriel Rossetti)

12. Full fathom five thy father lies;
    Of his bones are coral made;
    Those are pearls that were his eyes;
    Nothing of him that doth fade
    But doth suffer a sea-change
    Into something rich and strange.

—WILLIAM SHAKESPEARE, *The Tempest*

13. I strove with none, for none was worth my strife,
    Nature I loved, and next to Nature, Art;
    I warmed both hands before the fire of life,
    It sinks, and I am ready to depart.

—WALTER LANDOR, *On His Seventy-fifth Birthday*

14. Jenny kissed me when we met,
     Jumping from the chair she sat in;
     Time, you thief, who loves to get
     Sweets into your list, put that in:

     Say I'm weary, say I'm sad,
     Say that health and wealth have missed me,
     Say I'm growing old, but add
     Jenny kissed me.
                                    —LEIGH HUNT, *Rondeau*

15. Sunset and evening star,
     And one clear call for me!
     And may there be no moaning of the bar,
     When I put out to sea,

     But such a tide as moving seems asleep,
     Too full for sound and foam,
     When that which drew from out the boundless deep
     Turns again home.

     For though from out our bourne of Time and Place
     The flood may bear me far,
     I hope to see my Pilot face to face
     When I have crost the bar.
                     —ALFRED, LORD TENNYSON, *Crossing the Bar*

CHAPTER 8

Duration

Changes in duration, in the time given to the production of speech sounds and the time intervals between phrases, permit us to express feelings and to emphasize and subordinate meanings. On the emotional side, a markedly slow rate of utterance is associated with solemnity, depressed moods, and sadness and sorrow. A marked increase of rate is associated with happier states, with gaiety, and heightened feelings. The heightened feelings, however, need not always be pleasant. Anger is also expressed through an increased rate of utterance.

Changes in rate are associated with our physiological states and associated muscular activity. We behave more slowly when we are depressed and quickly when elated; we behave relatively slowly when our thoughts are solemn and more quickly when our mood is light or when we are excited. The muscles of our vocal and articulatory mechanism normally reflect these changes in our vocal tones and in our articulatory activity.

Changes in rate are, of course, correlated with changes in pitch and force. Heightened feelings are accompanied by increases in pitch level and force; depressed feelings by reduction in pitch level as well as by decreased force. These changes are summarized in Figure 8–1.

Changes in duration, as indicated earlier, are achieved through either variation in the rate of articulation or the use of pauses between groups of articulated sounds, or both. In general, content that is articulated slowly is considered more important—intellectually more significant—

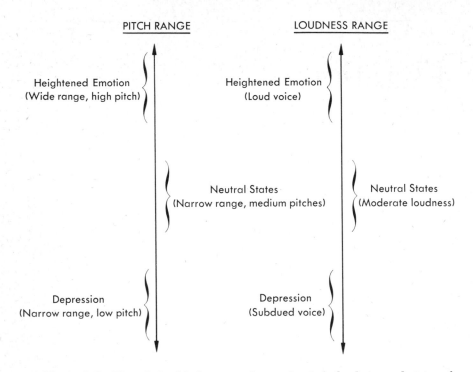

PITCH RANGE   LOUDNESS RANGE

Heightened Emotion   Heightened Emotion
(Wide range, high pitch)   (Loud voice)

Neutral States   Neutral States
(Narrow range, medium pitches)   (Moderate loudness)

Depression   Depression
(Narrow range, low pitch)   (Subdued voice)

Figure 8–1 The relationship between changes in pitch, loudness, and states of feeling.

than rapidly articulated content. If we listen to what is spoken slowly and are able to maintain attention while listening, we assume that what we have heard is more important than more quickly evoked content.

Some speech sounds—vowels and vowellike consonants—lend themselves to a varied and controlled rate of articulation. Words such as *alone, rarely, home, gone, away,* and *always* contain these sounds. They can be uttered quickly or slowly according to the will of the speaker. On the other hand, words such as *tip, stop, quick,* and *put* are necessarily articulated rapidly. In lyric prose and poetry dominant moods can be established through language that incorporates "slow" sounds and "rapid" sounds. Compare, for example, Coleridge's

> Alone, alone, all, all alone,
> Alone on a wide, wide sea!

with Milton's

> Come, and trip it as you go
> On the light fantastic toe

and the difference in mood becomes immediately apparent. The first couplet lends itself to a slow rate of articulation. But the lines from

Milton's *L'Allegro* have to be articulated quickly, or the result would be absurd.

RATE AND MEANING

We must of course, appreciate that when the rate of utterance is conspicuously changed to be either relatively rapid or relatively slow, the most significant word within the phrase, or the most significant phrase within the sentence, is usually spoken more slowly than the rest of the phrase or sentence. Any sustained, unvarying rate may become monotonous. Nothing of any considerable content that we say or read aloud should be uttered at the same rate, regardless of the feeling or mood.

The *use of pause* as a technique for varying rate is perhaps the best single indication of control and sophistication in speech. Both Winston Churchill and Franklin D. Roosevelt made considerable use of lengthened and intentional pauses to create dramatic effects and to emphasize ideas. When a speaker pauses at the end of a phrase, the listener waits. While waiting, he tends to fill in the time gaps with the last bit of content he heard. The inner listener repetition of what the speaker has last said reinforces this content. A pause before and after a word or a phrase sets either off from the rest of the context and so becomes a technique for the vocal underlining of an idea or a unit of thought.

A pause may also be used to indicate transition of thought in a larger context. This is the case when a speaker pauses after the evident completion of a thought. A short pause may separate sentences, a moderate pause may separate paragraphs, and a longer pause may prepare the listeners for a new line of thought.

Dramatic effects may be achieved by combining a pause with a rising inflection. If the phrase before the pause ends with an upward inflection, the result is the "suspension" of a thought. The thought is then completed in the content that follows. A similar effect may be achieved by pausing before and after a presented idea.

The speaker has an obligation, when he uses an intentional pause, to satisfy the expectation of his listeners. If what follows a pause is of no special importance or of no more significance than what preceded it, then the speaker has failed to meet his obligation and the listeners are likely to become disappointed and distrusting.

We all use pauses to separate or group our phrases. In conversational speech such word groupings come naturally with the flow of thought. When our thoughts do not flow as freely as we might like, when we search for words to communicate our thoughts, we reveal it in our unintentional pauses. Under pressure of a large or formal audience, we may become fearful and anxious about pausing, and fill in the gaps with *uh uh's* or their equivalent in nonverbal sounds to avoid moments of silence. The speaker who is poised enough to wait, who pauses with intent and without fear, who does not resort to repetitious fillers to avoid the void of silence will gain the respect of his listeners if what he has to say is worthy of the waiting and the listening. With these points in mind, the reader should find the exercises that follow of help in the practice of some of the uses of duration for vocal variety and as a technique for revealing feeling and communicating thought.

EXERCISES FOR PRACTICE OF CONTROLLED RATE

1. Read the following sentences so that full value is given to the italicized words. The sentences as a whole are to be spoken slowly, and the italicized words more slowly than the others.

    a. *Innocence* is *inconsistent* with the *acquisition* of *riches.*
    b. The *air* was *still,* the sea was *calm.*
    c. *All* rivers *find* their *way* to the *sea.*
    d. In *solitude* we may be *least alone.*
    e. *Life* is what the *living makes* it.
    f. The *snow* fell and *silently* concealed the *earth.*
    g. *Freedom* can *survive* only when it is *shared.*
    h. *Tomorrow* will *come* and pass into *yesterday.*
    i. Man's *inhumanity* to *man* makes *countless* thousands *mourn.*
    j. Through *memory* we can *recreate* a *yesterday,* and project a *tomorrow.*
    k. *Are* we *now* at a *time* when *knowledge* has *outrun wisdom?*

2. The next group of sentences should be spoken at a moderate rate, but the italicized words should be spoken somewhat more slowly for emphasis.

    a. *Mark Twain* held that *cauliflower* was *nothing* but *cabbage* with an *education.*
    b. It is *rare* for a man to be a *husband and hero* to his *own* wife.
    c. *Lawyers* soon *learn* that their *opinions* assume *value only* when they *exact* a fee.
    d. A *good listener* often achieves a *reputation* for being a good *conversationalist.*
    e. President *Coolidge* held that *one with the law* constituted a *majority.*
    f. *Cynics* hold that a *majority* is *almost always wrong.*
    g. To *study mankind* we must study *individual* man.
    h. It might be said of *Thoreau* that he loved not *man* the *less* but *nature* the *more.*
    i. *Muscles,* like *iron,* wear out *faster* with *disuse* than with *use.*

    j.   Montaigne observed that men are most apt to believe *what they least understand.*

    k.   Cervantes advised that a *closed* mouth *catches no flies.*

    l.   Bacon cautioned that *books must follow science,* and *not science books.*

    m.   *Centuries* ago *Plato* remarked that *man* is a very *inconstant creature.*

    n.   In his *Epistles, Seneca* noted, "It is *not* the *man* who has *too little,* but the man who *craves* more, that is *poor.*"

    o.   In *The Magic Mountain,* Thomas Mann wrote, "*Human reason* needs only to *will* more *strongly* than *fate,* and she *is* fate."

3.   Read the following excerpts at appropriate basic rates but with variation to emphasize the key words and so the essential ideas. The more serious or solemn the content, the slower the basic rate should be.

    a.   The childhood shows the man
        As morning shows the day.

                            —JOHN MILTON, *Paradise Lost*

    b.   For truth is precious and divine,—
        Too rich a pearl for carnal swine.

                          —SAMUEL BUTLER, *Hudibras*

    c.   Words are wise men's counters—they do but reckon by them; but they are the money of fools.

                          —THOMAS HOBBES, Leviathan

    d.   Man is his own star; and that soul that can
        Be honest is the only perfect man.

                   —JOHN FLETCHER, *Upon an Honest Man's Fortune*

    e.   Good thoughts his only friends,
          His wealth a well-spent age,
       The earth his sober inn
          And quiet pilgrimage.

                     —THOMAS CAMPION, *Integer Vitae*

    f.   You write with ease to show your breeding,
        But easy writing's curst hard reading.

                   —THOMAS MOORE, *Life of Sheridan*

4.   Read the following passages, using intentional pauses to set off the significant thought groups. Punctuation may help, but occasionally it may be misleading. Determine the units of thought, and pause whether or not the material is punctuated. Indicate pauses by inserting the sign ‖ at the end of thought units at which you intend to pause. Underline the words that carry the essential meanings in each selection.

    a.   The vagabond, when rich, is called a tourist.

                 —PAUL RICHARD, *The Scourge of Christ*

    b.   A man lives not only his personal life, as an individual, but also,

consciously or unconsciously, the life of his epoch and his con-
temporaries.

—THOMAS MANN, *The Magic Mountain*

c. . . . they shall beat their swords into plowshares, and their
spears into pruning-hooks; nation shall not lift up sword against
nation, neither shall they learn war any more.

—*Isaiah* 2:4

d. I live in the crowd of jollity, not so much to enjoy company as
to shun myself.

—SAMUEL JOHNSON, *Rasselas*

e. 'Tis known by the name of perseverance in a good cause—and
of obstinacy in a bad one.

—LAWRENCE STERNE, *Tristram Shandy*

f. There is no cure for birth and death save to enjoy the interval.

—GEORGE SANTAYANA, *Soliloquies in England*

g. There is nothing more tragic in life than the utter impossibility
of changing what you have done.

—JOHN GALSWORTHY, *Justice*

h. Volumes might be written upon the impiety of the pious.

—HERBERT SPENCER, *First Principles*

i. No man who has once heartily and wholly laughed can be alto-
gether irreclaimably bad.

—THOMAS CARLYLE, *Sartor Resartus*

5. The passages that follow call for more deliberate pauses to achieve
emotional impact or to heighten dramatic meaning. In many instances
these effects may be attained by pauses before as well as after the
significant words or phrases.

a. New opinions are always suspected, and usually opposed,
without any other reason but because they are not already
common.

—JOHN LOCKE, *Essay on Human Understanding*

b. The deepest thing in our nature is this dumb region of the heart
in which we dwell alone with our willingnesses and our un-
willingnesses, our faiths and our fears.

—WILLIAM JAMES, *The Will to Believe*

c. Men grind and grind in the mill of a truism, and nothing comes
out but what was put in. But the moment they desert the tradition for a spontaneous thought, then poetry, wit, hope, virtue,
learning, anecdote, all flock to their aid.

—RALPH WALDO EMERSON, *Literary Ethics*

d. Inferiors revolt in order that they may be equal, and equals
that they may be superior. Such is the state of mind which
creates revolutions.

—ARISTOTLE, *Politics*

e. Then darkness enveloped the whole American armada. Not a pinpoint of light showed from those hundreds of ships as they surged on through the night toward their destiny, carrying across the ageless and indifferent sea tens of thousands of young men, fighting for . . . for . . . well, at least for each other.

—ERNIE PYLE, *Brave Men*

f. I have learned silence from the talkative, toleration from the intolerant, and kindness from the unkind; yet strange, I am ungrateful to these teachers.

—KAHLIL GIBRAN, *Sand and Foam*

g. If we open a quarrel between the past and the present, we shall find that we have lost the future.

—WINSTON CHURCHILL, Speech, House of Commons, 1940

CHAPTER 9

Vocal Variety in Speaking and Reading

Although this chapter is specifically entitled "Vocal Variety," we have been anticipating and considering aspects and implications of this subject in several of the preceding chapters. When we discussed *loudness,* we considered first the fundamental need for the speaker to be heard if his intentions to communicate were to be fruitful. Beyond this we also considered the use of vocal force as related to word meanings, sentence meanings, and overall communicative efforts. *Pitch* was likewise considered as a basic attribute of voice that could be used to enhance vocalization *per se.* Pitch was also discussed in relationship to linguistic melody, to word and phrase meaning, and to the expression of states of feeling. Similarly, the vocal attribute *duration* was viewed in relationship to the speaker's physiological state, to feeling, and to semantic implications.

This chapter is in one sense a review and reconsideration of some aspects of vocal variety previously discussed. It also provides us with an opportunity to emphasize some aspects that were briefly touched on in the previous chapters that deal separately with individual attributes of voice.

Through the attributes of voice—pitch, quality, loudness, and duration—we tend as we speak to reveal our thoughts and our feelings or to express those thoughts and feelings we wish others to believe we entertain. The less inhibited we are, the more the component of feeling is expressed through our voice. When we were very young and had little or no awareness of cultural pressures, our voices reflexively indicated our changes in feelings and moods. As we matured, cultural pressures exerted increasing influence on us and we learned, almost always without awareness, of *how* we are expected to show our feelings in our overt behavior, including the way we give voice to our utterances. Pitch changes came under our voluntary control and conformed more and more to the pattern and the linguistic code of our culture. By the time we were of school age most of us spoke the sounds and the melody (intonation) of the language or languages of our culture. We learned also that American-English speech has syllable stress within a word and word stress within a phrase. So we became able to emphasize ideas as we spoke. Our tendencies to talk at changing rates according to mood, to talk more rapidly under heightened feelings, more slowly in the absence of heightened feelings, and quite slowly when sad or depressed, also became modified by cultural influences. Although these cultural modifications direct us toward norms of behavior, most of us still maintain and express our individualities. Sometimes we kick over the traces, and our voices minimize the influences and effects of environmental training and pressures. But usually we manage to conform to a sufficient degree to sound considerably like the people around us while still giving expression to our identifiable selves.

Igor Stravinsky, the noted composer, with considerably more sophistication and a much better than average ear for vocal nuances, listened carefully to how people talked. In one of his books Stravinsky presented graphic as well as verbal descriptions of the vocal characteristics of several of his friends.[1] Stravinsky described one friend as a "virtuoso talker who *likes* to talk, just as Rubinstein *likes* to play the piano." A second friend is described as "fast and funny." A third "talks in spurts like a ticker tape." Another "fishes . . . profoundly, between words." Still another is "too serenely high in tessitura and in volume too suavely soft."

IMPLICATIONS OF VOCAL ATTRIBUTES

With the possible exception of quality, each vocal attribute, as we have noted, is capable of revealing thought as well as feeling. Within a phrase, the important word is likely to be spoken more loudly, more slowly, and at a different pitch from the other words. These changes are paralleled for the phrase-sentence relationships, as well as for the sentence-paragraph, and so forth.

Through the use of vocal variety we are also able to capture attention and to maintain listener interest. In brief, through voice we are able to

[1] Igor Stravinsky and Robert Craft, *Dialogue and a Diary* (Garden City, N.Y.: Doubleday & Company, Inc., 1963).

Aldous:

Gerald: (Roman Candles)

Wystan:

Isaiah:

Figure 9–1 "Four Friends. Gerald [Heard] is a virtuoso talker, the most brilliant I have ever heard, and he *likes* to talk, just as Arthur Rubinstein *likes* to play the piano. Isaiah Berlin is even faster and funnier—an ironical gaiety underlies everything he says—but Isaiah tends to speak in spurts, like a ticker tape. Wystan Auden, by comparison, fishes, though profoundly, between words, and Aldous [Huxley] is too serenely high in tessitura, and in volume too suavely soft." (From *Dialogues and a Diary* by Igor Stravinsky and Robert Craft. Copyright © 1961, 1962, 1963 by Igor Stravinsky. Reprinted by permission of Doubleday & Company, Inc., and Faber and Faber, Ltd.)

reveal thought and feeling, to emphasize ideas, and to keep listeners attentive to our communicative efforts.

Quality

In our earlier discussions of quality, we considered its relationship to resonance and to the avoidance of undesirable vocal aspects such as excessive nasality and breathiness. At this time we consider quality as it is related to feelings and moods and as an aspect of vocal variety.

Although modifications in vocal quality take place as a result of inherent characteristics of our resonating cavities, except for those of us who tend to be either nasal or denasal, there is little that we normally should do consciously to bring about these changes. Normal changes in quality are related to feelings and moods, to the emotional rather than the intellectual aspects of our behavior. Unless we are dealing with a greatly inhibited individual, the feeling tone will be reflected and expressed in his vocal efforts. Usually, we have more difficulty in concealing our feelings than in revealing them. The speaker who does not strive to conceal his inner feelings, and yet does not make a point of putting them on display, will have no difficulty with quality changes. The normally responsive speaker who initiates tone properly and who uses an appropriate and flexible pitch range will do best with the quality that emerges reflexively and naturally.

Reading Aloud

When a speaker chooses to read material written by another person, he has the dual responsibilities of "translating" and transmitting thoughts and feelings that did not originate with him in the specific verbal formulations with which he must deal. The reader who is about to speak another's words, another's thoughts and feelings, must of course determine what these are. The reader-speaker must be certain not only that he knows the denotative or literal meaning of each word, but the *intentions* of the words—the verbal formulations—and their connotations and implications. He must be aware that the written material he is about to translate and transmit represents the feelings as well as the thoughts of another and that a reader, in expressing these feelings and thoughts, has an implicit obligation to be faithful to them. With such awareness of responsibility, and with such an appreciation of the task, the reader-speaker will set about to determine the dominant mood and nuances of feeling of each selection to be read aloud, as well as the underlying theme and specific thoughts to be communicated. Even the most proficient of professional actors—who are essentially readers because they are dealing with the verbal formulations of others—accept the need to study their lines carefully before they read them aloud. Such study is, of course, recommended to our student-readers.

When, as a reader, you are able to understand the mood, feelings, and thoughts inherent in the selections studied-to-be-read-aloud, you should begin to do your reading aloud. If at all possible, record and play back your efforts. Listen objectively and determine whether what you thought you thought, and felt you felt, is being expressed in your speaking of and with another person's words. Remember, you must have an overall appreciation of intention, mood, meaning, and meanings in dealing with another person's words just as you generally know how you think and feel or feel and think about what you are about to say in your own words before you start. With such preparation and appreciation, appropriate initial vocal qualities to establish the dominant mood, and changes in quality to suggest the particular feelings associated with particular ideas should take place "almost as spontaneously as if the words and feelings were initially your own." But because they are not your own, you will just have to work a bit harder to be effective in your role as a translator and transmitter of someone else's words.

EXERCISES FOR VOCAL QUALITY: ESTABLISHING MOOD

1. Somewhere—in desolate wind-swept space—
   In Twilight-land—no man's land—
   Two hurrying Shapes met face to face,
   And bade each other stand.

   —THOMAS BAILEY ALDRICH, *Identity*

2. During the whole of a dull, dark, and resoundless day in the
   autumn of the year, when the clouds hung oppressively low in the
   heavens, I had been passing alone, on horseback, through a singu-
   larly dreary track of country, and at length found myself, as the
   shades of evening drew on, within view of the melancholy House
   of Usher. I know not how it was—but, with the first glimpse
   of the building, a sense of insufferable gloom pervaded my
   spirit.
                             —EDGAR ALLAN POE, *The Fall of the House of Usher*

3. All sorts of things and weather
   Must be taken in together,
   To make up a year
   And a Sphere.
                             —RALPH WALDO EMERSON, *The Mountain and the Squirrel*

4. She left the web, she left the loom,
   She made three paces thro' the room,
   She saw the water lily bloom,
   She saw the helmet and the plume,
         She look'd down to Camelot.
                             —ALFRED, LORD TENNYSON, *The Lady of Shalott*

5. The centipede was happy quite
         Until a toad in fun
   Said, "Pray, which leg goes after which?"
   That worked her mind to such a pitch,
   She lay distracted in a ditch
         Considering how to run.
                             —MRS. EDWARD CRASTER, *Pinafore Poems*

6. Shall I, wasting in despair,
   Die because a woman's fair?
   Or make pale my cheeks with care
   'Cause another's rosy are?
   Be she fairer than the day
   Or the flowery meads in May,
         If she be not so to me,
         What care I how fair she be?
                             —GEORGE WITHER, *Shall I, Wasting in Despair*

7. A flock of sheep that leisurely pass by,
   One after one; the sound of rain, and bees
   Murmuring; the fall of rivers, winds, and seas,
   Smooth fields, white sheets of water, and pure sky;
   I have thought of all by turns, and yet do lie

Sleepless! and soon the small birds' melodies
Must hear, first uttered from my orchard trees;
And the first cuckoo's melancholy cry.

—WILLIAM WORDSWORTH, *To Sleep*

8. It is better to lose health like a spendthrift than to waste it like a miser. It is better to live and be done with it, than to die daily in the sickroom. By all means begin your folio; even if the doctor does not give you a year, even if he hesitates about a month, make one brave push and see what can be accomplished in a week. It is not only in finished undertakings that we ought to honour useful labour. A spirit goes out of the man who means execution, which outlives the most untimely ending. All who have meant good work with their whole hearts, have done good work, although they may die before they have the time to sign it. Every heart that has beat strong and cheerfully has left a hopeful impulse behind it in the world, and bettered the tradition of mankind.

—ROBERT LOUIS STEVENSON, *Aes Triplex*

9. No longer mourn for me when I am dead
Than you shall hear the surly sullen bell
Give warning to the world that I am fled
From this vile world, with vilest worms to dwell:
Nay, if you read this line, remember not
The hand that writ it; for I love you so,
That I in your sweet thoughts would be forgot,
If thinking on me then should make you woe.
O, if I say, you look upon this verse
When I perhaps compounded am with clay,
Do not so much as my poor name rehearse,
But let your love even with my life decay;
Lest the wise world should look into your moan,
And mock you with me after I am gone.

—WILLIAM SHAKESPEARE, *Sonnet 71*

The materials that follow will afford opportunities, some in depth, to employ knowledge and skill in the use of vocal variety. Be sure that you first read and understand the entire selection, and note the underlying, fundamental thought and mood as well as the nuances in feeling and thought. Experiment, using different techniques of emphasis—e.g., basic pitch change, force, or duration—and decide which of these is most appropriate to express the dominant meaning of each selection.

1. Veracity does not consist in *saying*, but in the intention of communicating *truth*.

—SAMUEL TAYLOR COLERIDGE, *Biographica Literaria*

2. As long as war is regarded as wicked, it will always have its
    fascination. When it is looked upon as vulgar, it will cease to be
    popular.
                                      —OSCAR WILDE, *The Critic As Artist*

3. O, who rides by night thro' the woodland so wild?
    It is the fond father embracing his child;
    And close the boy nestles within his loved arm,
    To hold himself fast and to keep himself warm.

    "O father, my father, see yonder," he says;
    "My boy, upon what dost thou fearfully gaze?"
    "O, 'tis the Erl-King with his crown and his shroud."
    "No, my son, it is but a dark wreath of the cloud."

    "O, come and go with me, thou loveliest child;
    By many a gay sport shall thy time be beguiled;
    My mother keeps for thee full many a fair toy,
    And many a fine flower shall she pluck for my boy."

    "O, father, my father, and did you not hear
    The Erl-King whisper so low in my ear?"
    "Be still, my heart's darling—my child, be at ease;
    It was but the wild blast as it sung thro' the trees."

    "O, wilt thou go with me, thou loveliest boy?
    My daughter shall tend thee with care and with joy;
    She shall bear thee so lightly thro' wet and thro' wild,
    And press thee, and kiss thee and sing to my child."

    "O father, my father, and saw you not plain,
    The Erl-King's pale daughter glide past through the rain?"
    "O yes, my loved treasure, I knew it full soon;
    It was the gray willow that danced to the moon."

    "O, come and go with me, no longer delay,
    Or else, silly child, I will drag thee away."
    "O father! O father! now, now keep your hold,
    The Erl-King has seized me—his grasp is so cold!"

    Sore trembled the father; he spurred thro' the wild,
    Clasping close to his bosom his shuddering child;
    He reaches his dwelling in doubt and in dread,
    But, clasped to his bosom, the infant was dead!
                                   —SIR WALTER SCOTT, *The Erl-King* (translation)

4.   Home they brought her warrior dead;
      She nor swoon'd, nor utter'd cry:
  All her maidens, watching, said,
      "She must weep or she will die."

     Then they praised him, soft and low,
       Call'd him worthy to be loved,
     Truest friend and noblest foe;
       Yet she neither spoke nor moved.

     Stole a maiden from her place,
       Lightly to the warrior stept,
     Took the face-cloth from the face;
       Yet she neither moved nor wept.

     Rose a nurse of ninety years,
       Set his child upon her knee—
     Like summer tempest came her tears—
       "Sweet my child, I live for thee."

—ALFRED, LORD TENNYSON,
Home They Brought Her Warrior Dead

5.   How doth the little crocodile
      Improve his shining tail,
  And pour the waters of the Nile
      On every shining scale!

     How cheerfully he seems to grin,
       How neatly spreads his claws,
     And welcomes little fishes in
       With gently smiling jaws.

—LEWIS CARROLL, *The Crocodile*

6.   Mycilla dyes her locks, 'tis said,
      But 'tis a foul aspersion;
  She buys them black, they therefore need
      No subsequent immersion.

—LUCILIUS, *On an Old Woman*
(Translated by William Cowper)

7.   They call thee rich; I deem thee poor;
  Since, if thou darest not use thy store,
  But savest only for thine heirs,
  The treasure is not thine, but theirs.

—LUCILIUS, *Treasure*
(Translated by William Cowper)

8. When all the world is young, lad,
        And all the trees are green;
    And every goose a swan, lad,
        And every lass a queen;
    Then hey for boot and horse, lad,
        And round the world away;
    Young blood must have its course, lad,
        And every dog his day.

    When all the world is old, lad,
        And all the trees are brown;
    And all the sport is stale, lad,
        And all the wheels run down:
    Creep home, and take your place there,
        The spent and maimed among:
    God grant you find one face there,
        You loved when all was young.
                        —CHARLES KINGSLEY, *Water Babies*

9. Remember me when I am gone away,
    Gone far away into the silent land;
    When you can no more hold me by the hand,
    Nor I half turn to go, yet turning stay.
    Remember me when no more, day by day,
    You tell me of our future that you planned;
    Only remember me; you understand
    It will be too late to counsel then or pray.
    Yet if you should forget me for a while
    And afterwards remember, do not grieve:
    For if the darkness and corruption leave
    A vestige of the thoughts that once I had,
    Better by far you should forget and smile
    Than that you should remember and be sad.
                        —CHRISTINA ROSSETTI, *Remember*

10. In the following excerpts from the speeches and writings of John
    F. Kennedy, esssential ideas are brought out by the balancing of
    phrases and by verbal contrasts resulting from positions of words
    within phrases. Often the same words occur in contexts which are
    almost but not quite the same. Be certain that in your study of the
    selections you anticipate and prepare to bring out the related yet
    contrasting thoughts and the subtleties and nuances in feeling as
    well as in thought by appropriate vocal changes.

    a. . . . democracy means much more than popular government
        and majority rule, much more than a system of political tech-

niques to flatter or deceive powerful blocs of voters . . . the true democracy, living and growing and inspiring, puts its faith in the people—faith that the people will not simply elect men who will represent their views ably and faithfully, but also elect men who will exercise their conscientious judgment—faith that the people will not condone those whose devotion to principle leads them to unpopular causes, but reward courage, respect honor and ultimately recognize right.
—JOHN F. KENNEDY, *Profiles in Courage*

b.   And thus, in the days ahead, only the very courageous will be able to take the hard and unpopular decisions necessary for our survival in the struggle with a powerful enemy—an enemy with leaders who need give little thought to the popularity of their course, who need pay little tribute to the public opinion they themselves manipulate, and who may force, without fear of retaliation at the polls, their citizens to sacrifice present laughter for future glory. And only the very courageous will be able to keep alive the spirit of individualism and dissent which gave birth to this nation, nourished it as an infant and carried it through its severest tests upon the attainment of its majority.
—JOHN F. KENNEDY, *Profiles in Courage*

c.   I want to be a President who responds to a problem not by hoping his subordinates will act, but by directing them to act.
When things are very quiet and beautifully organized I think it's time to be concerned.
—JOHN F. KENNEDY, Speech, 1960

d.   So let us begin anew—remembering on both sides that civility is not a sign of weakness, and sincerity is always subject to proof. Let us never negotiate out of fear. But let us never fear to negotiate.
Let both sides explore what problems unite us instead of belaboring those problems which divide us.
Let both sides, for the first time, formulate serious and precise proposals for the inspection and control of arms—and bring the absolute power to destroy other nations under the absolute control of all nations.
—JOHN F. KENNEDY, Inaugural Address

11. To every thing there is a season, and a time to every purpose under the heaven: a time to be born, and a time to die; a time to plant, and a time to pluck up that which is planted; a time to kill, and a time to heal; a time to break down, and a time to build up; a

time to weep, and a time to laugh; a time to mourn, and a time to dance; a time to cast away stones, and a time to gather stones together; a time to embrace, and a time to refrain from embracing; a time to seek, and a time to lose; a time to keep, and a time to cast away; a time to rend, and a time to sew; a time to keep silence, and a time to speak; a time to love, and a time to hate; a time for war, and a time for peace.

—*Ecclesiastes* 3:1–8

12.   The following short selections and excerpts require careful phrasing for their full import.

   a.   Nothing in life is so exhilarating as to be shot at without result.
   —WINSTON CHURCHILL, *The Malakand Field Force*

   b.   Dictators ride to and fro upon tigers which they dare not dismount. And the tigers are getting hungry.
   —WINSTON CHURCHILL, *While England Slept*

   c.   A truth that's told with bad intent
   Beats all the lies you can invent.
   —WILLIAM BLAKE, *Auguries of Innocence*

   d.   My only books
   Were woman's looks
   And folly's all they've taught me.
   —THOMAS MOORE, *The Time I've Lost in Wooing*

SUMMARY

Vocal variety may be used to express feelings, to communicate meanings, to hold attention, and to make speaking and listening interesting. Any of the attributes of voice—pitch, quality, loudness, or duration—may be used toward these ends. Rarely is a single attribute used alone. Changes in pitch and force are frequently made together. Usually words spoken slowly are also spoken with increased force. The effective speaker achieves his effects by a combination of vocal factors, but is able to control the factors according to the nature of what he has to say. The effective speaker is able to use a widened pitch range, appropriate inflection, modifications in vocal intensity, and changes in the tempo of his speech to indicate how he feels about his thoughts as he talks. Furthermore, he can use vocal variety as a means of pointing up essential ideas and subordinating less important ones.

Diction

PART TWO

CHAPTER 10

Our Changing Speech Patterns

Although we do not have to accept literally George Bernard Shaw's observation that "England and America are two countries separated by the same language," there is little doubt that from the time of the American Revolution to World War II, American English emerged as a language with enough divergence in pronunciation and word usage to require us to think of the differences in the English language spoken in the two countries despite the basic similarities between them. Interestingly, since World War II, the influences of improved communication, radio, television, and film have worked in the opposite direction.

American English is in a process of change because it is a living language. Classical Latin and Greek have become stabilized because they are "dead" languages that are no longer spoken by persons engaged in social or economic intercourse. As Whatmough observes "If language could not change, it would be incapable of coping with new demands, new concepts, new inventions. . . ."[1]

This chapter considers some of the factors and historical influences that resulted in English becoming the language of the United States, features that characterize American English and its dialectical variations, and some psychosocial forces that are currently and dynamically influencing the sounds, the lexicon, and even the syntax of our language.

[1] J. Whatmough, *Language* (New York: St. Martin's Press, Inc., 1956), p. 174.

129

ENGLISH HISTORICAL BACKGROUNDS

From the time of the ancient Romans until the eleventh century, the land masses known as the British Isles were successively conquered and occupied by peoples of many nations. Each of the conquering peoples left traces of influence on a language whose basic forms and structure were not to be determined until the sixteenth century.

The Romans under Caesar came to Britain in 55 B.C. and did not finally leave until about A.D. 400. The inhabitants who remained behind, other than the Romans, spoke a Celtic dialect but retained the use of Roman names for roads and many geographic locations (place names).

In the middle of the fifth century Angles, Saxons, and Jutes began to invade Britain and drove the Celts westward into Wales and Cornwall and northward toward what is now Scotland. The term *English* is used for the Germanic speech of these groups of invaders and their descendants. It is important to appreciate, however, that the earlier inhabitants of Britain did not suddenly change their speech habits, and those who stayed behind and were not pushed to the west or to the north continued to speak a language much as they had spoken, except that new linguistic forms—those of their conquerors—were incorporated and modified into their previous linguistic habits. Essentially, despite military conquests, the language of the conquered assimilated that of the conquerors.

Christianity came to Saxon England during the first half of the seventh century. With Christianity, Latin was introduced as the spoken and written language for religious and learned purposes. This influence on the common man, however, was not significantly reflected in his everyday speech.

Between the eighth and eleventh centuries, Scandinavians in increasing numbers came to Britain, and with it Scandinavian influences on what was to become English. The Scandinavians, for the most part Danes, also invaded and conquered the northeastern parts of France and ultimately became the ruling aristocracy of Normandy. During this period of achievement, the Scandinavians assumed Gallic ways, including French as a language, and their own Germanic speech was lost.

In the historically critical year 1066, the descendants of the Scandinavians, who now were Normans and who have become essentially French in culture and in their linguistic habits, invaded England under William the Conqueror, and became the established power in England. Although French then became the language of the ruling class in England, the masses continued to speak a Germanic language. In time the language of the Norman conquerors was reduced in influence, and all but disappeared, at least as far as the speech of the common man was concerned.

The English that most people in England speak today, and the American English that most Americans speak, are both derived from the speech of the inhabitants of the London area from the time of William the Conqueror through the Elizabethan period. But England throughout its history has never been free of divergent dialects. The Germanic groups— the Angles, Saxons, and Jutes—came from different parts of the continental lowlands. These groups spoke different dialects, settled in different parts of England, and left their linguistic influences where they settled. One important result is that the dialectical differences among the inhabitants of England today are greater and more divergent than are the regional-dialect differences in the United States.

It does not require an expert ear to discern differences between American and British speech, even assuming that the comparison is made between an educated Englishman who has lived most of his life in or near London and an educated American who has lived most of his life in or around Boston and is a Harvard graduate. These representative speakers are selected because, although the differences between American English and upper-class London English are comparatively few, yet differences exist. They exist in idiom and in specific words to denote situations and events as well as in word pronunciation and stress and in manner of articulation. Differences are also found in speech melody. The Londoner and the Bostonian are not likely to express their enthusiasms or their irritations with the same choice of words or the same manner of vocal melody. *A bloody American mess* has different connotations from a *bloody English mess*. The Bostonian gets about in *streetcars* or *subway* trains whereas his London cousin gets about in *trams* and by way of the *underground*. The Bostonian who does not own his own home lives in an *apartment;* his London counterpart lives in a *flat*. The Bostonian leaves his car in a ga*rage* rather than in a *ga*rage. He watches *TV* rather than "telly." The Bostonian law enforcer is a *policeman,* or a *cop*, rather than a *bòbby;* the Bostonian is entertained at the *movies* rather than at the *cinema*. The melody pattern of the Londoner, whether his utterance is intellectual or emotional, is likely to be characterized by wider inflectional changes than is that of the Bostonian. Articulatory differences may also be heard. The sound *t* in an unstressed syllable, as in *pity,* is likely to be more clearly and more lightly articulated by our English representative than it is by the American. Neither speaker is likely to pronounce an *r* when it is in a final position in a word, as in *dear* or *hear,* but the *r* would be articulated differently in words such as *very*. Our English representative pronounces the word *very* in a manner that phoneticians describe as a single flapped sound. Americans may think of it as approximating the pronunciation *veddy* as in "veddy nice," which of course it is not, except possibly to the prejudiced and motivated ear of an American comic strip artist trying to get across a notion of English pronunciation to an American comic strip reader.

STANDARD ENGLISH SPEECH?

If an American living in the first quarter of this century were to judge English speech by what he heard from Englishmen who were visiting in the United States, he might well have concluded that all Englishmen speak pretty much alike. Had he read Shaw's *Pygmalion,* he would have been puzzled by Professor Higgins' complaints. Yet both the American's and Professor Higgins' observations were correct. It is likely that the American, unless he happened to have traveled widely in England, would have been exposed only to the speech of British stage personalities, British political personages, members of the royal family, and well-to-do and well-educated Englishmen with public (really private) secondary school and Oxford or Cambridge backgrounds. Their speech is almost standard.

The speech of these groups is characterized by English phoneticians as *Received Pronunciation;* by *received* is meant "accepted in approved circles." This speech is described by the English phonetician Daniel Jones in his *An Outline of English Phonetics.*[2] Individual recommended pronunciations may be found in Jones' *Pronunciation of English.*[3]

Although "Received speech" was the one that Professor Higgins spoke as a matter of course and that Eliza Doolittle learned to speak after much rigorous training, but that broke down under emotional stress, it is not the standard for the speech of all Englishmen—not even for those with moderate amounts of education who live in or near the City of London. Members of the English Parliament, including those who represent the Conservatives, are today more likely to speak with the accents and pronunciations of the British Broadcasting Company than those identified with Eton and Oxford. A Labor member of Parliament is not likely to assume Tory accents, or even a Tory vocabulary, when he is aware that he may be on the air and his words heard by his constituents in the evening news broadcast. In brief, the forces of democracy in England, as well as the forces of the mass media of communicating, have worked in directions away from Received Pronunciation. Despite Professor Higgins, the English will go on being themselves and listening, so that they can appreciate British Broadcasting Company diction, American movies, and American television programs.

There are, of course, variances within the London area that are wide enough to require "translation" for many British as well as American citizens. Charles McCabe, an American journalist presents the following as an example of the Cockney dialect:

"A lorry pranged the banger in the boot and I hadn't the readies to

---

[2] Daniel Jones, *An Outline of English Phonetics,* 8th ed. (Cambridge, England: W. Hefner and Sons, 1956).
[3] Daniel Jones, *The Pronunciation of English,* 3rd ed. (Cambridge, England: W. Hefner and Sons, 1950).

get it out of the ricky, so do you fancy taking the tube to the cinema or slipping around to the pub for a pint." This translates to:

"A truck smashed into the trunk of my car and I didn't have the money to fix it, so do you want to take the subway to the movies or go to the neighborhood bar for a beer?" [4]

Despite variations in dialects "within cultures" we may conjecture with the popular linguist Mario Pei, who in 1949 predicted: "Granted a continuation of present historical conditions, the English language of two hundred years hence will be likely to represent a merger of British and American phonetic habits, with comparatively little in the way of morphological or syntactical innovations, but with a turn-over in vocabulary and semantics that would make it difficult, not to say incomprehensible, to the English speaker of today." [5]

AMERICAN BEGINNINGS

When, may we say, did American speech become sufficiently different from the English to give us the beginning of American English? What were the influences that produced and nurtured these differences? In what ways were they peculiarly a result of a new culture and new forces related to this culture? What forces, regardless of culture, continue to exert their effects on our ever-changing speech patterns?

At the opening of the nineteenth century, the United States had its critics and deplorers who raised the hue and cry, "What is happening to our language?" They were referring to English, and were warning Americans about the need to keep their language pure and free from new vulgarisms. John Witherspoon, a Scottish clergyman who came to the United States to become the president of Princeton, suffered considerable anguish at the thought of the development of an American language. Mencken, in *The American Language*, cites Witherspoon as being pained by what he heard in "public and solemn discourses." Said Witherspoon:

> I have heard in this country, in the senate, at the bar, and from
> the pulpit, and see daily in dissertations from the press, errors in
> grammar, improprieties and vulgarisms which hardly any person
> of the same class in point of rank and literature would have fallen
> into in Great Britain.[6]

But persons such as Witherspoon, however great their prestige, were opposed by such Americans as John Adams and Thomas Jefferson. Per-

---

[4] Charles McCabe, "The Fearless Spectator," *San Francisco Chronicle*, March 21, 1972.

[5] Mario Pei, *The Story of Language* (Philadelphia: J. B. Lippincott Co., 1949), p. 303.

[6] H. L. Mencken, *The American Language* (New York: Alfred A. Knopf, Inc., 1946), p. 5.

haps more realistically, as Mencken notes on the same page, Jefferson declared:

> The new circumstances under which we are placed call for new words, new phrases, and for the transfer of old words to new objects. An American dialect will therefore be formed.[7]

While the dispute between Americans for English English and those for American English was going on Noah Webster was busily at work on his *Grammatical Institute of the English Language* and, perhaps more importantly, on his *American Dictionary of the English Language*. Certainly, with the publication of the latter in 1828, American English achieved status and recognition, and became established as a major variant of the English language.

Even a cursory review of the forces that established American English as an independent variant of the English language would reveal the following: The American geography and physiography presented new features, new creatures, new ways of working for a livelihood, and with them the need for new words. Many of the words came from the Indians and had no competition from the mother tongue. Thus, words such as *skunk, hickory, moose, opposum, persimmon,* and *squash* came into our language. Place names, Mencken points out, also came from the Indians.[8] So did such names for articles of clothing and frequently used objects such as *tomahawk, wigwam, toboggan,* and *mackinaw*.

It would, however, be erroneous to conclude that the spirit of rebellion and the influence of the Indians were the only forces that shaped American English. The early colonists, from the very outset, had linguistic influences as a result of accretions from the languages of other colonizations. From the French came words such as *cache, portage,* and *voyageur,* as well as *prairie, bureau,* and *gopher.* From the Dutch in New Amsterdam, Mencken tells us, came such words as *cruller, cole-slaw, cookey, scow, patroon,* as well as *boss* and *Santa Claus.*[9] Many place names in the Hudson area containing *dorp, kill,* and *hook* are also directly from the Dutch. The word *Yankee,* according to Mencken (p. 110), is possibly the most notable of all contributions of Knickerbocker Dutch to the American language.

Spanish influences came later, at a time when American English had become well established as a variant of British English. Texas, the Southwest, and California had been colonized by the Spanish and were developed by Mexico when it won its independence from Spain. Spanish and Mexican contributions to American English are readily recognizable in place names, architecture, agriculture, and animal husbandry. Some of

[7] Ibid., p. 5.
[8] Ibid., p. 105.
[9] Ibid., p. 108.

the characteristic geographical features of the Southwest are known by Mexican-Spanish names such as *mesas, canyons,* and *arroyos.* The American, for the most part of Anglo-Saxon origin, who took over the Southwest not only learned how to construct buildings of mud and straw bricks but learned to call them *adobes.*

Many of the words that we now associate with cattle raising are also of Spanish origin. These include *ranch, lasso,* and *riata.* The *chaps* worn by cowboys to protect their legs are an abbreviation of *chaparajos.* The word *rodeo* has its English translation as roundup. It is now used as well to refer to an exhibition and competition in the skills that cowboys were and to some degree are still expected to perform in cattle raising. The word *ranch* has been extended to refer as a noun to an agricultural establishment and as a verb to farming activities.

The American colonists were ready borrowers of words from other languages, but they were also ready creators of words and phrases that were "coined in English metal" (Mencken, p. 113). Some of these words were a product of the new circumstances and conditions in which the colonists found themselves, but others reveal an underlying way people— any uninhibited and resourceful people—have with words. For a variety of reasons, words were invented. One of the reasons is that inventing words is fun. It is a kind of pleasure in which we indulged ourselves as very young children and again as adolescents. Word-inventing can be a sheer delight, and our American colonists needed to be delighted. Mencken reminds us that "the American, even in the seventeenth century, already showed many of the characteristics that were to set him off from the Englishman later on—his bold and somewhat grotesque imagination, his contempt for dignified authority, his lack of aesthetic sensitiveness, his extravagant humor" (pp. 113–114). Not restrained by grammatical awareness or a knowledge of the structure of their language, and largely illiterate, our uncouth and headstrong early colonists added words as the needs of the occasions demanded. So nouns such as *cowhide* and *logroll,* and adjectives and adverbs such as *no-account, no-how,* and *lickitty-split* became terms to reckon with and by in the utterances of our seventeenth-century Americans. These speakers also introduced such compound words as *bullfrog, hogwallow,* and *hoecake.* All of these are useful terms for persons who are busy working with or against the creatures and forces of nature in a new environment.

A living language shows the effects of a busy people. Early in our history the word *cent,* a verbal invention of Gouverneur Morris, was substituted for the two-syllable English word *penny. Dime* was a Jeffersonian invention derived from the French word *dixième.*

Later, we consider, in some detail, other examples of abbreviatory processes that have us riding in autos or cars rather than in automobiles, or watching TV rather than television.

ONGOING FORCES FOR CHANGE

Thus far we have traced the influences that created an American English and some of the differences in linguistic forms between British English and American English. Now we consider some of the forces that make any living language a changing language, constantly though slowly yielding to human inclinations and to changing verbal habits. To begin with, we should appreciate the effects of our contemporary ability for speed of movement and our general mobility as a nation of people on wheels or on wings. Washington and Julius Caesar traveled on state occasions in much the same kind of vehicles. Except for slight differences in styling and the addition of springs, similar vehicles were used by our presidents up to McKinley, although out of choice rather than of necessity, to ride to their inaugurations. Recent presidents are no longer earthbound. They may now move about with supersonic speed. What influence future presidents or future English-speaking citizens, American or British, or from other parts of the English speaking world, will have on American speech, or English speech, is a matter of conjecture.

Despite the efforts of some of our nineteenth- and early twentieth-century teachers of elocution and diction who considered British English a more genteel standard than the emerging American differences, the people of the United States do not observe or aspire to a single standard of what constitutes *good American speech*. Differences, however, at least among educated speakers, are relatively small. The members of Congress, regardless of the states they represent, have no difficulty in understanding one another because of differences in pronunciation or idiom. Nevertheless, as McDavid points out ". . . every speaker of American English knows that other varieties exist, different from the one he speaks, empirically he has learned to distinguish several of these varieties. . . ." [10] In 1958, C. K. Thomas identified ten major regional dialects in the United States.[11] The dialectical features, for the most part in pronunciation, enabled Thomas to "map" the United States into the following major areas (see Figure 10–1): "Eastern New England, New York City, Middle Atlantic, the South, Southern Mountain States, the North Central Area, the Central Midland, the Northwest, the Southwest Coastal Area, and Western Pennsylvania." [12]

[10] R. McDavid, in W. N. Francis, *The Structure of American English* (New York: The Ronald Press Company, 1958), p. 482.

[11] By dialect we mean a variety of language with features of pronunciation, grammar, or vocabulary that distinguish it from other varieties (dialects) of the same language.

[12] C. K. Thomas, *An Introduction to the Phonetics of American English*, 2nd ed. (New York: The Ronald Press Company, 1958), p. 232.

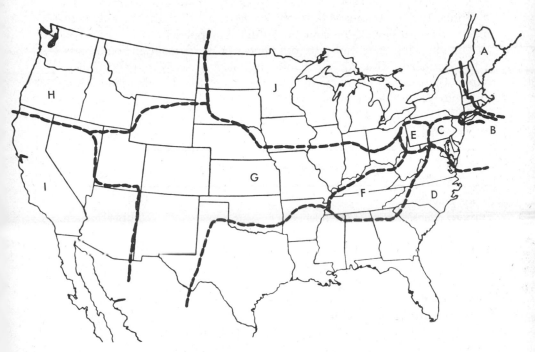

Figure 10–1 Map showing the major regional speech areas: *A:* Eastern New England; *B:* New York City; *C:* Middle Atlantic; *D:* Southern; *E:* Western Pennsylvania; *F:* Southern Mountain; *G:* Central Midland; *H:* Northwest; *I:* Southwest; *J:* North Central. (From Charles Kenneth Thomas, *An Introduction to the Phonetics of American English,* 2nd ed. Copyright © 1958 The Ronald Press Company.)

Regional Differences

In the continental United States, differences in pronunciation are most striking along the Atlantic Coast. As we move inland and westward, the differences, C. K. Thomas observes, ". . . become blurred. Over large areas, from the Connecticut Valley to the Oregon Coast, for instance, differences are so slight that casual listeners rarely notice them at all." Although differences are greatest along the Atlantic Coast, the merchant from Maine has no anxiety that he will not be readily understood if he speaks by telephone to a merchant from New York, or Maryland, or Florida.

Most students of American dialects agree with Thomas that "the most striking differences between the various regional pronunciations, and the difference around which the most lively, though inconclusive, arguments have revolved, is the nature of the sounds which correspond to the letter *r.*" [13]

[13] C. K. Thomas, *op. cit.,* p. 195.

Figure 10–2 is another dialect map of the United States. We may note that the western part of the country is still "unmapped."

The following chart indicates differences in word usage in some parts of the Northern, Midland, and Southern dialect areas within the United States. The reader may compare his own usage for the identified items with those of his friends or associates.

Dialect Area

ITEM	NORTHERN	MIDLAND	SOUTHERN
Paper container	bag	sack	sack
Type of cheese (cottage cheese)	Dutch cheese pot cheese	smearcase	clabber cheese
Bread	johnnycake corn bread	corn bread	corn bread corn pone
Valve mechanism over a sink	faucet	spigot spicket	spigot spicket
Small, striped, bushy-tailed animal	skunk	skunk polecat wood pussy	polecat
Cherry seed	pit stone	seed stone	seed stone
Container	pail	bucket	bucket

Adapted from R. W. Shuy, *Discovering American Dialects*, National Council of Teachers of English, Urbana, Illinois, 1967, pp. 26–27.

DIALECTS AND SOCIAL CLASS

Not all dialectical differences are limited to geographic regions. Within some regions there are dialectical differences related to social class and socioeconomic status. McDavid observes that "Social differences in language are usually more apparent in morphology and syntax. But in some communities, particularly in the South, they manifest themselves in pronunciation as well." [14] Many speakers, perhaps more so in the South than elsewhere in the United States, are bidialectal for both social and economic reasons. Certainly, many politicians—Huey Long and Eugene Talmadge may be cited as examples—were able to accommodate themselves to the dialect of their constituents as well as to the standards ordinarily observed in Congress without, of course, ever giving up the southern "flavor" of their speech.

[14] R. McDavid, *op. cit.*, p. 536.

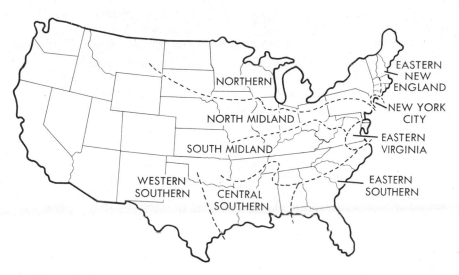

Figure 10–2 Some of the dialect areas in the United States. (From R. W. Shuy, *Discovering American Dialects*, National Council of Teachers of English, Urbana, Illinois, 1967, p. 47.)

Black English

Unlike dialects, which are "confined" to regions or characteristic of social classes within regions, contemporary Black English has no geographic boundaries. Black English is spoken or understood by a majority of persons in the United States who identify themselves as Blacks.[15] Despite its early origins and development in the southern colonies and states, Black English is now heard in most "inner cities" throughout the United States. In Chapter 11 we present some of the phonemic, morphemic, and syntactical features that have established Black English as a variant or dialect of "Standard" American English. Our concern in this chapter is to highlight some of the contributions of Black English to post-World War II American English as well as some of the dynamics behind these contributions.

In recent years, much American slang has been directly taken from Black English. The phrase *right on* may have achieved respectability beyond its usage as slang. It is heard in political speeches and in radio and television commercials. *Rip off* is a phrase with multiple meanings. When a friend has been *ripped off*, you have cause to worry whether he has been robbed, cheated, overcharged, arrested, or murdered. *Rap* is to talk or to argue. So, many of us have held *rap sessions*.

[15] J. L. Dillard, *Black English: Its History and Usage in the United States* (New York: Random House, Inc., 1972) claims that 80 per cent of American Blacks speak Black English.

There is considerable poetry in the vocabulary of Black English, in that words carry values and associations beyond their immediate meanings. For example, the substitution of *fox* for *woman* implies either an evaluation of women or a description of behavior. *Stone* is a *heavy* adjective, and a *stone fox* is *something else.* A *dude* is the successor of the *hip cat* of the 1950s. However, *dude* may refer to any adult male.

There are a number of speculations as to why Black English slang is entering and temporarily at least becoming part of contemporary American English. One possibility could be found in the identification or sympathy of a number of socially alienated white young people with the conditions and alienation of Blacks. Both white student activists and the late "hippie community" formed something of a counterculture, which adopted some Black terminology as its own, if not the syntax or phonology of Black English. Within this counterculture, skill at using Black English carried prestige, and both ends of this white counterculture received considerable coverage in the mass media in the late 1960s, and elements of Black English were literally broadcast as never before.

It should be noted that most of these lexical contributions come from poor and working-class Blacks. A few exceptions are those contributions made by Blacks who have been successful in the entertainment industry, where the use of Black English can be a professional asset. It is also generally assumed that the dialect of comparatively wealthy Blacks, the "respected speakers in the community," in the parlance of this book, is a variety of Standard English. It is possible to raise the question as to whether there is a "Black Standard English," and if so, who are its users. The Black clergy and some Black political figures have an oratorical style that is different from both White Standard English and the Black English of the poor and working classes. Much of the Black clergy was trained at all-Black seminaries. There were similarities in the diction and oratory of Dr. Martin Luther King and the union organizer A. Philip Randolph. King's diction differed from that of his contemporary, the late Bishop James Pike, and Randolph's style of speech is different from that of his contemporary, the late Walter Reuther. There may well be a Black Standard English or at least a "Standard English" as used by Blacks.

Who Determines Standards of Usage? The Dictionaries

Having briefly sketched some of the forces and influences that have given us American-English speech and its dialectical variations, both historical and contemporary, we return to Standard American English. Who determines when new words become respectable and older words become acceptable in regard to meanings they have assumed through usage? Who determines what are "proper" pronunciations? When does a slang term cease to be slang and become a "respectable" standard term?

One answer is, "when the educated, respected members of a culture use the terms." But the task still remains for terms and pronunciations to be recorded and for decisions for what is to be recorded. Because we have no equivalent of a French Academy whose members have stated meetings to make decisions and "fix the language," the responsibility inevitably falls on the editors of dictionaries. Fortunately, even Samuel Johnson noted in the preface to his famous *Dictionary,* published in 1755 that "words are the daughters of earth." Johnson opposed the notion of an Academy with the authority to determine what is correct and acceptable. Despite this, Johnson admits personal bias in his lexical selection. For example, he included words he recognized as obsolete "when they are found in authors not obsolete, or when they have any force or beauty that may deserve revival." Johnson's authorities were the English writers he respected. He recognized that "no dictionary of a living tongue ever can be perfect, since while it is hastening to publication, some words are budding, and some falling away."

Noah Webster published his *Compendious Dictionary of the English Language* in 1806. It acknowledged that current usage rather than prescription should determine lexical entries and their definitions and pronunciations. The title page of his *Compendious Dictionary* indicates that five thousand words were added "to the number found in the Best English Compends," and that definitions of many words were "amended and improved."

Contemporary dictionary editors are usually insistent that they record what is established and current, and are reluctant to accept the responsibility for establishing standards by virtue of printed and widely distributed publications. Harrison Platt, Jr., presents what we consider a fair view of the degree of responsibility and authority the editors of a respected dictionary cannot avoid. In an Appendix to *The American College Dictionary,* Platt says:

> What . . . is the rôle of a dictionary in settling questions of pronunciation or meaning or grammar? It is not a legislating authority on good English. It attempts to record what usage at any time actually is. Insofar as possible, it points out divided usage. It indicates regional variations of pronunciation or meaning wherever practical. It points out meanings and uses peculiar to a trade, profession, or special activity. It suggests the levels on which certain words or usages are appropriate. A dictionary . . . based on a realistic sampling of usage, furnishes the information necessary for a sound judgment of what is good English in a given situation. To this extent the dictionary is an authority, and beyond this authority should not go.[16]

[16] Harrison Platt, Jr., "Appendix," *The American College Dictionary* (New York: Random House, Inc., 1964), p. 1425.

In the light of this excerpt, we may reassess the significance of the entry on *ain't* in *Webster's Third New International Dictionary*. *Ain't*, according to the entry on page 45, is a contraction of *are not, is not, am not,* or *have not*. Further, we are told, *ain't* ". . . though disapproved by many, and more common in less educated speech [is] used orally in most parts of the U.S. by many cultivated speakers esp. in the phrase *ain't I*." Some critics of this dictionary have pointedly asked what is meant by "less educated speech" and imply that somewhere and somehow a comparison seems to be missing. On page 209, we learn that the entry *between* is no longer limited to an implication of two but may be used to suggest division or participation by two or more. The entry cites such usage by *Time Magazine* and by eminent scholars, including a linguist from Harvard University.

One of the supporters of the changes accepted, and so presumably given authority in the Webster's Third Edition, is Bergen Evans, who is recognized as a lexicographer and a language specialist, as well as the coauthor of *A Dictionary of Contemporary American Usage*. Professor Evans, in an informative and amusing article, opens with the suggestion to "Mind your language, friend: words are changing their meaning all the time, some moving up the ladder of social acceptability and others down."[17] In response to critics who accuse dictionary editors of condoning corruption and "low usage," Evans says: "Alas, the tendencies they deplore have been evident for as long as we have any record of language and are as indifferent to indignation or approval as the tides." As examples of changes in word meaning, Evans points out that the word *resentment* once could mean "gratitude"; in Samuel Johnson's time, it came to mean "a species of revenge" and now means "indignation." The word *censure* once meant simply "to pass judgment"; *censure* now implies "a judgment with negative criticism." The word *uncouth* once meant "unknown" (*couth* itself meant "known") without any contemporary implications of "a lack of polish or 'good' (approved) manners." Few of us are aware that *wench* could once (as late as 1200) be used to refer to "a child of either sex" or that *counterfeit* once had no implication of illegal reproduction but meant "to imitate" or "to model," even after a worthy ideal.

Sumner Ives, in an article reviewing as well as anticipating the controversy that followed the publication of *Webster's Third New International Dictionary*, makes a number of points relative to diction and grammatical usage that are decidedly worthy of our consideration.[18] Several of these points may be summarized as follows:

1. English has changed more during the past fifty years than during any similar period in the past.

---

[17] Bergen Evans, "Couth to Uncouth and Vice Versa," *New York Times Magazine*, (November 10, 1963), pp. 22ff.

[18] Sumner Ives, "A Review of Webster's Third New International Dictionary," *Word Study* (December 1961).

2. Language, any language, is a system of human conventions rather than a system of natural laws. . . .

3. A dictionary is reliable only insofar as it comprehensively and accurately describes current practices in a language, including community opinion, as to the social and regional associations of each practice described.

4. ". . . 'good' English is that which most effectively accomplishes the purpose of the author (or speaker) without drawing irrelevant attention from the purpose to the words or constructions by which this purpose is accomplished. Thus, for ordinary purposes, 'good' English is that which is customary and familiar in a given context and in the pursuit of a given objective."

5. Words may have more than one pronunciation. "Standards" of pronunciation must make allowances for regional variations and for differences related to specific contexts. *Webster's Third New International Dictionary* represents ". . . the normal pronunciation of English as it is spoken by cultured persons in each major section of the country—the 'language of well-bred ease,' culturally determined."

Slang and Argot

Argot is the special vocabulary and idiom of a particular profession or social group. Historically, argot is identified with the vocabulary of underworld characters, devised for "private" or ingroup communication and identification. Thus, we are informed by the *Random House Dictionary of the English Language* that *Beggar's Opera* by John Gay is "rich in thieves' argot." *The Random House Dictionary* defines *slang* as "very informal usage in vocabulary and idiom that is characteristically more metaphorical, playful, elliptical, vivid, and ephemeral than ordinary language."

McDavid in his discussion of usage, dialects, and functional varieties in the preface to the *Random House Dictionary* (page xxii) makes the following observation about slang and argot.

Slang was once a synonym for argot, the ingroup language used by those who participate in a particular activity, especially a criminal one. In fact, much slang still derives from small, specialized groups, some of it nursed along tenderly by press agents. Popular musicians have originated many slang expressions now in general use. The word *jazz* itself is a good example: a Southern term meaning to copulate, it was used by the musicians who entertained in New Orleans brothels to describe their kinds of musical improvisations and soon came into general use despite the horror of Southerners who had previously known the word as a taboo verb. Today much slang originates with narcotic addicts, spreads to popular musicians, and then gains vogue among the young while falling into disuse among its inventors. Other argot, however, is restricted to the practitioners of a particular field: *boff,* meaning variously "a humorous line," "a belly laugh," or "a box office hit," seems restricted in its use to theatrical circles; *snow,* as it means "cocaine or heroin," is a common term only among drug addicts.

The fate of slang and argot terms is unpredictable. Most of them disappear rapidly, some win their way into standard use, and still others remain what they were to begin with. *Mob,* deplored by Swift and other purists of 1700, would never be questioned today, but *moll,* meaning "a prostitute" or "the mistress of a gangster" has been in use since the early 1600's, and is still slang.

Technical terms arise because it is necessary for those who share a scientific or technical interest to have a basis for discussion. The difference between scientific and popular usage may be seen most strikingly in the biological sciences. A Latin term like *Panthera Leo* (lion) has a specific reference, while *cougar* may refer to any large wild American feline predator, or *partridge* may designate the bob-white quail, a kind of grouse, or some other game bird, according to local usage. Common words may be used with specific reference in a given field: *fusion* denotes one thing in politics, another in nuclear physics. As a field of inquiry becomes a matter of general interest, its technical terms will be picked up and used with less precision. Because of popular interest in Freudian psychology, such terms as *complex, fixation,* and *transference* are bandied about in senses Freud would never have sanctioned.

There is little question today that most of us employ slang and argot in both formal and informal speaking without any awareness of the origin of the terms or the semantic intentions of their originators. From contemporary learning theorists and *behavior shapers* we have such terms as *conditioning, reinforcement,* and *discriminative responses* as well as the abbreviated *S-R.* In our discussion of Black English we included some terms that are used by persons identified with the *counterculture* as well as by Blacks. It is too early to make any predictions about how many of these terms will become part of the everyday terminology of speakers of English or whether some terms will, because of frequency and wide distribution of usage, become entries in the dictionaries of the 1970s and 1980s.

Psychological Determinants

In concluding our discussion of changing speech patterns, some psychological factors that determine choice of words and the effects of such choice on our patterns of verbal behavior are reviewed. The words we use are generally selected according to our needs as speakers. The words we select to be impressive depend upon the situation and the person or persons we wish to impress. Not infrequently, this person may be the speaker himself rather than the listener. As speakers, we may have occasional need for a large mouthful of sounds and so speak polysyllabically and at length in a manner that would make Freudian listeners click their tongues and nod their heads with weighty surmises. More frequently, however, other factors determine the words we select. One such factor is *ease of pronunciation*. With few exceptions, short words are easier to pronounce than long words, and so, other things being equal, short words are likely to be chosen over long ones if they can be used effectively in communicating our thoughts and feelings. It is no accident that the most frequently used words in our language are shorter than the words that are less frequently used. George K. Zipf demonstrated that frequency of word usage is related to length (shortness) of words and that *words become shorter as spoken words* with increased frequency of usage. Zipf wrote, "There are copious examples of a decrease in magnitude of a word which results so far as one can judge solely from an increase in the relative frequency of its occurrence, as estimated either from the speech of an individual, in which the shortening may occur, or in the language of a minor group, or of the major speech group." [19]

We shorten words by processes of *assimilation,* by *truncation,* and by *abbreviatory substitution.* All three processes, incidentally, also result in ease of pronunciation. As examples of assimilation, we have dropped *p* from *cupboard* and most of us drop the *d* from *handkerchief.* Even short phrases are made shorter. For example, the modification of *goodbye* to *gdby,* or just *gby.*

Truncation can be exemplified by the change from *amperes* to *amps, elevator* to *el, telephone* to *phone* either as a verb or a noun, and *automobile* to *auto.* In California the Bay Area Transportation System is briefly referred to as the *Bart. TV* for *television* is an example of truncation by abbreviation.

Abbreviatory substitutions are exemplified by *car* for *automobile, juice* for *electric current,* and *prexy* for *president.* The last two terms happen to be usages within special groups, but the groups are large and influential. The word *cop* for *policeman* exemplifies the processes of truncation and abbreviation: from *copper* to *cop* as truncation, and *cop* for *policeman* as abbreviatory substitution. The processes of word shortening and the substitution of abbreviations exemplify Zipf's "principle of least effort." [20] According to Zipf, the changes that are associated with word-frequency usage are expressions of a general principle of human behavior that indicates that over a period of time we tend to minimize or reduce our average rate of work expenditure to accomplish an objective.

There are, however, counterforces that exert influence in preventing

[19] George K. Zipf, *Psycho-Biology of Language* (Boston: Houghton Mifflin Company, 1935), p. 29.
[20] George K. Zipf, *Human Behavior and the Principle of Least Effort* (Cambridge, Mass.: Addison Wesley Publishing Co., Inc., 1949).

overfrequent use of the same words and with it the process of word shortening. The most potent of these forces is the human drive for variety of experience, including our experience with the words at our command. To avoid monotony, we use synonyms that may be less precise in meaning than would be reiterations of the same word. Early in our school careers our teachers encouraged us to avoid the repeated use of a word merely because repetition is considered undesirable. Partly because of the authority of our teachers and partly because of our drive for variety, we go out of our way to use several different words to communicate an idea that might well be semantically more precise had a previously used word been used again (employed).

Until recently, verbal taboos and superstitions were cultural forces that worked against the use of some words, mostly of Anglo-Saxon origin, as expletives, adjectives, and verbs. Of late, our daily metropolitan newspapers and our magazines use rather than abbreviate the "four letter" words. Except for some senior citizens, these words have lost their shock value and are no longer taboo. We find also that there is less difference in the productive vocabularies of adolescent boys and girls, and young men and women in social situations. However, the grandparents if not the parents of the emancipated generation may continue to employ circumlocutions and euphemisms to suggest rather than forcibly say what they mean or intend. There are still some children who are *born out of wedlock* and so are *illegitimate*. People still *pass away* because speakers do not like to have them *die*. Undertakers are *morticians* whose establishments are *mortuaries*. Verbal habits and defensive attitudes persist, for at least part of the population, to maintain and even increase the use of terms that another part of the population may aggressively avoid.

These, briefly, are some of the forces and counterforces that have molded our language, influenced our verbal habits, and continue to modify our slow but ever-changing speech patterns. A living language is a growing language and one that changes forms, adds words and drops others, and modifies pronunciations. Some of the forces are global; others are peculiarly American.

CHAPTER 11

Introduction to the Study of American-English Speech Sounds

This part of the book has two related purposes. The first is to provide the reader with some fundamentals involved in the production of American-English speech sounds. The second is to provide specific information about the sounds of our language and practice materials for each of these sounds. Both purposes are intended to help the reader in his basic objective of becoming a more effective speaker.

IMPROVING DICTION

In this and the subsequent chapters we make no attempt to be prescriptive or to urge any one standard of diction (pronunciation) as either more desirable or "superior" to any other. We do, however, accept as a basic assumption that any manner or product of speech in a given community or environment that attracts attention to itself rather than to the intended message of its content deserves consideration as to the desirability if not the need for modification.

The sounds of speech, occasionally singly but usually in combination, constitute a symbol code that we use for oral and audible communication. We employ about forty-five distinctive sounds or *phonemes* in the symbol code of American-English speech. There are some variants in this code in different regions of the United States.[1] Major variants are pointed out, but they are relatively few and rarely so great as to prevent ready communication between good speakers from widely separated parts of our country. Poor speakers may have difficulty in communicating in their own areas; their difficulties tend to increase as they try to make themselves understood when they travel at distances from their homes. For the most part, however, the good speaker from New Orleans, Louisiana, may need a little time to "tune in" to the speech of the Bostonian, the New Yorker, or the resident of Chicago, but after a brief period all of these speakers should be able to understand one another despite some regional differences in pronunciation and occasionally in word usage.

DIALECTS

A *dialect* is a linguistic system within a system that is related to a special cultural group, a community of persons, or within an "identifiable" regional (geographic) area. Langacker (1967, p. 47) indicates that "The basis for distinguishing various dialects of a language is that the linguistic system used by speakers of one dialect differs in certain respects from that used by speakers of others." Differences may be ones of pronunciation (diction), vocabulary (word meaning),[2] and/or syntactic constructions. For example, American English speakers differ in the vowels used in words such as *roof, class, burn, after,* and *marry.* We *fetch something* in some parts of the United States that is *carried* in other areas; American English speakers go *to the hospital* or are *in the hospital* whereas those in England are more likely just to go *to hospital* or to be *in hospital.*

These dialectical variations are not likely to cause any difficulty in communication. However, there are dialects within the United States as well as within other parts of the English-speaking world where the differences are so great as to constitute barriers to communication. For example, speakers from the Appalachia region might have great difficulty in communicating with speakers from rural Maine or from southern Louisiana.

Black English

Black English is a dialect spoken by many Black children and adults in several geographic regions in the United States. Burling (1970, p. 118)

---

[1] There are perhaps even greater variants in different parts of the English-speaking world outside of the United States.

[2] Perhaps the selection of a word to indicate a meaning is a more appropriate statement relative to vocabulary differences.

points out that "The first and most obvious generalization about the English of many Negroes is that it shows abundant characteristics of the southern United States." With the migration of Negroes from the south to "northern" industrial areas (northeastern, north central, and western states), and because they became segregated in ghettos, their dialects are maintained in the speech of their "northern" born children. As a result "what had been geographically distinctive features have been converted into ethnic features."

Black English includes variations in phonology, word usage, and syntax. A readily recognized phonemic variation is the use of *d* in many words that in Standard English are pronounced with the voiced *th*, e.g., *the, them, they*. The final *ng* of Standard English is represented as *n*—a "substitution" by no means confined to the Black dialect. The use of multiple negatives, e.g., "I don't never have no luck nohow" is a syntactic feature of Black English. Another is the *absence* of *'s* to indicate possessive, e.g., "my uncle hat." The use of the verb *to be* is a special feature that permits distinctions of meanings in Black dialect that are not as readily made in Standard English. Thus, *Dey be walkin* means that some indicated persons are walking, according to their habitual inclination, whereas *Dey walkin* means that at a stated or particular time the indicated persons *are walking*. The use of *them* for *those, who* for *which*, and *she* for *her* are other characteristic lexical differences of Black English. However, Williamson (1971) points out that many of the characteristic differences between Black English and Standard English are also found in other dialects of English, and particularly in southern U.S. English.[3]

THE SOUNDS OF AMERICAN ENGLISH

Sound Representation

There are two ways of representing the sounds of our language: through spelling (orthographic representation) and through a system in which there is greater consistency between the visible symbol and the sound. It is obvious that a spoken language that has only twenty-six letter symbols and more than forty different sounds cannot have sufficient con-

[3] For a review of characteristics of Black English see C. Gifford, "Black English: An Introduction," *Acta Symbolica*, 1:1 (1970), 24–30. An excellent series of essays on dialects and their implications for attitudes, education, and social change may be found in F. Williamson ed., *Language and Poverty* (Chicago: Markham Publishing Co., 1970).

It is beyond the purpose of this book to take a position for or against the use of Black English or, for that matter, any recognized dialect of English. There is a considerable literature on the subject of Black English available to the interested student. Current bibliographic items may be obtained through the Center for Applied Linguistics, 1717 Massachusetts Avenue, N.W., Washington, D.C. 20036.

sistency between letter and sound to provide a reliable guide for articulation and pronunciation. Most of our dictionaries therefore employ a system of diacritical markings and symbols to help the reader appreciate how a word should be pronounced because of or despite its spelling. Unfortunately, even the use of diacritical markings fails to provide a clear one-to-one relationship between sound and symbol. Still another system, more consistent than either of the others, employs selected symbols of the International Phonetic Alphabet (IPA). In the IPA system one symbol is used for each distinctively different sound. Our approach emphasizes the use of the IPA system of representation. We shall, however, indicate the dictionary equivalents of the IPA symbols. Through this approach, we hope that it will become possible for the reader (1) to become aware of the sounds (phonemes) of our language, (2) to make distinctions according to the characteristics of the different sounds, and (3) to establish a visible basis to cue him on the manner of production for the individual sound, or for a series of sounds, in the contextual flow of speech.

The different sounds of American English speech and their phonetic symbol and dictionary symbol representations are shown in Tables 11–1 and 11–2.[4]

The Phoneme

We approach our study of the sound of American English through a consideration of the basic unit or sound family—the *phoneme*. Phonemes are distinctive phonetic (sound) elements of words. The phonetic elements are distinctive in that they incorporate sound features that enable us to distinguish between spoken words. For example, the word *bad* has three phonemes. If we change the first, we can distinguish between *bad* and *sad*. If we change the second, we can distinguish between *bad* and *bid;* if we change the last, we can distinguish between *bad* and *ban*. These changes of phonemes included ones with several different sound features that made the differences readily apparent. However, we can bring the phoneme "closer" by changing the *b* to *p* and so have *bad* and *pad*, or by changing the vowel and so have *bad* and *bed*, or changing the last sound and so have *bad* and *bat*. In regard to the consonants, our substitutions were of cognate sounds, ones that differed only by the feature of voicing. In contextual speech we might well need to depend upon the overall meaning of the utterance to perceive the differences in the consonants of the key words.

---

[4] The dictionary symbols are those used in *The American College Dictionary* (New York: Random House, Inc., 1958) and, with minor exceptions, those of the unabridged edition of the *Random House Dictionary of the English Language* (New York: Random House, Inc., 1966).

Allophones

A second aspect of the phoneme concept is variation. Speech sounds vary in production according to context. The /t/ in *tell* is somewhat different from the /t/ in *its* and *plate*. Despite the variations in sound, however, they are essentially more alike than different, and we respond to all of these words as containing a /t/. These sound variations, which do not affect our understanding of what we hear, constitute the members of the phoneme or sound family. The individual variants are called *allophones*.

If our pronunciations and articulatory efforts do not show regard for possible phonemic differences, our listeners may become confused. If the vowel of *bad* begins to approximate the vowel of *bed* we may be misunderstood if we utter a sentence such as *This will be bad for you.* Similarly, if an /s/ is produced so that it begins to suggest an /ʃ/ (sh), we may not know whether something is for *sipping* or *shipping*.

Some of the difficulty that foreign-born persons have in learning to speak English may be attributed to the fact that the phonemes in their native language are not always directly equivalent to ours. For example, we make a significant distinction between the vowels of words such as *heel* and *hill* and *seen* and *sin*. By way of television, radio, or movies, if not by direct experience, most of us know that many of our Mexican neighbors *think* with the vowel of *seen*. They may also have difficulty with the distinctions we make between *hail* and *hell*. We, of course, are not immune from these errors when we learn a foreign language. When speaking another language, we often produce vowels and some consonants of our closest phonetic equivalents and so manage to sound like foreigners.

Distinctive Features

Linguists view phonemes as sounds of speech, which, by virtue of the particular ways in which they are produced (articulated) and their associated acoustic consequences, comprise "bundles" of features that serve to distinguish (contrast) one phoneme from another. Thus, the stoppage of breath is a distinctive feature or characteristic of /p/, /t/, /k/, /b/, /d/, and /g/. In regard to breath stoppage, these sounds differ from all other sounds in a language system without this feature. The presence or absence of voice distinguishes the last three stops from the first three in the previous series. The sounds /m/, /n/, /ŋ/ (ng) are featured by intentional nasality. In this way, these speech sounds are distinctive, that is, they differ from all other phonemes in English speech.

Linguists such as Jakobson (1956), Fant (1962), and Chomsky and Halle (1956 and 1968) have "developed" distinctive feature systems that presumably permit a student of language phonology to distinguish among the phonemes of all natural languages. For our purposes, however, a more "modest" system such as that of Miller and Nicely (1955) or even the one used in this text is adequate to describe and distinguish one phoneme from the others in American-English speech. The descriptions for each of the sounds in the remaining chapters of this books may be considered to include phonetic distinctive features.[5]

CLASSIFICATION OF SOUNDS

The sounds of our language may be classified in three large groups: consonants, vowels, and diphthongs. All are produced as a result of some modification of the outgoing breath by the organs of articulation.

Consonants are speech sounds that are produced by either a complete or partial obstruction or modification of the breath channel by the organs of articulation. Aside from voice, the sound characteristics of each consonant result from the manner of vibration of the breath stream. This is determined by the way in which the breath stream is (1) modified by the closures produced by articulatory activity, (2) released by the activity of the opening of the closure, or (3) modified but not completely obstructed (stopped) by the narrowing of the breath channel.

Vowels are produced by articulatory movements of the speech organs without obstruction or interference of the vibrating breath stream in its passage through the breath channel. We determine the characteristic features of the vowels of our language by modifying the size and shape of the mouth cavity and by changing the position of the tongue within the mouth.

Diphthongs are voiced glides that are uttered in a single breath impulse. Some diphthongs are blends of two vowels. Most, however, represent an instability or "breakdown" of what at one time in the history of our language was one vowel. Regardless of historical development, a diphthong may be defined as ". . . a syllabic element, which begins with one sound and shifts to another, and we understand this to exclude consideration of those brief building-up and dying-out stages which characterize every speech sound." [6]

___

[5] The interested student may consult Winitz (1969, pp. 79–96) for a discussion of distinctive feature theory.

[6] R-M. S. Heffner, *General Phonetics* (Madison: University of Wisconsin Press, 1949), p. 112.

A diphthong may also be defined as a syllabic in which two vowel resonances are clearly identified, but with a *change of resonance* as an essential characteristic. See J. Carrell and W. R. Tiffany, *Phonetics* (New York: McGraw-Hill Book Company, 1960, p. 121).

TABLE 11–1. The Common Phonemes of American English (Consonants)

KEY WORD	DICTIONARY SYMBOL	IPA SYMBOL
1. pat	p	p
2. bee	b	b
3. tin	t	t
4. den	d	d
5. cook	k	k
6. get	g	g
7. fast	f	f
8. van	v	v
9. thin	th	θ
10. this	th	ð
11. sea	s	s
12. zoo	z	z
13. she	sh	ʃ
14. treasure	zh	ʒ
15. chick	ch	tʃ
16. jump	j	dʒ
17. me	m	m
18. no	n	n
19. sing	ng	ŋ
20. let	l	l
21. run	r	r
22. yell	y	j
23. hat	h	h
24. won	w	w
25. what	hw	ʌ or hw

Voice

All vowels and diphthongs, unless intentionally whispered, are produced with vocalization accompanying the articulatory activity. Consonants, however, may be produced with or without accompanying vocalization. Those that are produced with vocalization are known as *voiced* consonants, those produced without vocalization are referred to as *voiceless*.

Manner and Place of Articulation

In the individual descriptions of the consonant sounds that are presented later, the manner and place of articulation are considered for each

TABLE 11–2.   The Common Phonemes of American English (Vowels)

KEY WORD	DICTIONARY SYMBOL	IPA SYMBOL
26. fee	ē	i
27. sit	ĭ	ɪ
28. take	ā	e
29. met	ĕ	ɛ
30. cat	ă	æ
31. task	ă or à	æ or a depending upon regional or individual variations
32. calm	ä	ɑ
33. hot	ŏ or ä	ɒ or ɑ depending upon regional or individual variations
34. saw	ô	ɔ
35. vote	ō	o or ou
36. bull	o͝o	ʊ
37. too	o͞o	u
38. hut	ŭ	ʌ
39. about	ə	ə
40. upper	ər	ɝ by most Americans and ə by many others
41. bird	ûr	ɝ by most Americans and ɜ by many others
PHONEMIC DIPHTHONGS		
42. ice	ī	aɪ
43. now	ou	au or ɑʊ
44. boy	oi	ɔɪ

sound. Some consonants are described as stops, others as either *fricatives, glides,* or *nasals.* We anticipate some of the descriptions by defining a few terms at the present time.

Stop sounds are produced by a stopping of the breath stream. The stop sounds are /p/, /b/, /t/, /d/, /k/, and /g/.

Fricatives are produced by a partial closure of the articulators. This action results in the creation of a constricted passage through which the stream of air must be forced. The partial closures may take place as a result of the grooving of the tongue or of having other organs of articulation come close together. The distinctively fricative sounds are /f/, /v/, /θ/ (th), /ð/ (th), /s/, /z/, /ʃ/ (sh), and /ʒ/ (zh). The sound /h/ is produced with laryngeal constriction.

Nasal sounds are reinforced and emitted nasally. The three nasals are /m/, /n/, and /ŋ/ (ng).

Glides are sounds that are produced with continuous rather than fixed articulatory positions. The glide consonants are /w/, /j/ (y), and most varieties of /r/.

Affricates are blends of two sounds, one a stop and the other a fricative. There are two affricates, /tʃ/ (ch) as in *chum* and /dʒ/ (dzh) as in *jam.*

The sound /l/ is a *lateral* consonant. It is produced by the emission of vocalized breath at both sides of the tongue while the tip of the tongue is in contact with the gum ridge. The /l/ is designated as a *liquid* by some phoneticians and linguists.

SOUNDS IN CONTEXT

Although our approach to the study of diction begins with a descriptive analysis of the individual sounds of our language, speech does not consist of a series of individual sounds. Speech is a sequence or context of sounds. In context, individual sounds are modified and produced differently from what they would be in isolation. If one were to speak as though our linguistic symbols were a series of sounds, he would be uttering phonetic nonsense. In context, differences in force and duration to emphasize meanings, differences according to the formality or informality of the speech situation, and differences according to the size of the listening group all make for modifications of individual sounds in the flow of speech. Some of these differences are considered briefly.

ASSIMILATION

If asked for the pronunciation of the words *education, mature,* and *income,* many persons would carefully pronounce these words differently from their pronunciations in contextual speech. The word *education* may regularly be pronounced [ɛdjukeʃən] (ĕdūkāshən) by some persons, but most of us are likely to say [ɛdʒəkeʃən] (ĕjəkāshən) in talking about "the education of our children" or in asserting that "education means—." When we change from the careful but less usual pronunciation of words such as *educate, income, handkerchief* or phrases such as *don't you* and *meet you* to the easier and more usual ones, we are yielding to and demonstrating the effects of *assimilation in connected speech.*

Assimilation refers to the phonetic changes that take place when one sound is modified as the result of a neighboring sound or sounds in connected speech. Some of these changes become relatively fixed and so regularly influence the pronunciations of many words. Other assimilations depend upon particular verbal contexts and so influence the articulation and pronunciation of words only in these contexts. Examples of each are given in our brief discussions of some types of assimilative modifications.

Anticipatory Changes

Most assimilations reflect the influences of anticipatory changes. That is, the organs of articulation, in anticipation of a sound to follow, modify a preceding sound. The change tends to simplify or facilitate articulation. For example, in the word *congress,* the letter *n* is sounded as an /ŋ/ (ng) in anticipation of the sound /g/ that follows. It is easier to articulate /ŋg/ than [n + g] simply because both the /ŋ/ and the /g/ are produced with the same parts of the tongue and the palate. For the same reason *income* is pronounced with an /ŋ/ rather than an /n/ followed by a /k/. Similarly, it is easier to say *this shoe* with a lengthened /ʃ/ (sh) than with an /s/ followed by an /ʃ/. The pronunciation of *this shoe,* incidentally, is an example of contextual, temporary assimilation.

Voicing

Changes produced in voicing by assimilation are perhaps best exemplified in words that end with a final *s* or *d.* In the words *liked, heaped, rasped, guessed* and *ropes, takes,* and *plates* the next to the last produced sound is a voiceless consonant. (The letter *e,* in each case, is silent.) As a result, the final *d* is pronounced as /t/ rather than /d/ and the final *s* as an /s/ rather than /z/.

In words such as *passes, hedges, riches,* and *roses* the final *s* is produced as /z/ because the next to the last sound is a vowel and is vocalized. Similarly, *grounded, breaded,* and *heeded* are each pronounced with a final /d/. In the words *begs, seems, togs,* and *roams* the final sound is voiced because of the influence of the preceding voiced consonant.

Other Assimilations

In some cases assimilations may result in the complete loss of one or more sounds that are replaced by a third sound. This happens in the assimilated pronunciation of *picture, nature,* and *feature,* where the sound /tʃ/ (ch) is heard in the second syllable of each of the words.

STYLES OF SPEECH

In both manner and content, speech is appropriate or inappropriate, correct or incorrect, according to the circumstances and occasion. Despite possible differences in education, profession, and speaking ability, an individual's manner of communicating will or should vary according to the time, the place, and the speaking situation. The minister who feels the need to deliver a sermon to his family is likely to do so differently from the way he would speak to his congregation in church. The minister should certainly not converse at home, with members of his family or with visiting members of his congregation, as he would talk to them from his pulpit. The lecturer speaking to a large audience on a formal occasion is likely to use more elevated language than the same speaker at his club, on a picnic, with friends, or at a home social gathering.

Informal speech employs many contractions. We use more *he's, don'ts,* and *I'ms* when speaking informally and intimately than when speaking formally. We do not, however, usually employ contracted forms when emphasis is intended. Public addresses, with the exception of the humorous afterdinner speech, are generally delivered formally unless, for special purposes (usually political), the speaker wants his listeners to feel that he is "one of the boys."

SPEECH STANDARDS

Pronunciation Variants

In going over the list of consonants and vowel sounds some observations may be made relative to minor differences in pronunciation among Americans.

Many of us do not distinguish between the /hw/ in *what* and the /w/ of *watt* but pronounce both the way we do the first sound of *will.*

There is considerable variation as to the pronunciation of the vowel of the word *ask.* Most Americans use the same vowel in the words *ask* and *hat;* others broaden the vowel in *ask* to that of the /ɑ/ of *calm;* a smaller number of Americans use the vowel /a/, which is phonetically between /æ/ and /ɑ/.

Most Americans use the same vowel in *hot* as they do in *calm.* A few, however, use a vowel intermediate between the vowel of *call* and the vowel of *calm.*

There is considerable variation in the production of the vowel of words such as *bird* and *heard.* Some use the vowel /ɝ/, which has *r* coloring. Others include a clear-cut *r* preceded by a vowel much like the one in the word *bud.*

Paralleling the variations in the vowel of words such as *bird, heard, surf,* and *mirth* are those for the final sound of the words such as *after, supper,* and *thunder.* Most of us use the vowel /ɚ/, which is much like the first sound of the word *above* with the addition of *r* coloring. Others add a clear-cut /r/ sound after the same vowel, and a smaller number make no distinction between the first sound of the word *above* and the last sound of *after* and use /ə/ for both.

To this short list of variants in American pronunciation, we might add another relative to the articulation of the /r/ sound in words in which the spelling includes the letter *r.* We are in common agreement that an /r/ sound is produced whenever a word contains an initial *r* in its spelling, as in *rug, rice, rain,* and *runs* and in words in which the *r* is preceded by a consonant and followed by a vowel as in *tree, grease,* and *prize.* The /r/ is also pronounced in medial positions when it is followed by a vowel as in *forest* and *touring.* Practice differs, however, in words in which the *r* is medial in spelling and followed by a consonant as in *farm, card,* and *sharp* or final in the spelling as in *car, far,* and *soar.* These differences are considered again in our more detailed consideration of the /r/ phoneme.

Assimilations and Speech Standards

Most of the examples of assimilation given earlier are considered acceptable and in good standing by all except the most pedantic people. Some persons may prefer the unassimilated pronunciations of words such as *congress* and *income* and tax themselves to maintain the /n/ rather than yield to economy in articulation and produce an /ŋ/. Not all assimilations, however, are acceptable even to our liberal dictionary editors. For example, the word *open,* despite temptation and frequent pronunciation by small children, should still be produced with a final /n/ rather than an /m/.[7] The word *gas* is still better pronounced with a final /s/ than with a /z/, although the second pronunciation is frequently given by persons not habitually careless in their speech.

Criteria for Speech Standards

Speech in general and pronunciation in particular are appropriate if they are consistent with the objectives of the speaker in his role of communicator of ideas. The listeners, the occasion, and the speaker as a personality are some of the factors that determine appropriateness. What is appropriate may be accepted as standard. Speech becomes substandard if the pronunciations are such that they violate the judgments and tastes

[7] A. J. Bronstein in his *The Pronunciation of American English* (New York: Appleton-Century-Crofts, 1960), p. 212, recognizes that an *m* may be heard in the phrase "open the door" in assimilated colloquial educated speak.

of the listeners. We are likely to sense such violations if an official in high government office speaks to us as members of a large audience as he might to some of his initimate friends on a fishing trip. We might also sense some violation if a college president talking on the topic "The Need for a Liberal Arts Education" were to do so in the manner of a sports announcer.

Speech becomes distinctly substandard if it employs pronunciations that are not currently used by any persons whose backgrounds as speakers make their judgments as regards linguistic usage worthy of respect. Even a liberal attitude toward pronunciation would still not justify the pronunciation of *asked* as [æst] (ăst) or of *something* as [sʌmpɪm] (sŭmpĭm).

Pronunciations that reveal foreign language influence, such as the substitution of a sound that approximates the appropriate one in English, would also constitute substandard speech. The substitution of a /v/ for a /w/ in words such as *wife* and *went* or an /f/ for a /v/ in words such as *give* and *leave* are examples of substandard pronunciations frequently resulting from foreign language influence. Occasionally, they may reflect persistent foreign language influences in dialectal speech within this country.

The speaker who wishes to improve his speech, his articulation, and his pronunciation as well as his word usage, must be a good listener. He must listen with discrimination for what is best and current in the community in which he lives. He must listen to the educated and to the respected members of the community and use them as models but not imitate them slavishly. Above all, he should avoid trying to sound like somebody else, thus seeming to deny his individuality and his place of origin. This does not mean that he should maintain what may have been substandard in his background. It does mean that the man from New York should not consciously try to sound as though he were from Atlanta, Georgia, and that the speaker from Houston, Texas, should not try to sound like a Harvard-educated Bostonian. In time, if any of these speakers live long enough in an area, some of the flavor of the area's speech will naturally begin to appear. Careful listening is likely to translate itself into unconscious imitation of the speech of the immediate environment unless the speaker is negatively motivated toward the persons to whom he is listening.

REFERENCES

Bronstein, A. J. *The Pronunciation of American English.* New York: Appleton-Century-Crofts, 1960.
Burling, R. *Man's Many Voices: Language in Its Cultural Context.* New York: Holt, Rinehart and Winston, Inc., 1970.
Carrell, J., and W. R. Tiffany. *Phonetics.* New York: McGraw-Hill Book Company, 1960.

Chomsky, N., and M. Halle. *The Sound Pattern of English*, Chapter 7. New York: Harper & Row, Publishers, 1968.

Fant, G. M. "Descriptive Analysis of the Acoustic Aspects of Speech." *Logos*, 5 (1962) 3–17(a).

Gifford, C. "Black English: An Introduction." *Acta Symbolica* (1970), 1, 24–30.

Heffner, R-M. S. *General Phonetics*. Madison, Wisconsin: Universtiy of Wisconsin Press, 1949.

Jakobson, R., and M. Halle. *Fundamentals of Language*. The Hague: Mouton, 1956.

Langacker, R. W. *Language and Its Structure*. New York: Harcourt Brace Jovanovich, Inc., 1967.

Miller, G. A., and P. E. Nicely. "An Analysis of Perceptual Confusions Among Some English Consonants." *Journal of the Acoustical Society of America*, 27 (1955) 338–352.

Williams, F. (ed.), *Language and Poverty*. Chicago: Markham, 1970.

Williamson, J. V. "A Look at Black English." *Crisis* (1971) 169–173 and 185.

Winitz, H. *Articulatory Acquisition and Behavior*. New York: Appleton-Century-Crofts, 1969.

CHAPTER 12

Individual Study of American-English Sounds: The Vowels

Our study of American-English speech sounds is based on assumptions that knowledge of the sound (phonemic) system and the opportunity for application and practice will help toward attaining the objective of improving diction. Some sounds have been found to be more troublesome—more frequently produced in a faulty manner—than others. These sounds receive our major emphasis. They are treated in more detail, and a larger amount of practice-exercise material is provided for them than for those sounds that cause relatively little difficulty for the vast majority of speakers of American English.

Although we study the individual phonemes of American-English speech, we need to emphasize the point that sounds in context, in a flow of normal speech utterance, do not have all of the characteristics of the isolated phoneme. (See previous discussions in Chapter 11 of *sounds in context and assimilation.*) An utterance involves coarticulation. Both the acoustic and physiological characteristics of a sound in context are influenced by the preceding and succeeding sounds. Thus, the [s] and [t] in *stem* are produced somewhat differently from the [s] and [t] in *so to bed* or in *it's tight* or in *hats off*. Although it is obviously neither possible nor fruitful to consider all possible combinations of sounds in contextual utterance, we consider a number of frequently coarticulated sounds in our presentations of sound blends.

We begin our study with an analysis of the vowel sounds. Although differences in practice relative to the pronunciation of vowels are fairly wide in different parts of the country, most vowel sounds, because of their intensity and "open" manner of production, are comparatively easy to imitate. Pronunciation habits based upon regional practice may, however, result in the persistent use of one vowel in some words when most Americans use another. For example, there is considerable variation in the pronunciation of the vowel in the words *had, have, candy, bad,* and *sad,* depending upon regional custom. There is also a fair amount of regional variation in the pronunciation of the vowels in words such as *word, bird, heard, dearth, earth, curdle,* and *merge.* There is also some variation in the choice of vowel for words such as *path, ask,* and *dance.* Some of the variations in practice in different parts of the country are considered in the discussion of the individual vowel sounds.

VOWEL PRODUCTION

All vowels share several characteristics: (1) They are all voiced sounds; (2) all are articulated in essentially the same manner in that they are continuant sounds without interruption and without restriction of the stream of breath; and (3) although lip activity is involved, the activity of the tongue makes the essential difference in the production of the different vowel sounds.

Vowel Classification

Vowels may be conveniently classified according to the part of the tongue that is most actively involved in the production of the sound. If you concentrate on the vowel sounds of the words *me* and *moo,* you should be able to note that the blade of the tongue moves forward toward the hard palate for *me.* For *moo,* the back of the tongue moves toward the soft palate. Similar activity may be noted if you compare the vowels of *pet* and *paw.* For *pet,* the front of the tongue is most active, and for *paw* the back of the tongue is most active. For neither of the vowels, however, does the tongue move as high as for the vowels of *me* and *moo.* Comparable activity may be observed for all the other *front vowels* (those produced with the front or blade of the tongue most active) compared with the corresponding *back vowels* (those produced with the back of the tongue most active).

The approximate differences in tongue position for the front and back vowels are illustrated in Figures 12–1 and 12–2.

Figure 12–3 illustrates the position of the tongue for the central vowels, or midvowels (those produced with the middle of the tongue most active).

You may test these representative tongue positions with your own

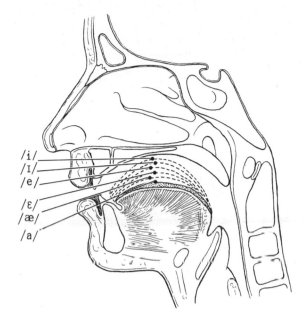

Figure 12–1   Representative tongue positions for front vowels.

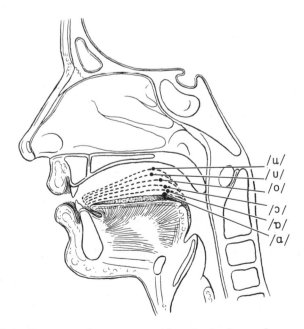

Figure 12–2   Representative tongue positions for back vowels.

Figure 12–3 **Representative tongue positions for the central vowels, or mid-vowels.**

articulatory behavior relative to these vowels by incorporating them in the following key words.

Front	*Central*	*Back*
me		boot
mit		book
made	mirth	boat
met	*a*bove, upp*er*	bought
mat	mud	box
mask		balm

On the basis of the production of the key vowels, a twofold basis for classification becomes possible.

First, vowels differ in production according to *place of articulation*—and so may be classified as *front, mid,* or *back* vowels according to the part of the tongue that is most actively involved in their production.

Second, vowels differ as to *height-of-tongue* position. The vowel of *me* is a high front vowel; the vowel of *moon* is a high back vowel. The vowel of *mask* is a low front vowel; that of *balm* is a low back vowel.

A *third basis* for the classification of vowels is *muscle tension.* If we compare the vowel of *peek* with that of *pick*, we should feel that the tongue is more tense for the vowel of *peek* than it is for the one in *pick.* Similarly, the vowel of *boat* is produced with the tongue somewhat more tense than in the production of the vowel of *book.* Tension may also be felt in the muscles behind the chin.

Before we go into our more detailed discussion of the individual

TABLE 12-1 Vowels of American-English Speech

FRONT VOWELS

	Phonetic Symbol	Dictionary Symbol
meet	i	ē
milk	ɪ	ĭ
may	e	ā
men	ɛ	ĕ
mat	æ	ă
ask*	a	à

CENTRAL VOWELS

	Phonetic Symbol	Dictionary Symbol
mirth	ɜ or ɝ	ûr
about	ə	ə
upper	ɚ	ər
mud	ʌ	ŭ

BACK VOWELS

	Phonetic Symbol	Dictionary Symbol
boon	u	o͞o
book	ʊ	o͝o
boat	o	ō
ball	ɔ	ô
bog	ɒ	ŏ
balm	ɑ	ä

* When the speaker compromises between the vowels of *mat* and of *balm*. This vowel is intermediate in placement as well as in sound between æ and ɑ.

165

sounds of our language, we might review briefly some features of vowel production. All vowels, unless intentionally whispered, are voiced, continuant sounds. When produced as isolated sounds, the tongue tip is usually placed behind the lower gum ridge. The vowel sounds are differentiated as a result of activity of the blade, the middle or the back of the tongue elevated to different positions (heights) within the mouth cavity. Some vowels are produced with muscle tension as an additional characteristic. The articulatory aspects that characterize the production of each of the vowels are now considered.

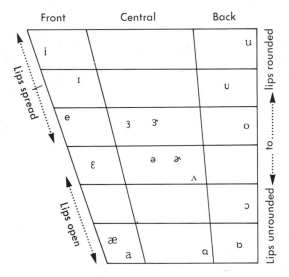

Figure 12–4 **Tongue and lip positions of the American-English vowels.**
The front vowels /i/, /e/, and /æ/ are produced with tongue and associated articulatory tension; the vowels /ɪ/, /ɛ/, and /a/ are relatively lax. The back vowels are produced with relatively lax tongue posture.

THE FRONT VOWELS

/i/ (ē) As in *See*

The vowel /i/ is a high front tense vowel.

An examination of the front-vowel diagram (Figure 12–1) will reveal that /i/ is produced with the blade of the tongue arched high in the front of the mouth. It is produced with a considerable degree of tongue tension and a lesser degree of lip tension. When /i/ is produced as an isolated sound, the lip position approximates a tight-lipped grin. Tension should also be present in the muscle bulge behind the chin.

Muscle tension is necessary to produce a clear /i/ and to distinguish it from the vowel /ɪ/ (ĭ), which is a more relaxed sound.

The sound /i/ has many different English spellings. The most frequent include *e, ee, ea, ei, i,* and *ie* as in *he, see, each, receipt, ski,* and *believe.*

PRACTICE MATERIALS

each	easy	eke	eerie
even	eager	equal	ego
ether	eel	eaves	Easter
east	eat	ease	edict
Eden	easel	eagle	Erie
beach	beast	appease	frieze
breathe	feast	conceive	machine
breed	meat	please	crease
cheese	sweet	breeze	team
heat	yield	intrigue	achieve
beet	steel	sneeze	tease
effete	creep	reed	speed
agree	pea	tree	sea
glee	flee	ski	spree
esprit	key	bee	lea
tee	she	we	knee
fee	dee	free	quay

Phrases

sleek fleet	sweet tea
beagle's fleas	believe and achieve
Pete is neat	steamed-up team
Oakie from Muskogee	eerie breeze
seasoned trees	gleeful tease

Sentences

1. The Marines seized the beach.
2. Steve said the steamy heat was a good enough reason to leap off the quay into the deep sea.
3. The chief was piqued because of his belief that the esprit of his police was not what it should be.
4. The machinist took a seat after cleaning his reamer.
5. Green peas and beans have as much protein as many pieces of beef.
6. MacNeal took a ball peen hammer and proceeded to beat the sheet of steel.
7. Anita was not pleased with Lita's teasing.
8. The sleek sneak thief beat his way up the creek.
9. Speed freaks are exceedingly heedless of their bodies' needs.
10. Snead, the weaver, believed in using green beads.

Selections

1. For truth has such a face and such a mien.
   As to be lov'd needs only to be seen.
   —JOHN DRYDEN, *The Hind and the Panther*
2. If there's delight in love, 'tis when I see
   That heart which others bleed for, bleed for me.
   —WILLIAM CONGREVE, *The Mourning Bride*
3. Even the weariest river
   Winds somewhere safe to sea.
   —ALGERNON CHARLES SWINBURNE, *The Garden of Proserpine*

/ɪ/ (ĭ) As in *Bit*

/ɪ/ is also a high, front vowel. /ɪ/ differs from /i/ in two respects; /ɪ/ is produced with a tongue position somewhat lower than is /i/ and *without articulatory tension.*

The lip position for /ɪ/ is approximately a relaxed smile in contrast with the tight-lipped grin for /i/. The difference in tension and lip may be observed by placing your hand behind your chin and looking in the mirror as you change from the word *heat* to *hit.*

The most frequent spelling for /ɪ/ is the letter *i* as in *sit, wit, fit,* and *lit;* other spellings include *u, ui,* and *e* as in *busy, build,* and *English.*

Some speakers use the vowel /ɪ/ for the final *y* in words such as *busy, city, petty.* Other speakers are likely to use a vowel somewhere between /i/ and /ɪ/. Still others may use a vowel closer to /i/ than to /ɪ/.

Determine your own practice by testing yourself with the following lists of words. The words are to be read across the page.

i   I

fleet	flitty	flit
scat	city	sit
peat	pity	pit
key	kitty	kit
meat	meaty	mit
cheese	cheesy	chit
we	weedy	wit
leak	leaky	lick

PRACTICE MATERIALS

ibid	idiom	ignite	igloo
ilk	its	ingot	infer
imp	is	Italy	intake
ink	itch	indicate	ignore
Indian	inch	inn	insert
into	imply	ignorant	image
imbue	ingrate	impale	impact

mist	list	fist	grip
business	tryst	strip	flick
differ	women	shrimp	whisk
fill	wishes	shrill	hymn
quick	drip	grill	quilt
wilt	mince	lick	think
eclipse	instill	bib	admit
addict	crib	simple	spin
frantic	abyss	aphid	antic
flint	frisk	ticklish	twitch

Sentences

1. Winter sits heavily on Minnesota.
2. The British ships drifted into the Atlantic slip.
3. Detective Investigator Hill built an illegal still.
4. Dr. Gilbert filled the prescription with a pharmacist's skill.
5. Dick Simpson made a quick trip to Riverton.
6. Simmons, who lives in Missouri, wished to be convinced of the merits of the bill.
7. "The wit is insipid," insisted the still livid critic.
8. The transit system claimed in a writ that the citizen's petition was illegal.
9. Mick whistles "Dixie" if he wishes to seem busy.
10. The kitten was sitting pretty in the kitchen cabinet.

Selections

1. The moving finger writes, and having writ,
   Moves on. Nor all your piety nor wit
   Shall lure it back to cancel half a line,
   Nor all your tears wash out a word of it.
   > —*The Rubáiyát of Omar Khayyám*
   > (Translated by Edward Fitzgerald)

2. Nick Machiavel had ne'er a trick,
   Though he gave his name to our old Nick.
   > —SAMUEL BUTLER, *Hudibras*

3. A tale without love is like beef without mustard; an insipid dish.
   > —ANATOLE FRANCE, *The Revolt of the Angels*

For persons who have difficulty in distinguishing between the tense vowel /i/ and the relaxed /ɪ/ the following material should be of help. Place your hand behind your chin and feel the tension for the vowel in the first word of each pair. The second word, in contrast, should have a relaxed chin.

i	ɪ		
seat	sit	leak	lick
beat	bit	sheep	ship
meat	mit	sleep	slip
heat	hit	peach	pitch
greet	grit	leap	lip
cheap	chip	green	grin
peep	pip	heap	hip
fleet	flit	peak	pick
reed	rid	greed	grid
feel	fill	heel	hill

In the following sentences the first italicized word has the tense vowel [i]; the second has the relaxed vowel /ɪ/.

1. They climbed to *reach* the *rich* mine.
2. The *beans* were stored in *bins*.
3. Much *steel* is *still* imported.
4. The *team* counted on *Tim*.
5. Ten *sheep* were sent by *ship*.
6. A rod and *reel* were lost in the *rill*.
7. The *deed* he *did* took courage.
8. At *least* ten items were on the *list*.
9. Her *feet* were the right size, the shoes didn't *fit*.
10. *Cheap* paint will *chip*.

/ɪ/ in Unstressed Syllables

The vowel /ɪ/ occurs rather frequently in many polysyllabic words as in add*ed*, frett*ed* *im*ply. In some instances the speaker may us /ɪ/ in the unstressed syllable. The following tice with the /ɪ/ in unstressed positions.

practice	wedded	impart	plosive
merit	sterile	instead	corrosive
encrusted	junket	inept	listed
frosting	rusted	immerse	watches
bursting	tempted	intend	matches

In the following lists, the /ɪ/ occurs in both the stressed and unstressed syllable or syllables.

implement	respective	imprinting	imagine
impending	politics	finicky	statistics
implicit	primitive	instinctive	simplify
intended	impinge	misgiving	activity
intuitive	kindling	consistent	indicate
impacted	thicken	picnic	syllabicate

/e/ (ā) As in *Mate*

/e/ is a midhigh, front vowel. Most Americans are more likely to produce the vowel /e/ as part of the diphthong /eɪ/ than as a pure vowel. Whether produced as part of a diphthong or as a pure sound /e/ is a tense, front, midhigh vowel (see front-vowel diagram, Figure 12–1).

Some speakers use the diphthongal form more or less regularly in a stressed syllable and the pure vowel form in an unstressed syllable. There are, however, no words in our language that would be distinguished in meaning from one another on the basis of the use of a pure vowel /e/ or the diphthongal form /eɪ/. We do not recommend the cultivation of either form for the sake of consistency. We do, however, recommend that excessive prolongation of the diphthong to a triphthong [eɪə] be avoided.

The vowel /e/ or the diphthong /eɪ/ is most frequently represented in spelling by the letter *a* as in *date, mate,* and *hate;* other frequent spellings include *ay, ai, ey,* and *ei* as in *say, mail, they,* and *vein.*

PRACTICE MATERIALS

ace	angel	aviary	ate
ail	April	ape	ache
age	aim	aviator	aid
apex	Asia	eighteen	aphid

base	brake	trait	braided
bait	crate	chaotic	fateful
bail	place	grate	station
deign	plate	lace	caged
date	rate	chaste	strafe
sake	flake	awake	failure
away	filet	sleigh	replay
dray	repay	dismay	relay
shay	delay	bay	ray
pay	hay	neigh	portray
day	may	betray	fray
weigh	they	play	display

Note whether you distinguish between the vowel and diphthong forms in the following sentences. Careful listening may help you to decide that sentence context may make a difference.

1. Peyton draped crepe paper around his place.
2. Jesse James was outraged by the railroad station's great unbreakable safe.
3. May has thirty-one days.
4. Nathan was fond of angel food cake or anything else that Jane would bake for him.
5. Casco Bay is in the state of Maine.
6. Dale won the relay race on Saturday.
7. Crane saw strange shapes riding in the gray mist.
8. Raymond gazed in dismay at stagestruck Rachel.
9. Grace watched the plane fly off into space.
10. *Arizona Ames* is a tale by Zane Grey.

Selections

1. Take, O take those lips away,
       That so sweetly were forsworn;
   And those eyes, the break of day,
       Lights that do mislead the morn:
   But my kisses bring again, bring again;
       Seals of love, but sealed in vain, sealed in vain.
                    —WILLIAM SHAKESPEARE, *Measure for Measure*
2. Let us have faith that right makes might.
                    —ABRAHAM LINCOLN, *Address*, Cooper Union
3. He left the name at which the world grew pale,
   To point a moral, or adorn a tale.
                    —SAMUEL JOHNSON, *The Vanity of Human Wishes*

/ɛ/ (ĕ) As in *Help*

/ɛ/ is a midfront vowel. The vowel /ɛ/ differs from /e/ in that the former is produced with a slightly lower front tongue position and *without articulatory tension.*

The most frequent spelling for the vowel /ə/ is the single letter *e;* other spellings include *a* as in *any, ay* as in *says, ai* as in *said,* and *ea* as in *bread.*

PRACTICE MATERIALS

In the lists of words for initial and medial /ɛ/ avoid any tendency to prolong the vowel into the diphthong /ɛə/.

edit	enemy	elegant	engineer
effort	emblem	enzyme	enterprise
ebb	empty	enter	engine
end	any	energy	exit
echo	elf	elk	elder
egg	elbow	edge	effort
etch	edible	entry	extra
else	edit	ensign	empire
attend	second	tether	trend
reckon	restless	festive	gender
beckon	said	jest	center
lend	gem	wren	theft
guess	thread	deaf	health
pleasant	meant	check	pensive
self	tent	ready	settler
friend	chest	descent	weather

Phrases

steady trend	desert weather
elfin jests	tense elders
edible eggs	pensive Frenchmen
ready guests	gentle echoes
enter and exit	thefts of gems
pleasant self	beckon the deaf
messy chest	lent the rent
bent head	spent wealth

Sentences

1. Betty sent a letter every day.
2. Ned, although wealthy, avoided getting into debt.

3. Men who are most deaf are those who will not attend.

4. General Westmoreland is descended from the well-known Nevilles of Britain.

5. Quentin said to send his regards to Betty but did not lend her a red cent.

6. Ben was energetic and often restless.

7. The ebb tide kept the ship from setting sail.

8. The empty room still held the scent of Beth's perfume.

9. The terrier was adept at picking up the scent.

10. Ted developed his method by careful measurements.

Selections

1. Truth is truth
   To the end of reckoning.
   —WILLIAM SHAKESPEARE, *Measure for Measure*

2. The rest to some faint meaning make pretence,
   But Shadwell never deviates into sense.
   —JOHN DRYDEN, *Mac Flecknoe*

3. And Marlowe, Webster, Fletcher, Ben,
   Whose fire-hearts sowed our furrows when
   The world was worthy of such men.
   —ELIZABETH BARRETT BROWNING, *A Vision of Poets*

Make certain that clear distinctions are made for the vowels in the italicized words in the sentences that follow.

1. The *pen* was placed next to the *pin*.
2. *Ed* called for *aid*.
3. *Fred* was seldom *afraid*.
4. *Ben*, where have you *been?*
5. The *men* were mean and *lean*.
6. The singer was *ready*, but her voice was *reedy*.

/æ/ (ă) As in *Bat*

/æ/ is a low front vowel. It is almost always produced with a lax tongue; occasionally some contexts call for a slightly tense tongue but emphatic tension should be avoided. The tongue is lower in position and the mouth wider open for /æ/ than it is for /ɛ/ (see front-vowel diagram, Figure 12–1).

The letter *a* as in *mash, pack, rack,* and *sack* is the most frequent spelling representation for the vowel /æ/.

In some parts of the United States the vowel blend /ɛə/ tends to be substituted for the vowel /æ/. In much of the United States a vowel closer to /ɛ/ than to /æ/ is heard in words in which the vowel is followed by the sound /r/as in *marry, parry, Harry,* and *Mary*.

PRACTICE MATERIALS

Determine your own practice for the following words in which the vowel /æ/ is an acceptable pronunciation. Doubts, if they exist, should be determined by usage of respected speakers in your community.

bad	ram	crab	slant
map	match	jam	grab
cap	shall	had	bag
can	carry	fact	trapped
cast	parrot	fancy	plant
back	drank	ham	sham
hag	Sally	lamb	path
asp	attic	after	ash
at	anthill	and	answer
angle	antler	act	add
apple	anchor	alkaline	aster
atom	agonize	ample	Alice
angry	abduct	annual	Alps
clash	slab	tagged	brash
crab	wrap	trapper	crash
crack	lacking	jagged	hack
stack	slapped	ragged	wax
mash	flax	flagging	hatched
pack	bagged	wrapped	satin

Phrases

Andy's antics	dappled band
candy and jam	ham sandwich
crack back	animal crackers
ragged and jagged crags	sagging flags
pack the bags	agonizing answer
apple mash	stand fast
wham bam	handstand

Sentences

1. Mack is a crackerjack at rock stacking.
2. Hank carried a bag of apples strapped to his back pack into the camp.
3. Fran was in a time jam and used Pam's notes to cram for the exam.
4. The Swiss Alps have many jagged peaks and crags.
5. Jam and pancakes make a snack for a boy and a meal for a man.

6.   Tad fancied himself a man of unflagging action.
7.   Alan went to California to enhance his acting career.
8.   A good match is preceded by a good catch.
9.   The cab's wheels sank deep into the sand.
10. Hatless and ragged, Calvin's spirits never flagged.
11. A hammer rather than an ax should be used for banging a tack.
12. Sam's ham sandwiches were wrapped in wax sacks.

In the following sentences be careful to avoid excessive tension or nasality for the vowels of the italicized words. Keep your jaw and tongue relaxed.

1.   *"Can Hank manage* the task?" asked *Nathaniel.*
2.   The *ban* on *canned ham* was dropped.
3.   *Dan* and *Sam* ran a fast race.
4.   Alfred had *random* thoughts when he *cat*napped.
5.   *Frank planned* to raise *Angus* cattle.
6.   *Andrew* enjoyed *active* sports.

Selections

1.   Clara planned a man to marry—
     A Sam, a Dan, perhaps a Harry—
     She asked, she prayed, he would not tarry
     And that her plan would not miscarry.
                                    —J. E., *Aspiration*

2.   Close to the sun in lonely lands,
     He clasps the crag with crooked hands;
     Ring'd with the azure world he stands.
                    —ALFRED, LORD TENNYSON, *In Memoriam*

3.   He casts off his friends, as a huntsman his pack,
     For he knew when he pleas'd he could whistle them back.
                    —OLIVER GOLDSMITH, *Retaliation*

/a/ (ȧ)

/a/ is a low, front, lax vowel.

We are intentionally excluding a key word for the vowel /a/ because most Americans do not use this sound as a pure vowel, but use it only as the first element of the diphthong /aɪ/ as in *I, my,* and *ice.* The pure vowel /a/ is used by a minority of American speakers, most of whom probably reside in the New England area. These speakers would use the vowel in words such as *ask, grass,* and *mask.*

In regard to tongue position the vowel /a/ is a compromise between the front vowel /æ/ and the low back vowel /ɑ/ (ä), as in *calm.*

There is, of course, no objection to cultivating the vowel /a/ if there is some cultural reason for doing so. We would suggest, however, that the cultivation of this vowel be accompanied by some degree of consistency and that the speaker avoid fluctuating between /a/ in *dance, craft,* and *mask* and /æ/ for *France, laugh,* and *ask.*

PRACTICE MATERIALS

Determine your practice in the use of the vowel /æ/ or /a/ for the following materials. Consistency of vowel pronunciation is recommended but not prescribed.

half	class	last	mast
ask	calf	advance	dance
grass	task	craft	demand
mask	laugh	France	bath
pass	staff	laugh	bask

Sentences

1. The birds took their bath in the moist grass.
2. We attended a dance wearing masks.
3. The craft took off for France.
4. The cowboy's task was to rope the calf.
5. Cass attended his last class at Harvard.
6. Claspell danced along the path when his Master of Arts degree was granted.
7. The command staff studied their plans on the top of a cask.
8. Branding of calves is a vanishing craft.

THE BACK VOWELS

/ɑ/ (ä) As in *Calm*

/ɑ/ is a low, back, lax vowel. The back vowels, we recall, are those that are produced with the back of the tongue most active (see Figure 12–2). In changing from the low front vowel /æ/ to the back vowel [ɑ] the tongue arching is moved from the front to the back of the tongue.

The vowel /ɑ/ is produced with the tongue in about as low a position as it is likely to assume without applying direct external pressure to the flat of the tongue. The mouth is open wide and the lips are unrounded.

In spelling, the /ɑ/ is most frequently represented by the letters *a* and *o*. In words such as *ah, alms, charm, psalm,* and *balm,* the sound /ɑ/ is consistently heard throughout the United States. In the words *hot, cot, cog, ox,* and *stock,* there is less consistency in pronunciation. Many speakers will use the /ɑ/ vowel, but others will use a variant with lip rounding /ɒ/ which is absent for /ɑ/.

Still others use the vowel /ɔ/, or one very close to it, in words such as *balm, calm,* and *psalm*.

PRACTICE MATERIALS

ah	Arnold	argyle	argosy
are	argue	arbor	ardent
alms	archer	army	Arthur
armor	artful	ark	archives
aqua	dark	harmed	father
alarm	hearten	qualify	balmy
calm	guard	sergeant	carved
cargo	bother	parked	partner

quality cargo	sergeant of the guard
calm charmer	smart partner
scarred farthing	artful archer
Arctic stars	charms of palms

Sentences

1. The armored guard was a part-time artist.
2. Acapulco and Acre are harbor cities, whereas Ankara is in the heart of Turkey.
3. The city fathers of Key Largo put an embargo on products from Fargo.
4. Mark Clark's 15th Army marched through Italy.

5. The stars arched between the palms, starkly guarding the harbor on balmy nights.
6. When Arthur became a father, he was alarmed to realize that he did not maintain the calm of a guardian angel.
7. Noah's ark had a well-guarded cargo.

Most speakers use the vowel /ɑ/ for the following words with *o* spellings. Others modify the sound by some lip rounding and so produce a sound that is or approximates /ɒ/ (ŏ).

Determine your tendency by looking at your mouth in a mirror as you practice with the following materials.

bog	odd	nod	pod	groggy
cod	option	cot	otter	docket
olive	cog	job	fodder	potted
occupy	frog	rob	locket	socket
ox	hot	hod	respond	rocket
got	golf	pocket	stop	topper

Sentences

1. Jock, an old Scotsman, carried a frog in the pocket of his golf bag.
2. Stockwell was shocked to learn that a robber stole his stopwatch.
3. *Lox* is a term for the liquid oxygen used as a fuel for rockets.
4. Robert sat calmly on the rock despite the hot weather.
5. Alfalfa is a crop used as fodder for stock.
6. Mollie, the fishmonger, sold cod and haddock.
7. Boswell was locked up for watering stock.
8. A frog may frighten an ox.

Selections

1. A pictur' that no painter has the colorin' to mock—
   When the frost is on the pumpkin and the fodder's in the shock.
   —JAMES WHITCOMB RILEY, *When the Frost Is on the Pumpkin*

2. Camelot, a dot
   Of space in time,
   Begot
   By need of man
   To spot and plot
   A dream
   Of what
   Man hopes of man:
   Of Lancelot

Tried by Guinevere,
Of Arthur
Tried by love and fear
And knowing
More than he could know.
Camelot, a dot
Of time that was, to be
A spot to plot
And prophetically, to see.

—J. E., Suggested by T. H. White's
The Once and Future King

3. Ev'n copious Dryden wanted, or forgot,
   The last and greatest art—the art to blot.

—ALEXANDER POPE, *Epistle I*

/ɒ/ (ŏ)

/ɒ/ is a low, back, lax, rounded vowel.

As noted earlier, the vowel /ɒ/ is used by some Americans in words in which the vowel /ɑ/ is used by others. The vowel /ɑ/ is also used as a variant for the vowel /ɔ/ (ô) as in *dog* and *cough*.

In manner of production and in acoustic impression, /ɒ/ is somewhere between /ɔ/ and /ɑ/. The vowel /ɒ/ is low and lax and is produced with slight rounding of the lips.

No list can be given of words for which the vowel /ɒ/ is consistently used throughout the United States, or even in any major area within the United States. Although not confined to eastern New England, the sound /ɒ/ is more likely to be heard there than elsewhere.

The vowel /ɒ/ may be heard in words in which the spelling includes the letter *o* followed by the consonants /f/, /θ/ (th), or /s/. It is not, however, limited to these spellings.

PRACTICE MATERIALS

In the practice materials that follow, determine what your pronunciation is for the key words and compare your pronunciation with that of the respected members of your community. First, however, you may wish to review the word list and sentences for the vowels /ɑ/ or /ɒ/ previously considered.

boss	froth	across	office
cloth	loft	along	aloft
cost	lost	glossy	choral
florid	song	moral	floral
floss	toss	mossy	wrongly

Phrases

costly crossing	frothy broth
flossy moss	odd job
lost officer	immoral choral
tossed aloft	sorry loss
soft morals	hot coffee

Sentences

1. A "coffin nail" can cost more than a cough.
2. Roth crossed the office to the coffee pot.
3. The men scoffed at the florid Bostonian officer's morals.
4. Foster tossed glossy paint on the canvas in his loft.
5. Rose walked softly across the mossy forest sod.

Selections

> The moonlight is the softest, in Kentucky,
> Summer days come oftest, in Kentucky,
> Friendship is the strongest
> Love's fires glow the longest
> Yet a wrong is always wrongest
>   In Kentucky.
>
> —JAMES H. MULLIGAN, *In Kentucky*

Additional practice material is provided following the consideration of the vowel /ɔ/ (ô).

/ɔ/ (ô) As in *Author*

/ɔ/ is a low, back vowel produced with definite lip rounding. The tongue is slightly higher for /ɔ/ than it is for /ɑ/ and /ɒ/ (see back-vowel diagram, Figure 12–2).

The most frequent spellings for /ɔ/ include *a* as in *ball, aw,* as in *lawful, au* as in *taught, ou* as in *bought,* and the letter *o* as in *horse.*

In many words, including some of those used as examples in the previous paragraph, the vowel /ɑ/, and less frequently /ɒ/, may be heard instead of /ɔ/. Some of the variations are more or less uniform according to geographic regions; others seem to be more individualized according to speaker choice.

PRACTICE MATERIALS

If you are not certain of your own pronunciation habits, practice before a mirror will help to distinguish the /ɔ/ from the /ɑ/ pronunciations. If you wish to establish a clear distinction make certain that your lips are rounded for /ɔ/; for /ɑ/ the lips are unrounded and the tongue is lax.

In the list that follows, the words of the first two columns are most likely to be pronounced with the vowel /ɔ/; the words of the other columns are likely to be pronounced with /ɑ/ or /ɒ/. The vowel /ɔ/ may, however, be used for any of the words.

hall	hawk	song	frog
ball	sawing	wrong	torrid
fought	call	soft	orange
taught	flawless	lost	foreign
wall	chalk	off	porridge
August	awesome	cost	forest
auto	claws	coffin	horrible

The words in the following list are most likely to be pronounced with the vowel /ɔ/ rather than either of the other back vowels we have studied.

author	calked	orphan	stall
awkward	yawn	north	organ
tall	falter	halt	thorn
nought	ordeal	shawl	horse
horn	fourth	reform	snort
corn	born	morbid	scorned
fortune	mourning	normal	storm

stalking horse   morbid author
August storm   law and order
normally warm   orphan of the storm
corn stalk   born to yawn
pause for nought   calked yawl
warm shawl   fourth brawl

Sentences

1. Dawson was taught to be a quarterback.
2. The cautious crew balked at manning the yawl into a squall.
3. Some politicians call for law and order, others are appalled with the ordeal of its responsibilities.
4. It was an ordeal to listen to the author's halting, faltering speech.
5. Morbid tall stories leave some people yawning.
6. Kansas is proud to be corny in August.
7. Quarter horses don't always cost a fortune.
8. Saul's widow wore a black shawl as a token of her mourning.
9. Paul called to inform us that automobile traffic was stalled on the northbound lanes, but normal toward the south.
10. Norman, a tall adolescent, was normally awkward.

/o/ (ō) As in *Mode*

/o/ is a midhigh, rounded back vowel. (See back-vowel diagram, Figure 12–2.) The tongue position is higher for /o/ than for the vowel /ɔ/. The vowel /o/ is only infrequently used as a pure sound. In most contexts, this sound is likely to be lengthened into the diphthong [ou].

The most frequent spellings of the vowel /o/ or the diphthong /ou/ are the letters *o*, *oe*, *oa*, and *ow* as in *no, foe, boat*, and *grow*.

There is no special value in working to maintain a distinction between the vowel /o/ and the diphthong variant /ou/. Phonetic context will generally determine whether the vowel or diphthong will be used. There is value in avoiding excessive prolongation so that a triphthong ending with a weak vowel /ə/ is produced and a word such as *hold* [hold] becomes [houəld].

PRACTICE MATERIALS

oak	ogre	Olympic	open
oath	okay	omen	opium
oboe	okra	omit	over
ochre	oleander	opal	owe
abode	cone	moat	scone
bloat	float	mowing	sole
bowl	grown	roast	stone
chose	hone	rote	tome
coast	lode	soak	towel
coke	lope	sold	whole
cold	lower	soap	zone
ago	follow	Ohio	sloe
beau	glow	potato	slow
doe	hollow	roe	though
ego	Joe	row	toe
flow	low	show	woe

Sentences

1. Yellow Hair's soldiers opened the road to the Dakota gold fields.
2. Jones had a toe hold on the steep slope, but still had to hold on to the rope.
3. Joe's host served a roast that was worthy of his boast.
4. Low clouds drifted over the coast.
5. Some folks make their homes in geodesic domes.
6. The old tug slowly towed the showboat down the Ohio.
7. Smoke from burning coke and coal rose into the ozone.

8. Homer's epic poetry told of hope and sorrow.
9. Hogan's goat loped over the frozen slope.
10. O'Neal was broke, but no one would float him a loan.

Selections

1. Rattle his bones over the stones.
   He's only a pauper whom nobody owns.
   —THOMAS NOLL, *The Pauper's Drive*
2. Death is a common friend or foe,
       As different men may hold,
   And at his summons each must go,
       The timid and the bold.
   —MICHAEL JOSEPH BARRY, *The Place Where Men Should Die*

/ʊ/ (o͝o) As in *Book* and /u/ (o͞o) As in *Pool*

/ʊ/ is a high, back, lip-rounded vowel. The tongue is lax and in a
higher position than for the vowel /o/.

The spellings for /ʊ/ include *u* as in *pull, full,* and *put, oo* as in *book*
and *cook, ou* as in *could* and *would,* and *o* as in *wolf.*

In many words of native English origin, especially those spelled with
oo, practice varies as to the use of /ʊ/ or the vowel /u/ (o͞o). For comparative purposes, therefore, we need to describe the vowel /u/.

/u/ (o͞o) is characterized by more lip rounding than any of the other
vowels in American-English speech. /u/ is the highest of the back vowels
(see back-vowel diagram, Figure 12–2, and compare /ʊ/ and /u/). The
tongue is tense in contrast with the lax tongue for /ʊ/. The most frequent
spellings for /u/ are *oo* as in *school, fool, ooze,* and *choose; o* as in *do;
u* as in *dupe;* and *ou* as in *coup* and *soup.*

The distinction between /ʊ/ and /u/ may be brought out by comparing the pronunciation of the following pairs of words.

/ʊ/	/u/	/ʊ/	/u/
book	boon	pull	pool
brook	bruise	roof	rule
crook	croon	shook	shoed
look	Luke	stood	stewed
nook	noon	wood	wooed

Determine your pronunciation of the following words. If your tongue
is tense and your lips rounded, you are using the vowel phoneme /u/; if
your tongue feels relaxed and your lips not so distinctively rounded, then
you are probably using the vowel phoneme /ʊ/. Do not be surprised that
you are not entirely consistent in vowel usage for the words that follow.

Many Americans vary according to the individual word. Make certain, however, that your pronunciation is distinctly either /u/ or /ʊ/.

roof	hoop
room	hooves
broom	root
group	rule

PRACTICE MATERIALS

The material that follows immediately is for practice wtih the vowel /ʊ/. Note its regular occurrence as a medial sound.

cushion	bullet	courier	footwear
would	bully	crooked	tourist
hook	bulwark	cuckoo	woody
boor	bushing	durable	woofer
moor	butcher	rookie	wool
booklet	bouillon	rural	goodness
Buddhism	boulevard	took	soot

Phrases

boorish moor	bushel of soot
good wood	wooden bookcase
rookie courier	Lynbrook boulevard
durable bulwark	took booklets
sugary pudding	neighborhood bulletin

Sentences

1. Goodman took Buddy Wolfe's hand and shook it.
2. No one could say whether the butcher was an unhooded crook.
3. The cook took the cookies from the oven and put in a well-seasoned pullet.
4. Woodville did not believe that good books could be misunderstood.
5. Brooks, a bulwark in his neighborhood, read the bulletin from the pulpit.
6. Cardinal Cook read the papal bull from the pulpit.
7. We took the rural path across the bushy moor.
8. They gave their neighbors a bushel of cookies.
9. Being hoodwinked means having the wool pulled over your eyes.
10. We pulled out of the woods when we saw a wolf.

The following material is for practice with the vowel /u/.

hoop	cool	doom	fruit
jubilee	raccoon	dual	gooey
junior	cooper	dues	goon
roost	coulee	duel	glue
womb	coupon	duke	goose
croup	croon	dune	hoot
boob	crouton	duty	July
boon	crude	fluid	loop
boot	clue	fool	loose
bouffant	crusade	frugal	rumor

booted fools	June moon
crusading duke	shrewd baboon
gloomy groom	soup spoon
womb to tomb	cool fruit
loose rumors	crude glue

Sentences

1. During July, Cooper cools off in the pool.
2. The duke led his troops in the crusade.
3. Ruth gets moody when someone croons "Blue Moon."
4. Lou said he is one who knew the plural of mongoose.
5. Fools in some groups prefer rumors to truth.
6. Newman did not choose the brew.
7. The shrew threw a soup spoon at the goose.
8. The overripe fruit oozed a sugary gooey fluid.
9. Cooper rued the day he played the buffoon.
10. June is a woman of many moods.

Many /u/ words are preceded by the sound /j/ (y) as in *you, youth, use,* and *hue.* In some of these words, the spelling y suggests the sound /j/, but in others the spelling is not a guide to the pronunciation. The following list contains some of the more frequent /ju/ words.

fuse	useful	feud	hew
you	utilize	cue	accuse
youth	mule	mute	huge
usury	hue	imbue	humor
unique	pupil	review	pew
eulogy	amuse	few	humid

Sentences

1. Few youths enjoy humid weather.
2. Our usury laws need review.

3. The mute mule carried a huge load.
4. Eulogies are not intended to be amusing nor unduly platitudinous.
5. The unique feud began over a ewe and was resumed every Tuesday.

There is considerable regional and individual variation as to the use of /ju/ or /u/ for some words. Tendencies exist on historical bases and may influence local and individual pronunciations. In general, our advice is to follow the pronunciations of persons in your community whose speech is deserving of respect. Do not strain for consistency for groups of words. Instead, work for consistency in the acceptable pronunciation of individual words.

ADDITIONAL PRACTICE MATERIALS

Sentences

1. There was much ado resulting from loose rumors about Hughes the recluse.
2. Lucy had to choose whether to buy good boots or new books.
3. A few groupings of everblooming bushes grew in the humid garden.
4. The detective reviewed his clues about the stolen jewels.
5. The well-ruled troops moved through the woods.
6. Too few students utilize the knowledge they accrue.
7. Rupert spooned out raccoon stew and put croutons in the soup.
8. Butcher saw a blue bull in the bushes.
9. The youths in the pew grew gloomy when the unmoving eulogy was read from the pulpit.
10. Ruth's hat was adorned with a blue goose plume.

Selections

1. Give me the room whose every nook
    Is dedicated to a book.
          —FRANK DEMPSTER SHERMAN, *The Library*
2. Every new movement or manifestation of human activity, when unfamiliar to people's minds, is sure to be misrepresented and misunderstood.
          —EDWARD CARPENTER, *The Drama of Love and Death*

CENTRAL VOWELS

The *central vowels* are those that are made with the middle of the tongue arched toward the palate. The central vowels include /ɝ/ (ûr), /ɜ/ (ûr), /ɚ/ (ər), /ə/ (ə), and /ʌ/ (ŭ) (see central-vowel diagram, Figure 12–3).

Carrell and Tiffany (1960, p. 98) point out that "stress plays a much more important part in differentiating the central vowels than it does in connection with the other vowels." Another characteristic is the presence or absence of *r* coloring. In our descriptions of the central vowels we emphasize the position of the vowel in regard to stress (accented or unaccented syllable) and the matter of *r* coloring.

/ɝ/ (ûr) or /ɜ/ As in *Bird, Curl*, and *World*

Most Americans use the vowel /ɝ/ in the previously indicated key words and in the accented syllable of words such as *avert, guerdon, journal*, and *unfurl*. Some phoneticians consider the /ɝ/ to be essentially a variety of the /r/ sound and suggest that the articulation of the sound can best be acquired by lengthening the initial /r/ of words such as *rose, red*, and *rim*. Such an /r/ might be produced with the tongue as a whole slightly retracted and the middle of the tongue raised toward the soft palate. We may think of the sound /ɝ/ as a vowel blended with the vowelized consonant /r/. The lips are unrounded for the production of /ɝ/.

Speakers who generally do not use the /r/ sound except when the letter *r* is immediately followed by a vowel are likely also to use /ɜ/ rather than /ɝ/ in the key words given in the preceding paragraph. The sound /ɜ/ is produced with a slightly lower tongue position, with the lips unrounded, and without the /r/ coloring of /ɝ/.

The use of /ɝ/ or /ɜ/ is largely a matter of regional practice. In the list of words that follows, most Americans would use /ɝ/. Many speakers in New England, New York City, and in the southern coastal states, however, use /ɜ/. Individual speakers who have been influenced by British speech or who were trained for the stage with eastern or British "standard" diction might also use /ɜ/ regardless of where they live.

We may note that the spelling of words in which /ɝ/ or /ɜ/ is used usually includes the letters *ur, or, ir*, or *ear*. The word *colonel* is one of the few exceptions in which the spelling does not include the letter *r*.

Some speakers substitute the diphthongal blend /ɜɪ/ for the vowel /ɜ/. The word *bird* may then become [bɜɪd] and *girl* may become [gɜɪl]. This diphthongal variant seems acceptable to many speakers in the South.

PRACTICE MATERIALS

earl	ergot	irk	urbane
early	ermine	Irma	urchin
earn	err	Irwin	urgent
erg	erstwhile	urban	urn
birch	germ	lurk	term
birth	gird	mirth	terse
curb	gurgle	nerve	turban
curt	herb	pearl	turf
dirge	herd	purse	turn
dirt	hurt	spurn	verse
tern	jerk	surge	virtue
flirt	learn	swerve	work
aver	deter	inter	sir
blur	err	occur	spur
burr	fur	purr	stir
cur	her	refer	were
demur	infer	shir	whir

Phrases

curved surface	certain person
terse sermon	earnest urging
affirm and aver	unfurl with a swirl
irksome urchin	avert being hurt
determined person	swerving skirts
shirk the burden	certain purpose
worried personnel	worthy circles

Sentences

1. Birds work to find worms lurking in turf.
2. The crew worked in earnest to avert collision with the iceberg.
3. Sir Bertram Burbank preferred to adjourn rather than demur.
4. Colonel Burton took his furlough in Berkeley.
5. Erwin was stirred by the fervent urge of the sermon.
6. The whirring turbine produced the urgently needed current.
7. It took courage for Curt to spur his pony into the whirling herd.
8. The customers were terse but the merchant far from taciturn.
9. A bird in the hand is worth a good deal on earth.
10. Shirley did not bestir herself to avert the falling urn.

Selections

1. Look round the habitable world:
    how few
    Know their own good, or knowing it,
        pursue.

    —JOHN DRYDEN, Juvenal

2. Werther had a love for Charlotte
        Such as words could never utter;
    Would you know how first he met her?
        She was cutting bread and butter.

    Charlotte was a married lady,
        And a moral man was Werther,
    And for all the wealth of Indies,
        Would do nothing for to hurt her.

    —WILLIAM MAKEPEACE THACKERAY, Sorrows of Werther

/ɚ/ /ər/ (ər) and /ə/ (ə) As in Unstressed Syllables of *Ever, Other, About,* and *Sofa*

The vowel /ɚ/ is the unstressed "equivalent" of /ɝ/. In words such as *earner* and *murmur* the first syllable vowels are stressed and so are pronounced as /ɝ/ by most American speakers. The second, unstressed, syllable is pronounced /ɚ/ by the same speakers—the majority of Americans who habitually pronounce medial or final *r*'s whenever the letter occurs in the spelling of the word.

/ɚ/ is a lax, unrounded, midvowel. It has a lower tongue position than /ɝ/. Because of its occurrence in the unstressed position, /ɚ/ is less intense and shorter in duration than its stressed counterpart.

/ə/ is a midvowel produced with a lax tongue and unrounded lips in a position slightly lower than /ɜ/.

/ə/ is probably the most frequently used vowel in our language for the following reasons:

1. It is the most frequently used vowel in unstressed syllables regardless of the spelling of the vowel. Some examples of the varied spellings are indicated in the italicized letters of the following: *a*lone, sof*a*, foc*u*s, lab*e*l, preci*ou*s.

2. In addition to its occurrence in unstressed syllables of polysyllabic words, /ə/ is also the most frequently used vowel when prepositions, articles, conjunctions, and auxiliary verbs are unstressed in sentence context. For example, in the sentence, "I *of*ten find it diffic*u*lt *to* believe *the* man," each italicized word or syllable may appropriately be pronounced with the vowel /ə/.

3. The vowel /ə/ also replaces /r/ in words such as *hear, dare,* and

cure for those speakers who do not pronounce final *r*'s or *r*'s in general unless they are immediately followed by vowels. These, of course, are the same speakers from New England, New York City, and parts of the South who use /ɜ/ rather than /ɝ/ in stressed syllables.

PRACTICE MATERIALS

Check the pronunciation in your community and decide whether you prefer /ɝ/ or /ə/ for the unstressed syllables of the following words and phrases.

after	collar	hunter	other
alter	dollar	junior	ponder
answer	drummer	learner	rather
baker	either	leisure	settler
center	further	matter	tether
cleaner	greater	nadir	whether

bother for mother   other brother
fender bender   proper neighbor
leather cleaner   roller coaster
letter opener   summer weather
modern actor   tender murmurs

Sentences

1. Miller's letter deserves a longer answer.
2. Basketball players are taller than most other athletes.
3. Miller's neighbors sent him flowers and hoped he would soon feel better.
4. Baker and Roberts left the poker table after they squandered their treasure.
5. Some reporters and editors believe that a newspaper is the mirror of its era.
6. Last December, Esther could not decide whether she enjoyed seeing herself more in a mirror or in a newspaper.

Note the occurrence of the "weak" vowel /ə/ in the unstressed syllables of the words in the list and in the sentences that follow.

above	annoy	tuba	American
about	agree	soda	urban
allow	anoint	data	surgeon
appoint	Texas	Canada	precious
avoid	assist	circus	stirrup
amiss	asunder	opera	typical

Sentences

1.   The American spoke with a typical Texas drawl.
2.   A tuba may be annoying to hear alone.
3.   Canada is north or above the United States of America.
4.   Vienna is the capital city of Austria.
5.   Sir Francis Bacon, the famous philosopher, was one of Queen Elizabeth I's most intelligent advisors.
6.   Edna liked bananas with her breakfast cereal.
7.   The Russians opposed every agenda item approved by the Americans.
8.   The baritone agreed to sing the aria when he learned that he would be accompanied by the Philadelphia Opera Orchestra.
9.   Ella advised Eva that she always avoided annoying gorillas who appeared to be asleep.
10.   Dillon was appointed Professor of Urban Studies at Metropolitan Junior College.
11.   Selma, a vegetarian, had an okra salad for luncheon.
12.   Emma was fond of flowers and especially of azaleas and petunias.

/ʌ/ (ŭ) As in *Cup*

/ʌ/ is produced with a relatively relaxed tongue arched a little bit toward the middle or back of the palate. If it is produced with the middle of the tongue arching, it is a midvowel. Many persons, however, produce the sound with the back tongue arching as a back vowel rather than a midvowel. Either way, the mouth is open fairly wide *without* lip rounding. The tongue should be arched higher for /ʌ/ than for /ɑ/ so that a clear distinction is made between these vowels and between words such as *sup* and *sop, suck* and *sock,* and *nut* and *not.*

The vowel /ʌ/ is represented by several letters in spelling, including *u* as in *cup, ou* as in *double,* and *o* as in *done.*

Except for the tendency of some speakers to produce an /ɑ/ instead of a /ʌ/, the vowel causes little difficulty. For those persons who may be inclined to make the /ɑ/ substitution, it might be of help to know that /ʌ/ is the vowel the American Indian is alleged to make when he grunts "Ugh."

PRACTICE MATERIALS

The first set of exercises should help to establish the distinction between /ʌ/ and /ɑ/.[1] Be certain to raise your tongue slightly higher for /ʌ/ than for /ɑ/. The mouth is somewhat more open for /ɑ/ than for /ʌ/. Note that /ʌ/ appears only in stressed syllables.

[1] The vowel /ɒ/ is also appropriate for many of the words in the /ɑ/ column.

/ʌ/	/ɑ/	/ʌ/	/ɑ/
come	calm	gut	got
done	don	color	collar
sup	sop	chuck	chock
dull	doll	bubble	bobble
ruck	rock	bum	bomb
shut	shot	lug	log
slug	slog	buddy	body

In the sentences that follow the first italicized word contains the vowel [ʌ], the second the vowel [ɑ].

1. Do *come* and *calm* down.
2. A job well *done* is what *Don* liked.
3. The *pup* was frightened by the loud *pop*.
4. It was poor *luck* to lose the key to the *lock*.
5. The bear *cub* was fond of corn on the *cob*.
6. The *duck* hunter fired from the *dock*.
7. The *hut* was exposed to the *hot* sun.
8. She *wondered* where he *wandered*.

ADDITIONAL PRACTICE MATERIALS FOR /ʌ/

ulna	umbrage	umpire	unctious
up	other	udder	upward
under	onion	utter	ulcer
us	ugly	uncle	Ulster
upper	usher	oven	ultimate
blubber	chunk	cucumber	discussion
blood	lunge	asunder	mud
blunder	mumble	assumption	much
brother	mutton	begun	rugged
bud	once	benumb	stuck
cub	rubber	instruct	tuck
club	supper	lump	won
done	punish	hungry	thunder
cuff	rough	enough	thumb
love	monkey	honey	funny
buck	bubble	trouble	rubble
buckle	double	thrust	rebuttal

Phrases

lucky hunch	hungry for money
hungry brother	month of Sundays
supper club	country cousin
double trouble	something for mother
munch for lunch	muddy lump
blunt instruction	rough monkey

Sentences

1. Buddy wanted to hunt for another buck in the upland country.
2. Uncle Chuck likes onions and mustard with his mutton.
3. "If that's your assumption," the judge instructed, "you are making an utterly foolish blunder."
4. Dudley hadn't had so good a supper in a month of Sundays.
5. Buckley had muddled his way out of dozens of troubles.
6. Duncan's uncle has ulcers.
7. The umpire raised his thumb and sent one of the benumbed players to the clubhouse.
8. Rough, troubled seas can make landlubbers blubber.
9. Mother sewed another button on her young son's cuff.
10. General "Blood and Guts" Patton was considered a blunt, rugged officer.

Selections

1. It's a song of a merryman, moping mum,
   Whose soul was sad, and whose glance was glum,
   Who sipped no sup, and who craved no crumb,
   As he sighed for the love of a ladye.
   —W. S. GILBERT, *The Yeoman of the Guard*

2. Life's a pudding full of plums;
   Care's a canker that benumbs.
   —W. S. GILBERT, *The Gondoliers*

3. Not a face below the sun
   But is precious—unto one.
   —SIR EDWIN ARNOLD, *Facies non Omnibus Una*

4. Double, double, toil and trouble;
   Fire burn and cauldron bubble.
   —WILLIAM SHAKESPEARE, *Macbeth*

5. The camel's hump is an ugly lump
   Which well you may see at the Zoo;
   But uglier yet is the Hump you get
   From having little to do.
   —RUDYARD KIPLING, *How the Camel Got His Hump*

CHAPTER 13

Diphthongs

Diphthongs are vocalic glides that are uttered in a single breath impulse within a single syllable. A superficial analysis of a diphthong, as well as a literal interpretation of the term, suggests that a diphthong is a combination of two sounds. Actually, a diphthong is a continuous change of sound from the first element to the second. The first phonetic symbol of a diphthong really represents the approximate initial sound, and the second element represents the approximate final sound. Thus, the diphthong /ɔɪ/ (oi) is initiated with the sound [ɔ]. The organs of articulation are then modified to produce a continuous change of sound until the diphthong is completed with what approximates the vowel /ɪ/.

We consider first three American-English phonemic diphthongs. Each represents a distinctive sound unit and each serves as a basis by which we distinguish between spoken words without depending upon context. The phonemic diphthongs are /aɪ/ (ī) as in *I* and *my;* /ɔɪ/ (oi) as in *boy* and *toy;* and /ɑʊ/ (ou) as in *house* and *out.*

Earlier, in our study of the individual vowel sounds, nonphonemic variants of the vowels /e/ and /o/ were considered.[1] Another group of

---

[1] The reference is to the use of /eɪ/ in words such as *ace, ale, tame,* and *base* and the use of /oʊ/ in words such as *oaf, node,* and *pole.* The meanings of these words would not change whether the vowel /e/ or the nonphonemic diphthong /eɪ/ is used for the first series of examples or the vowel /o/ or the diphthong /oʊ/ for the second series.

sounds that might be considered diphthongal variants are the sound combinations of persons who do not pronounce final *r*'s. This group of sounds include /ɪə/, /ʊə/, /ɔə/, and /ɛə/ as pronunciations for words such as *dear, poor, core,* and *care.*

/aɪ/ (ī) As in *Ice* and *Nice*

The diphthong /aɪ/ is initiated with a raising of the tongue in the front part of the mouth. It ends, as indicated, with the vowel /ɪ/.

The most frequent spellings for /aɪ/ are *i* at the beginning and middle of the words and *y* as the final letter of words as in *ice, spice, entice, my,* and *cry.*

PRACTICE MATERIALS

I	fine	bright	fired	apply
iambic	pipe	China	fight	astride
icicle	viaduct	cider	fly	beguiling
I'd	abide	citation	high	deny
Idaho	alive	cry	hind	espy
ideal	arrive	dice	mine	pantomime
identity	archive	dine	quite	remind
iodine	bias	dire	side	reply
ion	Bible	devise	pyre	required
ire	biceps	entire	strive	unsightly
ivy	by	file	style	untiring

type style	butterfly light
bright smile	ironic hindsight
iron biceps	refined designs
right height	rhyming iambs
sly guile	dire signs
drive by night	slice of pie
light eyes	admire kindness
frightful crime	iodine ions

Sentences

1. On Fridays, Mike liked to eat fried rice at the Chinese diner.
2. McBride invited Lyons to look at his diagrams of an iron pipe viaduct.
3. The night riders were frightened of a daylight flight.
4. Ty Cobb's spikes produced fright when he decided to slide into base.
5. However wise, the use of irony is often unkind.

6. A tiger without stripes is a dire sight.

7. The guide reminded us of the time our canoe quietly glided beside the island.

8. By midnight they had to drive another ninety-five miles.

9. *A Hard Day's Night* is a light, bright film produced in black and white.

10. Bribery and riot are high crimes.

Selections

1. Behold the child, by Nature's kindly law
   Pleased with a rattle, tickled with a straw:
   Some livelier plaything gives his youth delight,
   A little louder, but as empty quite
   —ALEXANDER POPE, *Essay on Man*

2. To make a happy fireside clime
   To weans and wife
   That's the true pathos and sublime
   Of human life.
   —ROBERT BURNS, *Epistle to Dr. Blacklock*

3. The ghosts of forgotten actions
   Came floating before my sight,
   And things that I thought were dead things
   Were alive with a terrible might.
   —CHARLES WILLIAM STUBBS, *Conscience and Future Judgment*

4. A silence in thy life when, through the night,
   The bell strikes, or the sun, with sinking light,
   Smites all the empty windows.
   —EDWARD ROBERT BULWER-LYTTON, *The Wanderer in Holland*

5. When I was five
   My father was the wisest man alive;
   At ten and five
   I wondered he had wits enough to thrive;
   At five and twenty
   He had acquired new brains a-plenty.
   —J. E., *Intellectual Evolution*

6. Virtue itself turns vice, being misapplied;
   And vice sometime's by action dignified.
   —WILLIAM SHAKESPEARE, *Romeo and Juliet*

7. Light seeking light doth light of light beguile.
   —WILLIAM SHAKESPEARE, *Love's Labour's Lost*

8. When your Imp of Blind Desire
   Bids you set the Thames afire,
   You'll remember men have done so—in the Files.
   —RUDYARD KIPLING, *The Files*

9. Though in silence, with blighted affection I pine,
   Yet the lips that touch liquor must never touch mine!
                    —GEORGE W. YOUNG, *The Lips That Touch Liquor*
10. Beyond the bright searchlights of science,
    Out of sight of the windows of sense,
    Old riddles still bid us defiance
    Old questions of why and of whence.
                    —WILLIAM DAMPIER,
                        The Recent Development of Physical Science

/aʊ/ (ou) /ɑʊ/ As in *Now* and *How*

Whether the speaker produces /aʊ/ or /ɑʊ/ in the indicated key word depends phonetically on whether the front or back of the tongue is elevated in the first part of the diphthong. It is likely that his articulatory habit is determined by what he hears in his community. Both pronunciations are used by cultured and educated speakers throughout the United States.

The tendency to substitute the vowel /æ/ for the first element of the diphthong is one we recommend avoiding or correcting. We also recommend avoiding or correcting the triple vowel combinations [æaʊ] or [æɑʊ] for either /aʊ/ or /ɑʊ/.

The most frequent spellings for the diphthong are *ou* as in *out, house,* and *mouse* and *ow* as in *cow, how,* and *brow.*

PRACTICE MATERIALS

ouch	cloud	douse	gout	anyhow
ours	clown	dowel	house	announce
hours	clout	down	howl	rebound
oust	couch	drought	jowl	allowance
outer	council	drown	mound	endow
blouse	county	flounder	mount	impound
bough	coward	flour	mouse	disavow
bounce	cowl	foul	mouth	uncrowded
bound	crouch	glower	plow	redoubtable
bower	crown	gouge	powder	astounding

powdery flour   carouse and shout
mound of flowers   crowd of thousands
hound's mouth   astounding rebound
drowning flounder   about to announce
stout plowman   tower of power

Sentences

1. The ball bounded off the tower and rebounded out of bounds as a foul.
2. Lowry was proud to announce that the crowd numbered about a thousand.
3. Astounded by a mouse, the hound aroused us with his howls.
4. Parts of the Southwest suffer from drought and powder-dry soil.
5. The count, who announced that he represented the crown, flouted his power before the stout councilmen.
6. McCloud frowned at the scoundrel lounging on the couch.
7. When asked, "How now," the brown cow did not know how to take a bow.
8. The hour-long shower drowned the flowers.

Selections

1. From a proud tower in the town
   Death looks gigantically down.
   —EDGAR ALLAN POE, *The City in the Sea*
2. Ye rigid Plowmen. Bear in mind
      Your labor is for future hours.
   Advance! spare not! nor look behind!
      Plow deep and straight with all your powers!
   —RICHARD HENRY HORNE, *The Plow*
3. He who doubts from what he sees,
   Will ne'er believe, do what you please,
   If the Sun and Moon should doubt,
   They'd immediately go out.
   —WILLIAM BLAKE, *Auguries of Innocence*
4. Time writes no wrinkle on thine azure brow—
   Such as creation's dawn beheld, thou rollest now.
   —GEORGE GORDON, LORD BYRON, *Childe Harold's Pilgrimage*
5. The strongest castle, towers and town,
   The golden bullet beats it down.
   —WILLIAM SHAKESPEARE, *Sonnets to Sundry Notes of Music*

/ɔɪ/ (oi) As in *Boy, Soil,* and *Noise*

The diphthong /ɔɪ/ is appropriately produced by beginning with the back, rounded vowel /ɔ/ and ending with the front vowel /ɪ/. The most frequent spellings include *oi* and *oy* as in *oil, boil, toy,* and *boy.*

Some speakers tend to substitute /ɜɪ/ for /ɔɪ/. This tendency is generally considered substandard and we recommend that it be avoided or corrected. Another tendency to be avoided is the substitution of /oɪ/ for /ɔɪ/.

PRACTICE MATERIALS

boiler	hoist	noisy	anoint
boisterous	hoyden	oily	annoy
boycott	join	ointment	despoil
cloister	joist	point	embroil
coin	loin	quoits	employ
coy	loiter	roister	recoil
foible	loyal	royal	exploit
goiter	moist	soy	rejoice

boisterous roisterers	soiled coin
loyal to royalty	poisoned oyster
soybeans and poi	toy boycott
noisy boys	annoying foibles
broiled loin	exploited loyalty

Sentences

1. McCoy ran a noisy, boisterous joint.
2. Roy exploited the oil that lay beneath his soil.
3. Doyle's voice sounded as if he were poised, but his words were annoyingly poignant.
4. Royal heads were anointed with oil.
5. Lloyd joined the floorboards to the joists.
6. She may look coy when embroidering doilies but she is often a roisterous hoyden.
7. Spoiled oysters are poisonous.
8. The little boy avoided stepping on the toys in the foyer.
9. Few enjoy being employed as decoys or foils.
10. The villain's ploy to purloin the coins was foiled.

Selections

1. The very honey of all earthly joy
   Does of all meats the soonest cloy.
   —ABRAHAM COWLEY, *The Wish*
2. Joy is the sweet voice, Joy the luminous cloud—
   We in ourselves rejoice.
   —SAMUEL TAYLOR COLERIDGE, *Dejection*
3. She was a hoyden,
   Yet could play coy

As practiced maiden
Not boisterous boy.

—J. E., *Tried and Untrue*

4. The long guns poised
Exploded and recoiled
From fire and burst of noise
And what they had despoiled.

—J. E., *Annoying Toys*

/ɛə/ (åə) As in *There*

The nonphonemic diphthong /ɛə/ is used instead of the more frequently heard /ɛr/ or /ɛɚ/ by persons who omit *r*'s in their pronunciations except before vowels. It is heard in such words as *air, their, fair, care, dare, chair,* and *pear.*

/ɛə/ is also heard as a not entirely approved substitution for the vowels /æ/ or /a/ in words such as *ask, last, class,* and *bath.*

Speakers who generally pronounce their *r*'s when the letter *r* occurs in the spelling are likely to use the combination /ɛr/ or /ɛɚ/ rather than /ɛə/ in the words that follow:

PRACTICE MATERIALS

air	lair	compare	repair
bear	fair	declare	unaware
care	their	chair	heirloom
dare	wear	forbear	heiress
flair	affair	prepare	impair
hair	beware	welfare	despair
spare	scarce	square	scared

air fare	undeclared warfare
scared hare	their welfare
scarce hair	dared to forbear
pared pears	bears and mares

Sentences

1. Few dare to impair a bear's welfare.
2. Mary carried the heirloom chair upstairs.
3. Claire rode her mare to the dairy fair.
4. "Beware, this is not your affair," Blair said with a cold stare.
5. The daring are often scared, despite their devil-may-care airs.

Selections

1. Fair tresses man's imperial race ensnare,
   And beauty draws us with a single hair.
   > —ALEXANDER POPE, *The Rape of the Lock*

2. Away from the world and its toils and its cares
   I've a snug little kingdom up four pairs of stairs.
   > —WILLIAM MAKEPEACE THACKERAY, *The Cane-Bottomed Chair*

3. Shall I, wasting in despair,
   Die because a woman's fair?
   Or make pale my cheeks with care,
   'Cause another's rosy are?
   Be she fairer than the day,
   Or the flowery meads in May,
   If she be not so to me,
   How care I how fair she be?
   > —GEORGE WITHER, *The Author's Resolution*

4. Said Dairlington to Fairlington,
   "However various
   You're reliably nefarious."
   Said Fairlington to Dairlington,
   "Were you not undarious
   You too might be nefarious."
   > —J. E., *Point-Counter Point*

/ɔə/ and /oə/ (ôə)

The diphthongs /ɔə/ and /oə/ are used by persons who are inclined to omit the /r/ from their pronunciations except before vowels. Practice in regard to /ɔə/ and /ɔr/ or /oə/ and /or/ varies along the following lines.[2]

In words such as *horse, lord, accord,* and *north,* usage is fairly uniform throughout the United States. The pronunciation is /ɔr/ for most Americans and /ɔə/ in the "r-dropping" sections of the country.

Usage varies between /o/ and /ɔ/ pronunciations for the words *board, mourning, course,* and *more.* These words are pronounced with either /o/ or /or/ by most American speakers. In the New York City area these words are pronounced with /ɔ/ by "native" speakers. Thus, except for the New York City area, most Americans make distinctions between the words *horse* and *hoarse, for* and *four,* and *cord* and *cored.* The sound /ɔ/ is more likely to be used for the first word of these pairs and the /o/ for the second.

---

[2] The transcriptions [ɔɚ] and [oɚ] are alternatives for [ɔə] and [or].

PRACTICE MATERIALS

Determine your own practice by comparing the pronunciation of the following pairs of words.

border	boarder
horse	hoarse
morning	mourning
war	wore
coarse	course

Sentences

1. Guns were stored in the fort.
2. Each pull on his oars brought McCord closer to the shore.
3. Four hours of riding on his horse brought him to the border.
4. The lion roared himself hoarse because he wanted more food.
5. The owner of the resort inn was noted for being in accord with forty different points of view.

Selections

1. Cruel Remorse! where Youth and Pleasure sport,
   And thoughtless Folly keeps her court—
   —ANNA L. BARABAULD, *Ode to Remorse*

2. Come in the evening, or come in the morning,
   Come when you're looked for, or come without warning,
   Kisses and welcome you'll find here before you,
   And the oftener you come here the more I'll adore you.
   —THOMAS O. DAVIS, *The Welcome*

3. He will hold thee when his passion shall have spent its novel force,
   Something better than his dog, a little dearer than his horse.
   —ALFRED, LORD TENNYSON, *Locksley Hall*

4. Three poets, in three distant ages born,
   Greece, Italy, and England did adorn.
   —JOHN DRYDEN, *Under Mr. Milton's Picture*

5. Society is now one polish'd horde,
   Formed of two mighty tribes, the *Bores* and *Bored*.
   —GEORGE GORDON, LORD BYRON, *Don Juan, Canto XIII*

6. What care though rival cities soar
   Along the stormy coast,
   Penn's town, New York, and Baltimore,
   If Boston knew the most.
   —RALPH WALDO EMERSON, *Boston*

7. Forms more real than living man
   Nurslings of immortality.
                    —PERCY BYSSHE SHELLEY, *Prometheus Unbound*
8. Love, sole mortal thing
   Of worth immortal.
                    —COVENTRY PATMORE, *The Angel in the House, Prelude I*

/ɪə/ (ĭə) As in *Dear* and *Year*

The diphthong /ɪə/ (ĭə), as noted earlier, is used by persons who omit medial and final /r/ sounds from the pronunciation of such words as *dear, fear, hear, beard, cheerful,* and *earful*. Throughout most of the United States, all of these words are more frequently pronounced with the combinations [ɪr] or [ɪɚ] rather than with the diphthong /ɪə/.

PRACTICE MATERIALS

Determine your own pronunciation for the following words and compare them with the pronunciation of respected speakers in your community.

beard	pier	gear	piercing	earwig
beer	cheer	queer	seared	nearly
dear	arrear	cheerful	fierce	sincere
fear	mere	earful	spear	tearful
hear	drear	fearful	bier	Shakespeare
merely	clear	we're	year	sneering

fearfully dear	steer clear
eerie bier	year's arrears
we're here	tearful earful
queer gear	fiercely pierced
near and dear	appeared sincere

Sentences

1. Geary's beard appeared to be seared.
2. The hunter's gear included a fearful-looking spear.
3. The trees looked dreary because of the sere leaves.
4. A fierce fire destroyed the pier.
5. Beardsley was not considered a cheerful person because of his habit of crying in his beer.

Selections

1. But at my back I always hear
   Time's wingèd chariot hurrying near;
                    —ANDREW MARVELL, *To His Coy Mistress*

2. We're tenting tonight on the old camp ground,
   Give us a song to cheer,
   Our weary hearts a song of home
   And friends we love so dear.
   —WALTER KITTREDGE, *Tenting on the Old Camp Ground*
3. The skies they were askew and sober;
   The leaves they were crisped and sere—
   The leaves they were withering and sere;
   It was night in the lonesome October
   Of my most immortal year.
   —EDGAR ALLAN POE, *Ulalume*
4. Damn with faint praise, assent with civil leer,
   And without sneering, teach the rest to sneer;
   —ALEXANDER POPE, *Prologue to Satires*

/ʊə/ (o͝oə) As in *Poor*

The diphthong /ʊə/ is likely to be used by speakers who are inclined to pronounce /r/ only in contexts in which the letter *r* is immediately followed by a vowel. These speakers would probably use /ʊə/ rather than [ʊr] or [ʊɚ] in words such as *poor, sure,* and *tour.*

PRACTICE MATERIALS

Determine your own pronunciation for the words that follow and compare each with what is current in your community.

poor	allure	assure	fury
sure	moor	jury	endure
tour	boor	ensure	touring

Sentences

1. Be he rich or poor, there is little that is alluring about a boor.
2. What we cannot cure we must learn to endure.
3. If you're surely poor, you can hardly afford to tour among the Moors.
4. The jurymen had to control their fury to ensure a fair and enduring verdict.
5. Though Moore was a poor man, he felt socially secure.
6. The cat's nine lives was no insurance against curiosity.
7. The seamen were glad to have their ship securely moored after enduring the fury of the storm.
8. As the touring boorish actor sawed the air in fury, the director told the producer, "Rest assured, this ham will never be cured."

Selections

1. "I'll be judge, I'll be jury," said cunning old Fury.
   —LEWIS CARROLL, *Alice's Adventures in Wonderland*
2. I'll make assurance doubly sure,
   And take a bond of fate.
   —WILLIAM SHAKESPEARE, *Macbeth*
3. How small of all that human hearts endure
   That part which laws or kings can cause or cure.
   —SAMUEL JOHNSON, *Lines Added to Goldsmith's Traveller*

/eɪ/ (ā) As in *Gale*

Earlier we discussed /eɪ/ as a nonphonemic variant of the vowel /e/. At this point, we merely present additional practice materials that include words that may be appropriately pronounced with the diphthong /eɪ/.

PRACTICE MATERIALS

aid	blade	nail	wane
ale	blaze	pace	weight
aim	braise	skate	await
bail	cape	tame	detain
bait	hail	taint	dismay
bane	mail	trait	waiver

Sentences

1. After his zany escapade, Ray was detained in jail without bail.
2. Brady labored at the mason's trade.
3. Rick Blaine told his famous friend that fate was about to play a painful hand.
4. Blaine asked whether Major had to take the late plane to Spain.
5. The stranger paid the bill that the waiter had placed on the table and went on his way.
6. Jay weighed his mail on the postal scale.
7. Crayton did not hesitate to use the radio-telephone to relay weighty news.
8. Kate waved to Sadie as they made their way through the shady dale.
9. Lady Grey had a quaint way of betraying her famous status.
10. Rain came with daybreak, as if nature did not want the croquet game to be played on the graded field.

Selections

1. Said Grayson to Payson,
   "By the way that you behave
   I cannot help but assay you
   As primate trained to shave."

   Said Payson to Grayson
   "The way in which you rave
   Makes primate seem ascendant
   However you behave."

   —J. E., *Evolution*

2. All human things are subject to decay,
   And, when fate summons, monarchs must obey.

   —JOHN DRYDEN, *Mac Flecknoe*

3. What of the faith and fire within us
   Men who march away
   Ere the barn-cocks say
   Night is growing gray?

   —THOMAS HARDY, *Men Who March Away*

/oʊ/ (ō) as in *Bone, Prone*

Earlier we discussed /oʊ/ as a nonphonemic variant of the midhigh, rounded back vowel /o/. We now present some additional practice materials in which /oʊ/ may be appropriately used. We should have in mind, however, that words such as *bone, home,* or *grow* do not change in meaning whether they are pronounced with the vowel /o/ or the diphthong /oʊ/.

bone	goal	alone	acetone
bonus	hold	although	bestow
bowl	knoll	cyclone	regrow
cone	loan	Dover	resole
drone	moan	below	unknown
ghost	prone	enroll	homely

Sentences

1. Joan made her home in the adobe hut on the knoll.
2. The troll was prone to fall into the old moat.
3. Although he kept his hold on the controls, the captain broke his nose when the ship almost rolled over.
4. Greta Garbo boldly chose to lead her own life over the moans of nosy reporters.

5. The old rover warmed his hands over the coals glowing in his host's golden bowl.

6. The wind blows and moans across the road to Nome.

7. Rose told Mona that she preferred older and homely men because they were supposedly easier to control.

Selections

1. I know a bank wheron the wild thyme blows,
    Where oxlips and the nodding violet grows.
    —WILLIAM SHAKESPEARE, *A Midsummer Night's Dream*

2. I'm growing frugal of my gold;
    I'm growing wise, I'm growing—yes—
       I'm growing old.
    —JOHN GODFREY SAXE, *I'm Growing Old*

3. Avenge, O Lord, thy slaughtered saints whose bones
    Lie scattered in the Alpine mountains cold;
    Ev'n them who kept thy truth so pure of old
    When all our fathers worshiped stocks and stones.
    —JOHN MILTON, *On the Late Massacre in Piedmont*

4. I know his name, I know his note,
    That so with rapture takes my soul;
    Like flame the gold beneath his throat
    His glossy cape is black as coal.
    —WILLIAM DEAN HOWELLS, *The Song the Oriole Sings*

CHAPTER 14

Consonants: The Lip (Bilabial) Sounds

Consonants, we recall, are speech sounds produced as a result of the modification of the outgoing breath stream by the organs of articulation. The form of modification produces the characteristics (features) peculiar to the various consonants. Unlike vowels, which are all voiced sounds unless the speaker is intentionally whispering, some consonants are appropriately voiced and others are appropriately voiceless.

The description and manner of production of each of the consonant sounds are considered individually. Precautions to be observed and the pitfalls to be avoided are indicated for those sounds that some American-English speaking adults find difficult.

THE FAVORED ARTICULATORY CONTACT

Many languages seem to have a favored place of articulatory contact. In French, Spanish, and Italian many sounds are produced by contact between the tongue tip and the upper teeth. In German the point of contact is a bit lower. In American English, the favored contact area is the upper gum ridge. At this point, by contact with the tongue tip, the sounds /t/, /d/, /l/, and /n/ are articulated. A fraction of an inch behind the gum ridge, articulatory placements are made for the sounds /s/, /z/,

/ʃ/ (sh), /ʒ/ (zh), /tʃ/ (ch), /dʒ/ (j), and for one of the varieties of /r/.

Because of the proximity of articulatory positions for the American-English sounds and those much like them in Spanish, French, Italian, and German, the tendency to carry over foreign language speech habits is understandable. We should also be able to appreciate the need for special precautions and considerable practice to overcome these foreign language influences. A good beginning in correcting such influences, and in establishing awareness of the favored place of American-English articulation, is to study the diagram of Figure 14–1.

Figure 14–1   Diagram indicating the "favored contact area" for American-English consonants. The upper gum ridge is the contact point for /t/, /d/, and /l/. Essentially the same tongue-tip and gum-ridge contact is made for /n/.

The consonant sounds are presented approximately according to the place of major articulatory activity proceeding from the front to the back of the mouth (see Table 14–1). This order of presentation is not to be interpreted as necessarily the most desirable or the prescribed one to be followed. We believe that the specific order of consonant study should be determined by the instructional needs of the students or the philosophy of the teacher. An individual student, aware of his own limitations in diction, or striving for improvement in a given direction, might well begin with the sound, or one of the sounds, requiring attention. An instructor might determine the order of consonant study based on a screening of his group of students. The sound most in need of improvement for the largest

TABLE 14-1 Classification of Consonants of American-English Speech

MANNER OF ARTICULATION	LIPS (BILABIAL)	LIP-TEETH (LABIO-DENTAL)	TONGUE-TEETH (LINGUA-DENTAL)	TONGUE-GUM-RIDGE (ALVEOLAR)	TONGUE-HARD PALATE (POST-ALVEOLAR)	TONGUE-BLADE-PALATE (PALATAL)	TONGUE-VELUM (VELAR)	LARYNX (GLOTTAL)
Voiceless stops	p			t			k	ʔ
Voiced stops	b			d			g	
Voiceless fricatives	ʍ (hw)	f	θ (th)	s	ʃ (sh)			h
Voiced fricatives		v	ð (ŧh)	z	ʒ (zh)			
Nasals (voiced)	m			n			ŋ (ng)	
Lateral				l				
Glides (vowel-like consonants)	w				r*	r j (y)		
Voiceless affricate					tʃ (ch)			
Voiced affricate					dʒ (dzh)			

* In our discussion of the /r/ phoneme, the variable characteristics of /r/ are considered.

number of students in his class may then be selected as the one with which to begin. If the instructor believes that it is better to teach a relatively difficult sound by contrasting it with another easier sound for the student, then this may become the proper initial sound to be studied. An instructor who has many students coming from a given speech region and who, on the basis of his experience, is able to anticipate frequent consonant difficulties, may choose to begin his improvement program in the light of his anticipations. He will soon learn whether the students are living up to his expectations or whether his own program for his particular group of students is in need of modification. Such an approach will afford the individual student and the class as a whole the greatest amount of instructional time and the opportunity for work on common problems and for frequent review during the course of a term.

An alternate rationale for the order of presentation of the consonants is one based on a knowledge of normal speech sound acquisition in children. This approach would call for approximately the following order:

1. /m/, /p/, /b/
2. /n/, /f/, /h/, /ŋ/ (ng)
3. /w/, /j/ (y)
4. /k/, /g/
5. /t/, /d/, /l/, /r/
6. /s/, /z/, /ʃ/ (sh), /tʃ/ (ch)
7. /θ/ (th), /ð/ (th), /v/
8. /ʒ/ (zh), /dʒ/ (dz) and /hw/.

THE BILABIAL SOUNDS

/p/ As in *Pea*, *Soap*, *Separate*, and *Spy*

/p/ and /b/ are bilabial, closed lip, stop consonants. These sounds are produced as a result of a lip-closing action that momentarily stops the flow of breath. Both of these sounds require a raised soft palate so that after the lip action, the sound produced is emitted orally rather than nasally.[1]

The sound /p/ in initial or stressed positions, as in *pea* and *plate*, requires considerable breath pressure. The lips must be tightly compressed to permit the production of a vigorous /p/. In unstressed positions there is considerably less breath pressure and less vigorous lip action. In

[1] All but three American-English sounds are normally produced with an elevated soft palate. Except for the three nasal consonants /n/, /m/, and /ŋ/ (ng), the reader should assume that the directions for the production of a sound include the one to *elevate the soft palate.*

all positions, /p/ is a voiceless sound. When /p/ is followed by a vowel, a distinct puff of breath (plosion or aspiration) should accompany the completion of the sound. In final positions /p/ may not be "exploded."

PRACTICE MATERIALS

pea	pool	person	pound
peat	pull	pert	pout
peel	poor	purse	powder
pill	poke	pun	power
pit	pole	put	peace
paid	paltry	pike	pitch
pay	paw	pile	peg
pen	park	pine	patch
pat	pond	point	pack
path	pot	poise	poem

When a medial /p/ is followed by a stressed vowel, a distinct puff of air should accompany the completion of the /p/. In combinations preceded by an /s/, however, the aspirate quality is considerably reduced.

Medial (Stressed Positions)

appeal	rapport	apart	rupee
appease	repair	repay	turnpike
repeat	repartee	upon	repugnant
repeal	impact	apology	umpire
unpin	report	deport	suppose
repaid	repatriate	despair	epistle
repent	repose	support	inspire
repel	oppose	superior	inspect
repast	appoint	superb	respite

For a medial /p/ in unstressed positions lip activity is less vigorous and there is less accompanying breath puff in anticipation of the sound following the /p/.

Medial (Unstressed Positions)

aped	stupor	rapier	napping
happy	sweeping	steeple	chopping
carpet	champion	taper	clapped
typify	grapple	stepping	flippant
tipped	hoping	clipping	wrapper

[pl] *and* [pr] *Blends—reduced aspiration for the* [p]

plea	plume	plight	place
please	Pluto	pliant	play
plenty	plot	plow	pleasure
plate	plum	applaud	plural
plain	plug	aplomb	plunder
plan	pluck	plausible	plunge
preen	prune	price	spread
pray	reprove	pride	sprite
prick	proof	proud	sprawl
press	prawn	prow	sprain
prank	prod	praise	spree
prattle	prolix	approve	prized

[p] *followed by* [t]—*little or no aspirate quality for the* [p]

aped	escaped	hoped	rapped
apt	gaped	lapped	reaped
capped	gapped	leaped	roped
caped	heaped	loped	soaped
draped	hipped	mapped	yapped

[p] *followed by* [s]—*little or no aspirate quality for the* [p]

apes	flaps	jumps	pops
beeps	flips	lapse	pups
capes	gaps	loops	raps
cops	hopes	mops	ropes
dips	hops	napes	tapes

Sentences

1. President Nixon welcomed Peking's championship Ping-Pong players in the spring of 1972.
2. Pickled jalapeno peppers were too potent for Peter Piper.
3. Paul put a pippin apple into the piglet's mouth.
4. Peterson produced a sample of a protective paint that was presumed not to chip.
5. Some companies employ Pinkerton operatives to prevent predators from plundering their premises.
6. Springer polished the pistons of his "chopper."
7. "Spot" is not an appropriate appellation for springer spaniels, poodles, or Pekingese, but is perfect for plain, dappled pups.
8. Pete wrapped the snappers he caught in a piece of newspaper.
9. Some people are pleased to see ships pulling out of port to the open sea.

10. With practice Plunkett can put his powerful passes precisely where he pleases.

11. The proud prince placed too low a price on the approval of the people.

12. *Pippa Passes* is a poem by Browning.

Selections

1. By heaven, methinks it were an easy leap
   To pluck bright honour from the palefaced moon,
   Or dive into the bottom of the deep,
   Where fathom-line could never touch the ground,
   And pluck up drowned honour by the locks.
   —WILLIAM SHAKESPEARE, *Henry IV*

2. When the hounds of spring are on winter's traces,
   The mother of months in meadow or plain
   Fills the shadows and windy places
   With lisp of leaves and ripple of rain.
   —ALGERNON CHARLES SWINBURNE, *Atalanta in Calydon*

3. Now when a doctor's patients are perplexed,
   A consultation comes in order next—
   You know what that is? In a certain place
   Meet certain doctors to discuss a case
   And other matters, such as weather, crops,
   Potatoes, pumpkins, lager-beer, and hops.
   —OLIVER WENDELL HOLMES, *Rip Van Winkle, M.D.*

/b/ As in *Bean, Rabid,* and *Robe*

/b/ is a voiced, lip-stop, unaspirated consonant produced with less lip and breath pressure than /p/. Lip activity should be precise so that there is a clear-cut stop and release action for the /b/ even though it is less vigorous than for the /p/.

By way of review, /b/ is articulated with (1), a firm closing of the lips, (2) a compression of air behind the lips, and (3) a sudden parting of the lips to release the *vocalized sound*. Final /b/ may be articulated without the explosive or release phase.

PRACTICE MATERIALS

Make certain that you show a clear distinction between /p/ and /b/ in the following words and sentences.

peak	beak	prick	brick
pay	bay	peen	bean
pane	bane	punk	bunk

paste	baste	plank	blank
pare	bare	planned	bland
paid	bade	pass	bass
pace	base	pat	bat

Figure 14–2 Articulatory positions for /p/ and /b/. The lips are tightly compressed and the soft palate is raised.

Sentences

1. Pete Brady bastes his roast beef with tomato paste.
2. Paula bailed the boat with a pail.
3. The punted ball bounced against the goal post.
4. Buck packed his bags and paid his bill.
5. Better peach pies are baked without pits.
6. The belt was made of leather pelt.

ADDITIONAL PRACTICE MATERIALS

Initial

bean	boon	burn	broom
bill	bull	bud	bruise
bale	boor	breach	brought
beg	boat	bring	brain
back	ball	bread	brine

bask	bog	brass	brown
busy	bulk	bleed	bloom
bunch	burrow	blink	blue
base	bird	black	block
blame	burst	breath	blurt

Medial

about	table	somebody	disturbing
abate	feeble	habit	rubber
abbey	stable	noble	ribbon
abet	number	tumble	tribute
abhor	lumber	fumble	robust

Final

rib	tube	disturb	curb
crab	nub	cube	jibe
web	rub	hob	daub
stab	robe	sob	cob
dab	lobe	rob	mob

Sentences

1. Bill is fond of brown berries and broiled bass.
2. Ben abhorred boasting but liked to be busy.
3. Bacon and beans were a habit with Bess and Bob.
4. Benton played a brass tuba in the Boys Band.
5. Somebody permitted the black horse to break out of the barn.
6. Few buds bloom in February to attract bees.
7. The stable was swept with a bulky, brown broom.
8. Lobsters and crabs were brought in on the old, flat-bottomed boat.
9. Bricks and boards are basic building materials.
10. Brad hit the ball for a three-base hit.

Selections

1. But far on the deep there are billows
   That never shall break on the beach.
   —A. J. RYAN, *Song of the Mystic*
2. This truth within thy mind rehearse,
   That in a boundless universe
   Is boundless better, boundless worse.
   —ALFRED, LORD TENNYSON, *The Two Voices*

Figure 14–3   Articulatory positions for /m/. Note lip-contact and lowered soft palate.

/m/ As in *Me, Summer,* and *Plum*

/m/ is one of the three nasal, continuant consonants. As such, it is produced with a lowered soft palate, nasal cavity reinforcement, and nasal emission. /m/ is articulated with the lips in relaxed contact and the teeth slightly parted. Vocal fold vibration is a necessary accompaniment for the /m/ as well as for the other two nasal sounds. As indicated in Figure 14–3, the tongue usually lies at the bottom of the mouth in the production of the /m/.

The sound /m/ is usually represented by the single letter *m*. Occasionally, the *m* is followed or preceded by a "silent" letter as in *lumb* and *dumb, psalm* and *calm*. The sound is found in initial, medial, and final positions. Unless hurried, slurred, or produced with the lips too tight, the /m/ is a relatively easy sound to produce. As suggested in our discussion on nasal reinforcement (see pages 76–86), the /m/ lends fullness and roundness to the voice. The material and exercises for /m/ in the section on voice should now be reviewed.

PRACTICE MATERIALS

me	main	most	mirth
meek	mend	mode	murky
meal	met	mote	murder

mean	mess	motive	mud
meat	man	motor	moist
middle	map	mourn	mouth
milk	mash	mortar	mount
mist	mask	mauve	mouse
make	mass	mock	my
mate	match	month	might
mail	mood	mob	mine
made	moon	monk	mile

Medial

demean	ember	foaming	human
seemly	emanate	reformed	humor
seamstresss	embank	informing	grimy
dreaming	embassy	armor	slimy
remit	embattle	termed	omit
permit	cement	termite	remind
simple	amnesty	terminal	remedy
Amy	remove	grumble	remark
emblem	emote	stumble	almond
empty	bemoan	umbrella	lament

Final

beam	game	groom	worm
seem	gem	tomb	term
team	stem	tome	drum
theme	phlegm	comb	hum
dream	lamb	dome	I'm
dim	ham	home	dime
trim	tam	form	climb
slim	sham	dorm	grime
aim	slam	calm	crime
same	doom	farm	prime
tame	room	alarm	column
blame	broom	bomb	autumn

In final, unstressed position, the final /m/ may sometimes have syllabic value. What is your pronunciation for the words that follow?

chasm	schism	spasm	bedlam
bottom	rhythm	theism	bosom
prism	atom	truism	column

In the following material, work for a light, sustained /m/. At first exaggerate the length of the /m/ and avoid carrying over nasal quality to proximate nonnasal sounds.

Sentences

1.   Moss covered the bottom of the maples in the Maine forest.
2.   Miniver mourned for memories that might have been.
3.   Termites undermined the dismal mansion.
4.   Mamie grumbled because she stumbled over her umbrella.
5.   Mason was phlegmatic about matters that made most ill-humored men storm in anger.
6.   Mending and making neat seams were Amanda's prime ways of staying calm.
7.   The monk remained in good humor as he informed his friends about the grimy tomb.
8.   Mortar, a material employed for masonry, is made by mixing lime or cement with sand.
9.   Man maintains continuity by making note of his memories.
10.   Emily, broom in hand, was in no mood to be stymied by a mouse in either animal or human form.
11.   Man is mighty in his ability to transform molehills into mountains by mentation, mendation or imagination.
12.   Morton dreamed that no mound was too high for him to climb nor chasm too wide for him to jump.
13.   Emerson held that each mind has its own method.
14.   Men with empires in their minds cannot long remain humble or calm.
15.   Many monuments to men in time need their own memorials.
16.   The moon may look on many men, but a man has but one moon.
17.   Remembrance, and repentance, often come together in the morning.
18.   Lamb and ham make fine mincemeat.
19.   Simmons climbed up from the bottom of the chasm.
20.   Rhyme and rhythm do not necessarily produce a truism.

Selections

1.   No coward soul is mine,
      No trembler in the world's stormed-troubled sphere:
      I see heaven's glory shine,
      And faith shines equal, arming me from fear.
                                          —EMILY BRONTË, *Last Lines*

2. Neil Armstrong, on landing on the moon, summed up his thinking and his mood with the statement: "One small step for man, one giant leap for mankind."
3. Terence manifest his understanding of humanity and his insight into himself when he noted that: "Nothing which is common to mankind is foreign to me."
4. I have thought some of Nature's journeymen had made men and not made them well, they imitated humanity so abominably.

—WILLIAM SHAKESPEARE, *Hamlet*

5. Go! You may call it madness, folly;
   You shall not chase my gloom away!
   There's such a charm in melancholy,
   I would not, if I could, be gay.

—SAMUEL ROGERS, *To——*

6. In his *Maxims* Nietzsche remarked, "Many a man fails to become a thinker for the sole reason that his memory is too good."
7. And frame your mind to mirth and merriment,
   Which bars a thousand harms and lengthens life.

—WILLIAM SHAKESPEARE, *The Taming of the Shrew*

8. The worst part of an eminent man's conversation is, nine times out of ten, to be found in that part which he means to be clever.

—PHILIP H. STANHOPE, *Caxtonia*

9. We are the music-makers,
   And we are the dreamers of dreams,
   Wandering by lone sea-breakers,
   And sitting by desolate streams;
   World-losers and world-forsakers,
   On whom the pale moon gleams:
   Yet we are the movers and shakers
   Of the world for ever, it seems.

—A. W. E. O'SHAUGHNESSY, *Ode*

10. He left a Corsair's name to other times,
    Linked with one virtue, and a thousand crimes.

—GEORGE GORDON, LORD BYRON, *The Corsair*

The Bilabial Glide Consonants: /ʍ/ or /hw/ (hw) As in What and When and /w/ As in Will and Wit

The consonants /ʍ/ or /hw/ and /w/ are *glide sounds*. Such sounds are produced with the organs of articulation in movement from an initial, determinate position to a final position determined by the sound that

Figure 14–4 Initial articulatory position for glide sounds /ʌ/ and /w/. Note that the back of the tongue is raised.

immediately follows. The sound /ʌ/ or /hw/ is voiceless; /w/ is voiced. Both are initiated with the lips rounded in a close, pursed position as for the vowel /u/. The tongue is raised in back toward the soft palate. Study Figure 14–4 for the initial position for the lip glide sounds. Note that the lips do not touch the teeth, as they necessarily do for the sounds /f/ and /v/. The palate is raised for the bilabial glide sounds, and the sounds are emitted orally.

/ʌ/ (hw) occurs in words spelled with *wh* initially or medially. Many speakers, however, use the voiced /w/ rather than the /ʌ/ in words such as *why, what,* and *when.* The /ʌ/ also occurs in contexts following a /t/, /s/, or /k/ as in *twine, swim,* and *quit.*

PRACTICE MATERIALS

To determine whether you use a /hw/ or /w/, place your hand in front of the mouth for the trial words *what* and *where.* The /hw/ should begin with a definite stream of unvocalized breath. In contrast, /w/ is vocalized and there is no obvious stream of breath. The word pairs that follow should help to make the distinction between the two sounds.

/hw/	/w/	/hw/	/w/
whither	wither	while	wile
where	wear	white	wight

/hw/	/w/	/hw/	/w/
wheel	weal	whether	weather
whet	wet	whacks	wax
what	watt	whirled	world
which	witch	whine	wine
when	wen	Whig	wig
whirred	word	whish	wish
whale	wail	whist	wist
whey	way	whoa	woe

Initial /hw/

wheat	whistle	wharf	whiting
wheedle	whelp	whimper	whittle
wheeze	whence	whimsy	whipsaw
whiff	whirl	whiskey	whang
whim	whistling	whiffle	wheal
whip	whop	whinny	whetstone
whisper	whorl	whisker	whelp

Medial /hw/

pinwheel	somewhat	meanwhile	unwholesome
anywhere	awhile	bobwhite	buckwheat
nowhere	somewhere	freewheeling	erstwhile
elsewhere	bullwhip	flywheel	everywhere

Sentences for /hw/ and /w/ Contrast

1. Do you prefer the song of the bobwhite or the whippoorwill?
2. What was Wilson's whispering about?
3. Walt Whitman was somewhat wordy.
4. The Whig thought it whimsical to wash the Tory's wig in whiskey.
5. Wallace yelled "whoa" and whistled, but his horse went for the wheat.
6. The *White Witch*'s engines whirred as the steamer went off on the whaling voyage that would take her around the world.
7. The bewhiskered old man whet his knife and whittled away on a piece of wax.
8. Management was whipsawed, with the white collar workers on one side and labor on the other, and there was no way in which either could win or persuade the other.
9. Winton wished to go back to Wichita and hear the wind wail through the Western Union wires.
10. Wiggins whispered that he was ready to go somewhere, anywhere, away from where he was.

ADDITIONAL PRACTICE MATERIALS FOR /w/

wad	wall	web	wide
wade	walk	we'd	wield
wafer	wan	wed	wife
waffle	wander	week	will
wager	want	weigh	window
waif	ward	weird	wing
wail	wash	weld	woman
wait	wean	wen	won't
wake	wear	wet	wood
waive	weave	wick	worst

Medial /w/ (Note That the Spelling May Be u *and* o *as Well as* w)

biweekly	await	inward	unworthy
unwieldy	reweigh	unwavering	rewed
bewitch	away	awoke	earthworm
unwitting	awake	unworn	reworked
unwary	bewail	rewarned	anyone
unwept	byway	onward	everyone
unwelcome	unwilling	reweave	everyway
unwise	unworldly	reward	inquire
bewilder	unwanted	unwind	liquid
unwell	unwonted	reweb	require

Sentences

1. Wales has many rewarding and wonderful sights.
2. Kingsley wrote that "men must work, and women must weep."
3. Wilton walked west through the quagmire to earn one reward.
4. New York's Broadway, once a cowpath, is now known as the Great White Way.
5. Woodrow Wilson was president when the U.S. entered World War I, "the war to end all wars."
6. During World War II, General Dwight Eisenhower once was reputed to have wept while reviewing his troops.
7. Willy walked away into the woods unaware that wolves and quagmires lay that way.
8. In weaving, the woof thread goes between the warps to form a web.
9. Watson wondered whether the equation would work out.
10. The lawyer winked unwisely at the bewildered witness.
11. The Westerner wasted his wages on unwise wagers.
12. Whiskey is a liquid that can bewilder one in the worst way.

13. Welch wound up and swatted the wasp on the window.

14. Wanda tripped over a wet twig and twisted her ankle.

15. The once bright flame waxed and waned and diminished into nothingness.

Selections

1. Christmas is here:
    Winds whistle shrill,
    Icy and chill,
    Little care we;
    Little we fear
    Weather without,
    Shelter about
    The Mahogany Tree.
    —WILLIAM MAKEPEACE THACKERAY, *The Mahogany Tree*

2. When you wander, as you often delight to do, you wander indeed, and give never such satisfaction as the curious time requires. This is not caused by any natural defect, but first for want of election, when you, having a large and fruitful mind, should not so much labour what to speak as to find what to leave unspoken. Rich soils are often to be weeded.
    —SIR FRANCIS BACON, *Letter of Expostulation to Coke*

3. There's hardly anything so small,
    So trifling or so mean,
    That we may never want at all,
    For service unforseen;
    And wilful waste, depend upon't,
    Brings almost always, woeful want.
    —ANN TAYLOR, *The Pin*

4. Wandering between two worlds, one dead,
    The other powerless to be born.
    —MATTHEW ARNOLD, *Stanzas from the Grand Chartreuse*

5. An honest Ale-house where
    We shall find a cleanly room,
    Lavender in the Windows, and twenty
    Ballads stuck about the wall.
    —IZAAK WALTON, *The Compleat Angler*

6. For it so falls out
    That what we have we prize not to the worth
    Whiles we enjoy it, but being lack'd and lost,
    Why, then we rack the value; then we find
    The virtue that possession would not show us
    Whiles it was ours.
    —WILLIAM SHAKESPEARE, *Much Ado About Nothing*

/w/ and /v/

Some persons, probably because of foreign language influence, tend to confuse the bilabial /w/ with the labiodental (lip-teeth) /v/. The following word pairs should help to establish the distinction between these two sounds. Observe the lip action in a mirror and make certain that there is no contact of the teeth and lips for the /w/.[1]

PRACTICE MATERIALS

wane	vein	wend	vend
wary	vary	worse	verse
west	vest	wine	vine
weld	veld	wiper	viper
wiser	visor	wow	vow
went	vent	wile	vile
wet	vet	wail	veil

Sentences

1. It is wise not to get caught in a vise.
2. Wine is made from the fruit of the vine.
3. William West was fond of his velvet vest.
4. As the vain writer grew older, his ability was on the wane and his verse became obviously worse.
5. To vend his various wares he had to wend his weary way and be wary of wily customers along the wayside.
6. The knight looked wiser behind his visor.
7. We were puzzled at the witch's vow never more to use her wiles for vile purposes.

Selections

1. There is not in the wide world a
       Valley so sweet
   As that vale in whose bosom
   The bright waters meet.
                      —THOMAS MOORE, *The Meeting of the Waters*
2. No longer mourn for me when I am dead
   Than you shall hear the surly sullen bell
   Give warning to the world that I am fled
   From this vile world, with vilest worms to dwell.
                      —WILLIAM SHAKESPEARE, *Sonnet 71*

[1] See subsequent discussion for /v/ in Chapter 15.

The Lip-Teeth Sounds

The lip-teeth (labiodental) consonants /f/ and /v/ present little or no difficulty for native English speakers. Persons for whom Spanish is a first language may carry over a tendency from their native tongue and use the sounds /b/ and /v/ interchangeably. Another tendency of these speakers is to substitute a sound intermediate between /b/ and /v/.

Speakers with a Germanic background may confuse /v/ and /w/ because the letter *w* is pronounced /v/ in German. Fortunately, the pronunciation of the letter *v* as /v/ is consistent in English so that spelling serves as a reliable guide. Speakers whose first language is German need also to overcome their native inclination to pronounce the letter *f* as /v/.

/f/ As in *Feel, Fun, Afraid,* and *Enough*

/f/ is a voiceless, fricative, lip-teeth (labiodental) consonant. It is made by pressing the lower lip against the upper teeth and forcing a stream of breath between the narrow spaces of the upper teeth or between the lower lip and upper teeth. The soft palate is raised to prevent nasal emission of breath.

In spelling, the sound is most frequently represented by the letter *f*. Other spellings include *ph* as in *phrase* and *gh* as in *rough*. The sound occurs in initial, medial, and final positions.

Figure 15–1   Articulatory position for /f/ and /v/.

PRACTICE MATERIALS

feed	fad	fob	fire
feel	fan	fog	fowl
fib	food	fox	foible
fin	fool	firm	foil
fit	full	first	foist
fail	phobia	fudge	feud
fame	photo	fuss	fume
fed	falter	fight	fuse
felt	fork	file	future
fence	fought	find	few
coffee	defect	afford	afar
enfeeble	after	effort	stuffing
effete	aft	soften	rifle
sphere	raft	affirm	trifle
efficient	raffle	refurbish	stifle
sphinx	laughed	unfurl	sapphire
swift	refuse	roughen	refute
chafed	effuse	shuffle	prophet
effect	careful	sofa	reference
defend	barefoot	loafer	breakfast

beef	skiff	chafe	half
chief	cliff	deaf	staff
reef	whiff	chef	graph
belief	stiff	chaff	enough
thief	strafe	laugh	tough
tiff	safe	calf	golf

[fl]

flee	fluke	flirt	flutter
fleet	flute	flourish	flight
flip	flood	flurry	fly
flame	flaw	flub	flounder
flu	floral	flunk	flour
float	Florence	flush	flout

[fr]

free	fret	frozen	afraid
frill	frank	fraught	affray
fray	France	frolic	affricate
freight	frugal	front	affront
freckle	fro	fry	infringe

Sentences

1. Despite Freya's fickleness, she gave no obvious offense to her friends.
2. Phil Philbrick was considered a diamond in the rough.
3. After the fog lifted, the fast planes took off for foreign lands.
4. Coffee, although not a food, is a favorite breakfast drink for many of us.
5. Frank and his father are very fond of golf and fishing.
6. "Fair, fat, and forty" although no longer in fashion is still fraught with folly for many females.
7. Fran went to her physician because of her frequent sniffles.
8. The chef served the roast pheasant on a fancy chafing dish.
9. The thief came to grief over the theft of the sapphire.
10. Farnum had a phobia of fire even in a fireplace.

Selections

1. The painful warrior famoused for fight,
   After a thousand victories, once foil'd,

Is from the books of honor razed quite,
And all the rest forgot for which he toil'd.
—WILLIAM SHAKESPEARE, *Sonnet 25*

2. Time stoops to no man's lure;
    And love, grown faint and fretful,
    With lips but half regretful
    Sighs, and with eyes forgetful
        Weeps that no loves endure.
    —ALGERNON CHARLES SWINBURNE, *The Garden of Proserpine*

3. A faithful friend is a strong defence: and he that hath found
    such an one hath found a treasure.
    —*Ecclesiasticus*, 6:14

4. Fare thee well! And if forever,
    Still forever, fare thee well.
    —GEORGE GORDON, LORD BYRON, *Fare Thee Well*

5. When tillage begins, other arts follow. The farmers therefore
    are the founders of civilization.
    —DANIEL WEBSTER, *Remarks on Agriculture*

/v/ As in *Vie*, *Provoke*, and *Live*

/v/ is the voiced cognate of /f/. It is, of course, produced like the /f/
except that the /v/ is voiced and requires less breath pressure than the /f/.

Except for the *f* of *of*, /v/ is spelled as it is sounded.

The sound /v/ causes little or no difficulty for American-English
speakers. As we have noted, some foreign-born speakers may have difficulty because they confuse the /v/ and /w/. (See discussion and practice
material for /v/ and /w/, page 226.)

In context, when it is immediately followed by a voiceless consonant
as in "I've ten cents" or "Give Tom the book," the /v/ is normally produced with partial devoicing. It is also partially devoiced when it occurs
at the end of a phrase or sentence such as in "I had five" or "We enjoyed
the drive."

PRACTICE MATERIALS

Venus	valley	vault	visit
veal	van	vaunt	vile
venal	value	varnish	vine
veer	vend	varlet	vital
vigor	very	verse	vulgar
vim	vary	virtue	vulture
victor	voodoo	vernal	volume
vein	vogue	voice	volunteer

vale	vote	void	Volga
vapor	voracious	vice	vowel
evening	paved	proven	reverse
Eva	shaved	grooved	nervous
even	revel	hooves	convert
believing	event	roving	jovial
given	prevent	clover	revile
livid	having	Dover	trivial
evil	gavel	marvel	avoid
devil	travel	carving	invite
raving	ravel	starving	lover
staved	avid	avert	cover
deceive	delve	mauve	dive
receive	shelve	starve	strive
heave	have	carve	alive
sleeve	salve	nerve	hive
give	move	curve	naïve
live	groove	swerve	resolve
gave	prove	glove	revolve
knave	rove	above	twelve
slave	stove	shove	love
stave	strove	dove	trove

Sentences

1. Victor, for fear of becoming a victim, would not volunteer to test the voodoo.

2. Eve, an avid traveler, began her voyage from Dover to the Everglades.

3. The devil, for his evil purposes, can be a scrivener as well as a quoter of scriptures.

4. It is naïve to approach a beehive without a veil for covering.

5. Jovial conversation accompanied Vera's carving of the turkey.

6. Some have tried to improve the figure of Venus with drapes, but very few have tried gloves.

7. Twelve Javanese were found roving through the river valley.

8. Valentine banged his gavel to put a stop to the verbalization at the convention.

9. The thieves found it of value to cultivate a Harvard accent.

10. Vinson resolved to give up his vain ways and to live a life of value.

Selections /f/ and /v/

1. Ever let the Fancy roam,
   Pleasure never is at home!

. . . .
Where's the eye, however blue,
Doth not weary? Where's the face
One would meet in every place?
Where's the voice, however soft,
One would hear so very oft?

—JOHN KEATS, *Fancy*

2. For a man can lose neither the past nor the future; for how
can one take from him that which is not his? So remember
these two points: first, that each thing is of like form from
everlasting and comes round again in its cycle, and that it
signifies not whether a man shall look upon the same things
for a hundred years or two hundred, or for an infinity of time;
second, that the longest lived and the shortest lived man,
when they come to die, lose one and the same thing.

—MARCUS AURELIUS, *Meditations*

3. All is ephemeral—fame and the famous as well.

—MARCUS AURELIUS, *Meditations*

4. Back of the sound broods the silence,
   back of the gift stands the giving;

Back of the hand that receives thrill
   the sensitive nerves of receiving.

—RICHARD REALF, *Indirection*

CHAPTER 16

The Tongue-Teeth Sounds

The tongue-teeth consonants /θ/ and /ð/ present some difficulties for native speakers of English as well as for persons with foreign language backgrounds. The causes of these difficulties and exercises for overcoming them are presented in individual considerations of these sounds.

/θ/ (th) As in *Thin, Thank, Theory; Anything, Truthful; Faith, Earth*

The /θ/ is a voiceless fricative. It is produced by placing the tip of the tongue lightly against the back of the upper teeth or slightly between the teeth. Air is forced through the place of contact to produce the characteristic fricative quality. In spelling, the sound is represented by the letters *th*. The sound /θ/ may occur initially, medially, or finally.

/θ/ tends to be a somewhat troublesome sound for many speakers. Native-born Americans exposed to substandard or dialectal speech influences may substitute a /t/ for the initial /θ/ so that words such as *thin* and *three* are pronounced as though they were *tin* and *tree*. Foreign-born speakers who do not have the /θ/ in their native language tend to substitute their nearest approximation for it. Frequent substitutions include a dentalized /s/ and a dentalized /t/. A comparison of Figures 16–1 and 17–1 for the /θ/ and /t/ and practice with the material that immediately follows should help to establish the distinctions between /θ/ and /t/ and /θ/ and /s/.

Figure 16–1   **Representative articulatory positions for /θ/ and /ð/ as post-dental sounds.**

PRACTICE MATERIALS

Distinguish between /θ/ and /t/:

thank	tank	theme	team
thin	tin	thought	taught
through	true	deaths	debts
thread	tread	ether	eater
thrill	trill	sheaths	sheets
thick	tick	forth	fort
thrips	trips	bath	bat
thorn	torn	oath	oat
wrath	rat	hearth	heart
wraith	rate	Gertha	Gerta
faithful	fateful	ruthless	rootless
myths	mitts	booth	boot

Distinguish between /θ/ and /s/:

theme	seem	thought	sought
think	sink	thumb	sum
thick	sick	thigh	sigh
thing	sing	thin	sin
thank	sank	kith	kiss
thaw	saw	myth	miss

faith	face	moth	moss
truth	truce	bath	bass
mouth	mouse	math	mass
worth	worse	fourth	force

Sentences for /θ/, /t/, and /s/ Contrast

1. We felt a thrill to hear the trill of the thrush.
2. Theodore was regarded as being a man true blue, all through.
3. The tick was found in the thick woods.
4. Ted, a good student, thought that he had been well taught.
5. Thelma heard the story through and thankfully believed it to be true.
6. Catherine could sing about almost anything.
7. The ache in Matthew's thigh brought forth a deep sigh.
8. The thick, acrid smoke made Thaddeus feel sick.
9. Miss Thornton declared the story to be a myth.
10. Few traces are left of what was once the region of Thrace.

ADDITIONAL PRACTICE MATERIALS FOR /θ/

three	through	thud	thousand
theme	throe	thunder	thymus
thesis	throat	thump	theory
thimble	throne	third	threat
thicken	thrall	Thursday	throttle
theft	thought	thirst	thrust
thalamus	thwart	thirteen	thicket
thank	thaw	thigh	theology
thread	thrash	thrush	thyroid
thrips	thrive	thrum	Thrace

ether	pathos	enthusiasm	lengthen
breathy	pathetic	author	strengthen
anything	bathtub	orthodox	earthy
nothing	wrathful	orthopod	forthright
healthy	ruthless	slothful	toothless
wealthy	truthful	mirthful	atheist
stealthy	ethyl	toothache	method
rethread	birthday	mythical	lethargy
deathly	earthquake	synthetic	panther
youthful	hawthorn	arithmetic	Cathay
frothy	fifths [1]	sixths [1]	months [1]

[1] Speakers should guard against a tendency to substitute a /t/ or omit the /θ/ in these words.

wreath	booth	month	hearth
beneath	uncouth	mouth	sleuth
myth	both	warmth	troth
pith	oath	south	froth
kith	fourth	growth	length
faith	north	eighth	fifth
death	moth	ninth	breath
zenith	cloth	path	truth
wrath	dearth	mammoth	Ruth
stealth	earth	worth	Beth

Sentences

1. Arithmetic is thought to be the most elementary form of mathematics.
2. *Thank you's* are better than threats in strengthening associations.
3. Matthew learned how to be thoughtful rather than ruthless in telling the truth.
4. The warmth of the day made Theodore lethargic.
5. Thelma, unlike her brother Thaddeus, enjoyed a bath.
6. The famous author Shaw thought that youth is wasted on the youthful.
7. Ruth considered the eighth day of the month her thoroughly lucky one.
8. Beth spotted the panther creeping stealthily through the thicket.
9. There was no dearth of growth from the fertile soil of the South.
10. Thursday is the fifth day of the week.

Selections

1. The youthful Keats was the author of many famous lines. Among the best known are the following from *Endymion* and *Ode on a Grecian Urn:*

   A thing of beauty is a joy forever:
   Its loveliness increases; it will never
   Pass into nothingness.

   "Beauty is truth, truth beauty"—that is all
   Ye know on earth, and all ye need to know.

2. In *My Lost Youth*, Henry Wadsworth Longfellow, often called the poet of the hearth, wrote:

   A boy's will is the wind's will,
   And the thoughts of youth are long, long thoughts.

3. In his *Resignation,* Longfellow wrote of death. Perhaps most famous are the lines:

> There is no Death! What seems so is transition;
>> This life of mortal breath
> Is but a suburb of the life elysian,
>> Whose portal we call Death.

4. Thomas Moore is probably best known to us for his tender song themes. He was also the author of the following prophetic and almost wrathful verse taken from his poem *Lalla Rookh:*

> And from the lips of Truth one mighty breath
> Shall like a whirlwind scatter in its breeze
> That whole dark pile of human mockeries—
> Then shall the reign of mind commence on earth.
> And starting fresh as from a second birth,
> Man in the sunshine of the world's new spring
> Shall walk transparent like some holy thing!

5. Said Bertha to Gertha
You seem full of mirth;
Does your ungentle laughter
Endanger your girth?

> Said Gertha to Bertha
> I am full of mirth
> And my broad, healthy laughter
> Is good for my girth.

> —ANONYMOUS, *Envious Interchange*

6. Lay not up for yourselves treasures upon earth, where moth and rust doth corrupt, and where thieves break through and steal.

> —*Matthew,* VI:19

7. For wrath killeth the foolish man, and envy slayeth the silly one.

> —*Job,* V:2

/ð/ As in *That, Those; Either, Weather; Bathe, Breathe*

/ð/ is the voiced cognate of /θ/. It is represented by the letters *th* and may occur initially, medially, or finally as in *these, bathing,* and *wreathe.* The /ð/ is produced with light tongue-tip contact either behind the upper teeth or between the cutting edges of the teeth. Air is forced through the place of contact while the vocal folds are in vibration.

There is no certain way of determining whether a particular word should be pronounced with a /θ/ or a /ð/. We may note a tendency, in initial positions at least, for words that are stressed and significant in a sentence, such as nouns, verbs, and adjectives, to be pronounced with the voiceless /θ/. Pronouns, articles, and conjunctions, which are more likely to be unstressed and weak in sentence context, tend to be pronounced with a /ð/. Because of this the /ð/ tends to occur more often than the /θ/ in our speech.

Persons who are inclined to substitute a /t/ for a /θ/ are also likely to substitute a /d/ for a /ð/. The first set of practice materials should help to establish a clear distinction between the /d/ and /ð/. (See page 248 for description of /d/.)

PRACTICE MATERIALS

Distinguish between /ð/ and /d/:

thee	dee	their	dare
they	day	thence	dense
then	den	lather	ladder
than	Dan	lathe	laid
though	dough	loathe	load
those	doze	seethe	seed
thy	dye	other	udder
thine	dine	worthy	wordy

Sentences for /ð/ *and* /d/

1. Dan was taller than his brother.
2. Most men loathe a heavy load.
3. There are few children who can resist a dare.
4. They devoted the day to thinking worthy thoughts, but did few worthy deeds.
5. Ted thought that even though he could not help make the dough, he could enjoy the bread.

ADDITIONAL PRACTICE MATERIALS

these	than	the	thine
this	those	thus	them
then	though	thy	therefore
they	there	that	therein
either	weather	although	mother
neither	feather	loathing	bother
heathen	lather	brother	logarithm
leather	rather	father	further

breathe	soothe	scythe	swathe
bathe	scathe	writhe	teethe
wreathe	blithe	tithe	with

Sentences

1. Although he was loathe to speak his mind, father often knew best.
2. Neither mother nor brother enjoyed foggy weather.
3. The word *thine* is the possessive form of *thou.*
4. *This* and *that* are demonstrative pronouns.
5. Mother is fond of feathered creatures.
6. The ghosts gathered among the other blithe spirits.
7. Leather is being replaced by plastic in the making of clothing.
8. The heather withered in the field.
9. The heathen considered it a bother to bathe.
10. Although the birds were of a feather, they preferred not to flock together.

Selections for /θ/ and /ð/

1. Let us crown ourselves with rosebuds before they be withered.
   —*Wisdom of Solomon, 2:8*
2. At the door of life, by the gate of breath,
   There are worse things waiting for men than death.
   —ALGERNON CHARLES SWINBURNE, *The Triumph of Time*
3. But he who loveliness within
   Hath found, all outward loathes,
   For he who colour loves, and skin,
   Loves but their oldest clothes.
   —JOHN DONNE, *The Undertaking*
4. Fame sometimes hath created something of nothing.
   —THOMAS FULLER, *Of Marriage*
5. Rather than love, than money, than fame, give me truth.
   —HENRY DAVID THOREAU, *Conclusion*

CHAPTER 17

The Tongue-Tip to Gum-Ridge and the Postdental Sounds

A glance at the consonant chart will reveal that the tongue-tip to gum-ridge (lingua-alveolar) and the postalveolar sounds include a third of the American-English consonants. The lingua-alveolar and the postalveolar articulatory positions are distinctive for our language. For this reason the sounds in these groups are given detailed consideration.

THE TONGUE–TIP TO GUM–RIDGE SOUNDS

We begin our study of the tongue-tip to gum-ridge consonants with the [t] as in *tea, ton,* and *too.* If the contact point and manner of articulation for this [t] are mastered, the speaker will have an excellent point of reference for the production of other American-English alveolar speech sounds.

/t/ As in *Ton, Until,* and *Boat* [1]

To produce the [t] as in *ton* or as an isolated sound, the tongue is raised so that the tongue tip comes into contact with the upper gum ridge

[1] In this section, devoted to the phoneme /t/, we present separate materials for several of the allophones of /t/. The allophones, in keeping with phonetic practice, are indicated in brackets [ ].

240

(See Figure 17–1). The soft palate is raised to prevent nasal emission of breath. The sides of the tongue near the tip are in contact with the upper molars. The tongue, tense and extended, is held in this position for a fraction of a second. Then, quickly and as completely as possible, the tongue is retracted with a resultant slight "explosion" of air at the tongue tip. This should be felt as a puff of breath if you hold your hand in front of your mouth.

The [t] as just described occurs whenever the sound appears in a stressed syllable and is immediately followed by a vowel. The [t] in such contexts is a lingua-alveolar (gum ridge), stop-plosive consonant. In producing this [t] the following cautions should be observed:

1. Make certain that the tongue tip is in contact with the gum ridge and *not the upper teeth*. The contact, when broken, should be quick and complete.

2. Do not permit the tongue to slide so that contact is made between the front surface of the tongue and the gum. If this happens, a [ts] blend is likely to be produced.

PRACTICE MATERIALS

Establish the contact position for the stressed [t] by practice with the material that follows. Repeat each of the words of the list at least three times.

Figure 17–1 Articulatory position for /t/ and /d/.

Initial

tea	take	too	tole
tee	ten	tube	talk
tip	tell	took	taught
tell	tag	tomb	tog
tape	tap	toe	top
turn	type	town	tone
Turk	time	tower	team
tub	tide	toy	teach
ton	tile	toil	tease
tie	tire	towel	tool

Medial (Followed by a Vowel)

attend	interne	Utopia	partake
atone	iterate	Utah	pitied
attack	deter	intake	rotate
attempt	detect	eternal	entire
attach	until	retool	historical
attain	utensil	retook	intone
entire	intense	return	intend

Phrases

take your time	talk and tell
tip to top	took the tea
ten and ten	ten times ten
twenty and two	turn the tape
tap the top	take a turn
the town tower	tie the tag

Sentences

1. Tom played a tuba to tease Ted.
2. Ted's toe was taped.
3. Tell Tillie the time when it is 2:00 P.M.
4. Tea was served privately for the two who wanted to be entirely alone.
5. The tower was attacked and attained.
6. Time and tide are eternal verities.
7. Tuesday was made tag day in town.
8. Utah was named for the Ute Indians.
9. The interne detected a contagious tic.
10. Tom turned detective to test his attainments at detection.

Final [2]

bait	fat	dote	but
eat	bat	note	cut
it	boot	bought	hut
ate	emit	blot	hurt
might	foot	right	naught
out	flout	might	suit
quoit	incite	sought	root
sight	blight	fort	shoot

Sentences

1. We will eat at eight.
2. Football is a favorite American sport.
3. Nat was hurt by the split bat.
4. Mint and fruit juice make for a pleasant drink.
5. The boat was lost in the mist at night.
6. Naught could induce Chet to emit a sound.
7. Most adolescent boys like to eat things that are sweet.
8. The note was brought by a servant who wore a blue suit.
9. The quoit contest was won by the Ute.
10. A well-fitted boot will not hurt the foot.

[t] As in *Safety*

The sound [t] in an unstressed syllable followed by a vowel is produced in a less vigorous manner than when it occurs in a stressed syllable. The contact between tongue tip and gum ridge is not held as long as for a stressed [t] and there is less breath puff following the breaking of the contact. Avoid assimilating the unstressed [t] either in the direction of substituting a [d] for it or omitting the sound entirely.

PRACTICE MATERIALS

The words that follow provide practice for the unstressed [t].

pity	hatter	hefty	jetty
city	latter	utter	tempted
plenty	faulty	bitter	twenty
better	mountain	fifty	written
letter	scatter	thirty	litter

[2] A final [t] is exploded when it is followed by a vowel in the next word within the same phrase, as in *the cat is here.* Most persons do not explode the final [t] at the end of a sentence as in *I'll come at eight.*

Practice in discriminating between the unstressed [t] and [d] in the following pairs of words:

latter	ladder	wetting	wedding
betting	bedding	written	ridden
heated	heeded	butting	budding
bitter	bidder	tenting	tending
rating	raiding	contented	contended
shutter	shudder	writer	rider

The following words provide practice for [t] followed by a vowel and/or in the final position.

tell	waste	fateful	bit	tat
ten	last	inter	flat	tent
till	quite	contain	flute	taste
time	after	rotary	hoot	tight
told	comet	twine	root	taught
tab	lout	twist	tote	toot
tangle	between	twig	wart	tort
toll	return	palliate	what	twist
at	continue	unite	flirt	twit
boat	atone	beet	wheat	tossed

Sentences

1. Ten and ten and two count up to twenty-two if counted right.
2. Tom Tucker will have to be told to wait for tomorrow.
3. Ted, please put the cat and the light out before you take off.
4. The tidings of the times portended that temptation was to be avoided at all cost.
5. On his trip to Utah, Thomas sat next to a taciturn gentleman from eastern Texas.
6. The stars twinkled brightly in the Oriental sky.
7. Thomas learned that it was easier to start than to stop a fight.
8. Thomson could not take being twitted, although he was expert at taunting others not quite his size.
9. We had to wait for twenty minutes between the acts of the play.
10. Too few learn in time that it is for them that the bells toll.

Selections

1. Temptation can be many different things to different men. It has been a time-honored subject for the poet, the moralist, the dramatist, and the timeless philosopher. Some views of temptation are presented in the quotations that follow.

a. "I can resist everything except temptation," Oscar Wilde had one of his characters protest.

b. In contrast, the ever optimistic Robert Browning asserts in his *The Ring and the Book:*

Why comes temptation but for man to meet
And master and make crouch beneath his foot,
And so be pedestaled in triumph?

c. Finally, for the moment at least, we have the terse statement of the British humorist and poet Douglas Jerrold who in his *The Catspaw* contends: Honest bread is very well—it's the butter that makes the temptation.

2. Take hands and part with laughter;
    Touch lips and part with tears;
Once more and no more after,
    Whatever comes with years.
    —ALGERNON CHARLES SWINBURNE, *Rococo*

3.   O, it is excellent
To have a giant's strength; but it is tyrannous
To use it like a giant.
    —WILLIAM SHAKESPEARE, *Measure for Measure*

4. Sweet courtesy has done its most
    If you have made each guest forget
    That he himself is not the host.
    —THOMAS BAILEY ALDRICH, *Hospitality*

[t] As a Final, Morphemic Sound As in *Chased* and *Lunched*. Note its consistent representation in spelling by the letters *ed.*

chased	branched	lunched	grossed
faced	lanced	munched	crossed
graced	bunched	tossed	nursed
laced	hunched	bossed	trooped

Sentences

1. Ted munched as he lunched.
2. Tom hunched in pain when his finger was lanced.
3. They trooped to the right of the triple branched route.
4. Theresa was faced with the need to be chased so that she might be caught.
5. It was once common practice for ladies to be tightly laced.

Other Varieties of /t/

As indicated earlier, the consonant /t/ varies somewhat in manner of production and acoustic end result according to speech context. Some of the more frequent variations are now considered.

[t] Followed by /θ/ (th) or /ð/ (th) As in *Right Things* and *At The*. In combinations such as *at the, hit that, light things,* and *eighth,* the [t] is produced by contact between the tongue tip and the upper teeth rather than at the gum ridge. The dentalized [t] in these combinations is produced as a result of the assimilative influence of the next sound /θ/ or /ð/ which is articulated dentally.

This variety of /t/ is least likely to be produced defectively by persons with foreign language backgrounds. It is the variety most likely to be produced habitually by speakers whose English speech is influenced by French, Spanish, Italian, or German.

PRACTICE MATERIALS

eighth time	sweet thoughts
hit the ball	right thinking
swat the fly	bright theorist
light the lamp	slight theme
stout thump	correct theory
went there	hurt Thelma

Sentences

1. Bright theories make for right thoughts.
2. Tom struck out the eighth time at bat.
3. Tess could not bear to swat the fly.
4. The poet thought in slight themes.
5. Ted liked to light the lamp.
6. Shelley wrote that our sweetest themes for songs are those that tell of saddest thoughts.
7. Burt thanked Thelma for her right thinking.
8. After the sixth try, Nat hit the ball and no longer felt thwarted.

[t] Followd by /l/ or /n/ As in *Little* and *Button*. When the [t] sound is immedaitely followed by an /l/ or /n/ it is not necessary to remove the tongue tip from the gum ridge to complete the sound. Instead, the sides of the front part of the tongue break contact with the side teeth to permit a *lateral* escape or explosion of breath. When the [t] is followed by [l], as in *little, battle, settle, kettle,* and *mortal,* the breath of the explosion is emitted orally.

In words in which [t] is followed by /n/, as in *written, button, cotton,* and *rotten,* the tongue position is maintained in going from the [t] to the

/n/. When the velum is lowered for the /n/ a nasal rather than an oral explosion takes place. If you place your hand just below the nostrils, you should be able to feel a nasally emitted puff of air.

There is a marked tendency to substitute a throat or glottal (laryngeal) click sound for the [t] when it is followed by /l/ or /n/. This substitution, in American speech, is generally considered substandard. You may check your tendency for glottal substitution by placing your hand at the larynx while speaking the list of words and sentences that follow. If you feel a click, it is likely that you are using a glottal (laryngeal) catch sound instead of the [t]. To avoid this tendency, pay special attention to the prescribed manner of articulation for the [t] in [tl] and [tn] combinations.

PRACTICE MATERIALS

beetle	mortal	bitten	rotten
battle	glottal	button	fountain
metal	bottle	cotton	written
whittle	scuttle	gotten	fatten
settle	rattle	mountain	mutton

Sentences

1. Morton was in fine fettle as he filled the kettle.
2. The mutton chops were too tough to be eaten.
3. The ill-gotten gains were hidden in the mountain.
4. Little by little Benton analyzed the contents of the bottle.
5. The buttons were whittled out of wood.
6. The kitten played with the cotton ball.
7. Skelton hoped to become immortal by well-written words.
8. A metal figure of Triton dominated the fountain.
9. Martin found it difficult to fatten his mutton.
10. On his climb up the mountain, Fenton stopped to fill his metal bottle.

[t] Followed by /s/ and Preceded and Followed by /s/ As in *Pets* and *Posts*. In contexts in which the [t] is immediately followed by an /s/, the tip of the tongue is permitted to slide forward in anticipation of the /s/. Care should be taken not to omit the [t] entirely, especially in combinations in which the [t] is medial between two /s/ sounds. The fine articulatory movements required for the [sts] combination increase the tendency for the omission of the [t].

PRACTICE MATERIALS

Practice with the words and sentences that follow should help to focus attention on the precise articulation that is required for [ts] and [sts].

pets	pots	insists	pests
lots	flights	breasts	ghosts
gates	paints	posts	resists
facts	mists	rests	persists
lasts	jests	masts	tests

Sentences

1. The last acts of plays should be the playwright's best.
2. Painted pots were placed next to the fence posts along the streets.
3. Gray mists stopped the planes' flights.
4. The hard facts of life may interfere with the attainments of the heart's desires.
5. Birds' nests were found on the masts.
6. Stone persists in presenting lots of facts at times when jests or stories of ghosts are more to listeners' tastes.

Selections

1. Hope springs external in the human breast:
   Man never is, but always to be, blest.
   —ALEXANDER POPE, *Essay on Man*
2. Now cracks a noble heart. Good night, sweet prince,
   And flights of angels sing thee to thy rest.
   —WILLIAM SHAKESPEARE, *Hamlet*

/d/ As in *Done, Ado,* and *Glad*

The consonant /d/ in *done* is articulated in essentially the same manner as the /t/ in *ton* except that the /d/ is voiced. The /d/, like the /t/, is a variable sound. The varieties of /d/ parallel those for /t/. Faults in articulation of /d/ also parallel those for /t/, the chief one being the tendency for dental articulation. A second tendency to be avoided is the substitution of a /t/ for a /d/ in words in which the final /d/ should be voiced. This fault may be especially noted in the speech of German-born persons or of persons for whom German was and perhaps continues to be a strong influence. The probable reason for this is that the final /d/ does not occur in German.

PRACTICE MATERIALS

The first set of materials should help establish a clear distinction between /t/ and /d/. Make certain that the /t/ is voiceless and the /d/ is voiced.

Distinguish between initial /t/ and /d/:

tame	dame	tuck	duck
teem	deem	tune	dune
tip	dip	tomb	doom
tail	dale	toe	doe
ten	den	taunt	daunt
tan	Dan	tot	dot
time	dime	town	down
too	do	touch	Dutch

Distinguish between final /t/ and /d/:

seat	seed	brute	brood
bit	bid	note	node
ate	aid	naught	gnawed
late	laid	not	nod
mat	mad	coat	code
let	led	writ	rid
bat	bad	cart	card
set	said	stunt	stunned
cat	cad	hurt	heard
beat	bead	curt	curd

Initial

deal	daze	dart	dire
deep	duel	dark	dear
din	dough	dirt	dean
day	dote	dearth	dream
debt	dawn	dub	drip
dance	dock	dike	drain
dew	dog	doubt	draw
dale	damp	dull	does

Phrases

deep in dew	dull and damp
dance till dawn	daily dozen
day by day	duel in the dew
dark and dreary	due date
din at daybreak	dull ditty
dry desert	denizen of the deep
dog at the dock	delicate dough
dearth of dough	dire dream

Medial

adder	adduce	bedding	gander
admit	fading	bedlam	hinder
ardent	hidden	candor	needed
oddly	eddy	splendor	indoor
edict	adverse	random	odious

Final

add	amid	said	spade
crowd	old	lead	code
rude	bald	heed	abode
hoard	fraud	reed	node
heed	curd	rod	aloud
ode	brood	toad	cloud
mode	Druid	mood	mold

Sentences

1. Undaunted by earlier failures, Diane led a dozen determined ladies to begin a ten-day diet.

2. Dan claimed that frequently he could not distinguish between Dick's candor and his rudeness.

3. As the day was dying, a deep-red cloud rested on the mountain top.

4. The dog's barking at dawn warned Daniel and helped him to undo a dastardly plot.

5. Duncan brooded over the fraud that deprived him of his gold and his abode.

6. Daybreak is considered the correct if not the good time for undertaking duels.

7. The crowd did not heed the warning to disperse.

8. London is a city of dense fog and bright-minded traders.

9. The drug made Dick's head droop as he dropped off to sleep.

10. Matilda married her admiral who wrote an ode to his bride.

11. David took heed of every detail as he decoded the note.

12. Druidism is a religion that was once prevalent in the lands that are now England and Ireland.

[dz]

adds	cards	reeds	fords
beads	fades	steeds	raised
beds	heads	rides	hazed

bends	deeds	loads	pleased
buds	meads	roads	teased

[d] *followed by* [θ] *or* [ð]

had that	herd the cattle	ride through
hid the ball	sad thoughts	width and breadth
heard the call	rid the land	ford the stream

Selections for /t/ *and* /d/

1. But when I tell him he hates flatterers,
   He says he does, being then most flattered.

   —WILLIAM SHAKESPEARE, *Julius Caesar*

2. Cowards die many times before their death;
   The valiant never taste of death but once.

   —WILLIAM SHAKESPEARE, *Julius Caesar*

3. My true-love hath my heart, and I have his,
   By just exchange one for the other given;
   I hold his dear, and mine he cannot miss,
   There never was a better bargain driven.

   —PHILIP SIDNEY, *The Bargain*

4. When Adam was created,
   He dwelt in Eden's shade,
   As Moses has related,
   Before a bride was made;
   Ten thousand times ten thousand
   Things wheelèd all around,
   Before a bride was formed
   Or yet a mate was found.

   —GEORGE PULLEN JACKSON, *Wedlock*

5. No living man can send me to the shades
   Before my time; no man of woman born,
   Coward or brave, can shun his destiny.

   —HOMER, *Iliad*

6. Said Trixon to Dixon
   You look full of thought
   I'll offer you tuppence
   Though it may be worth nought.

   Said Dixon to Trixon
   Your offer's quite tempty
   But not for ten tuppence
   Would my mind for you empty.

   —J. E., *A Thought's a Thought for All That*

7. The day is done, and the darkness
    Falls from the wings of Night
    As a feather is wafted downward
    From an eagle in his flight
                  —HENRY WADSWORTH LONGFELLOW, *The Day Is Done*

8. In his sixth *Meditation,* and elsewhere, Descartes led himself
    to conclude that what distinguished man from the other ani-
    mals was that the human one consisted of two quite unlike
    substances. One of them was a substance, the major, if not
    sole, attribute of which was thought. The other was a sub-
    stance with, among others perhaps, the attributes of length,
    breadth, and width, that is, an extended substance. The first
    was an unextended, but thinking, substance, while the second
    was an extended, but unthinking, substance. The first was, of
    course, the soul or mind, while the second was body. The
    problem was how two such unlike substances could possibly
    influence one another.
                  —JAY N. EACKER, *On Some Elementary Philosophical*
                  Problems of Psychology
                  (*American Psychologist,* June 1972)

/s/ As in *Sea, Asleep, Icy, Best,* and *Less*

The consonant /s/ is a high-frequency, voiceless, tongue-tip fricative
that requires careful and precise articulatory action for its production.
The adjustments involve the following:
1. The tongue is raised so that the sides are pressed firmly against the
inner surfaces of the upper molars.
2. The tongue is slightly grooved along the midline. Air is forced
down along this groove.
3. The tip of the tongue is placed about a quarter of an inch behind
the upper teeth. The tongue tip is almost in position for a /t/. (Persons
not able to attain this adjustment will probably find it easier to place the
tongue tip close to the lower gum ridge.)
4. The teeth are brought in line, with a very narrow space between
the rows of teeth.
5. The breath stream is directed along the groove of the tongue
toward the cutting edges of the teeth.
6. The soft palate is raised to prevent nasal emission of the sound.

Use a mirror to see the articulatory adjustments for the /s/. The
recommended articulatory position is represented in Figure 17–2.
In producing the /s/, exercise special care to avoid having the tongue
tip touch either the upper teeth or the gum ridge. Neither should you
permit the tongue tip to slide down so as to protrude between the rows

Figure 17–2   Articulatory adjustments for /s/ and /z/.

of teeth. The first articulatory error will result in the production of a [ts] blend or in a lateral sound resembling a voiceless [l]. The second fault will result in the production of an infantile lisp resembling a [θ] (th).

Persons who habitually produce /t/ and /d/ sounds with dental rather than gum-ridge contacts are likely to lower the tongue tip for the production of /s/. The result, in most instances, is the production of a dull, low-pitched sibilant.

In some instances, the articulatory adjustments just described do not help to produce the desired result of a high-frequency, sibilant sound. Occasionally, the person, possibly because of his unusual mouth structure, must make individual adjustments to arrive at the same acoustic end result. With some articulatory adjustments, a low-pitched sound may be the best that the individual can achieve. Most persons, however, regardless of articulatory mechanism, can learn to produce an /s/ that acoustically resembles the high-pitched fricative just described.

Apart from the manner of articulation, the sound /s/ in American-English speech may present some difficulty for the foreign-born speaker because of the varied spelling representations for the sound. The most frequent representation is the letter *s;* other representations include the *ss* as in *less, sc* as in *scene, c* as in *race,* and *x* as in *hoax.* The foreign-born speaker of English may be forgiven his failure to know when to produce the sound /s/ if we realize the many ways the letter *s* may be pronounced. In addition to the /s/ we have /ʒ/ (zh) as in *treasure,* /ʃ/ (sh) as in *sure,* and /z/ as in *his*. To add to the consternation of the foreign-born speaker, we also have the "silent" *s* as in *island* and *aisle*.

PRACTICE MATERIALS

Because of the frequency of the /s/ in American-English speech, we recommend that a considerable amount of attention be given to this sound. Practice first to produce the sound in isolation until a clear, high-frequency sibilant can be articulated at will. Then incorporate the sound in nonsense syllables. The advantage of nonsense syllable practice in the early stages of establishing or correcting a sound lies in the avoidance of habits of articulation that may be faulty. Suggested nonsense syllable combinations precede the word lists.

seef	sif	sef	saf	sek
sah	sof	soo	sook	sawp
sut	sug	sul	sool	sipe

ahsah	ahsaw	eesaw	aysaw
ohso	ohsoo	ooso	oosoo

Initial [3]

see	sew	suck	circuit
seat	soak	seal	cease
say	saw	sale	citric
sane	sought	ceiling	cinch
sin	sog	sigh	scenic
sit	sop	cite	scent
set	song	civil	sceptre
sell	sock	cider	science
sat	sir	cigar	scion
sag	certain	cinder	screen
sue	soil	cipher	screw
soot	sun	circle	scratch

Medial

asleep	boost	essay	tracing
mist	rooster	icy	trousseau
hasten	boast	pressing	bracer
pest	bossy	blessing	hoist
last	twosome	history	peaceful

[3] Additional word lists are provided for [s] blends. Some of the words of the early lists may again be used when the frequent [s] blends are presented.

Final

crease	loops	choice	loss
leaps	loose	voice	dross
miss	dose	terse	hiss
kiss	horse	verse	hex
pace	Norse	curse	fix
race	bus	fuss	tricks
bets	truss	mouse	cheeks
debts	puss	house	plates
pass	worse	dress	waits
caps	hearse	niece	fleets
farce	entice	boss	keeps

[s] *Preceded and Followed by a Vowel*

deceive	casing	assume	gusset
acetic	assay	twosome	russet
precede	resale	isobar	assign
acid	assemble	isolate	nicety
assimilate	assent	isotype	oscillate
asymmetry	asset	assault	ossify
aseptic	brassy	assort	ascend
essay	glassy	asunder	assail
lacing	messy	assert	asylum

Sentences

1. Six swift horses started in the historic race.
2. Sue, a suave, slim lass, wore a silk dress.
3. Selma Sweet fussed about the small squeaking mouse.
4. Simon insisted that clever verse must be terse.
5. Simson had a steady fondness for sweet cider.
6. The storm-tossed sloop sank beneath the spray.
7. Stevenson was a scientist who liked to be certain of his evidence.
8. Stella was enticed by the high ceilings of the house.
9. "Puss in Boots" is a story for small children who like to listen.
10. Some historians say that there is no such thing as a bad peace.

If the /s/ sound cannot be mastered directly, it may be of help to begin with a /t/ and to work initially for a [ts] blend. This is especially helpful for persons who have no difficulty with the /t/ but do have some with the /s/. The words that follow should be useful for this approach.

cleats	meats	fats	kites
heats	mats	yachts	riots

beats	cats	divots	hurts
bits	hoots	blots	nights
gets	notes	ruts	blights
debts	floats	hurts	weights
hits	thoughts	flights	quoits
fights	lights	nuts	rates

/θ/ (th) and /s/

Some speakers must exercise caution not to confuse the voiceless /θ/ (th) with the /s/. The /θ/ is properly produced with the tip of the tongue in contact with the back of the upper teeth or slightly protruded between the teeth. This contact is to be avoided for the /s/.

PRACTICE MATERIALS

The following pairs of words should help to establish the difference between articulatory positions and acoustic results.

thin	sin	think	sink
theme	seem	thaw	saw
thick	sick	thuds	suds
thank	sank	thought	sought
thigh	sigh	thong	song
thumb	sum	third	surd
Thane	sane	thunder	sunder
path	pass	worth	worse
bath	bass	kith	kiss
truth	truce	myth	miss
math	mass	Beth	Bess
faith	face	wraith	race

Make certain that the distinction between the /θ/ and the /s/ is made clear in the following material.

Sentences

1. In counting the sum, the boy used his fingers and his thumb.
2. The thick smoke made us feel sick.
3. The lightning that tore the sky asunder was followed by thunder.
4. Because the cook did not think, she clogged the sink.
5. No thinking man can win a race with a wraith.
6. Though not a sin, it is a thin faith that is limited to saving face.
7. Although Sam did not catch the bass, he enjoyed a bath in the stream.
8. The path led over the mountain pass.

Frequent [s] Blends and Clusters

Initial [sk]

scheme	scalp	score	sky
skiff	scab	scorch	scare
skin	scan	scorn	scallop
skill	scandal	skirt	scamp
skip	scant	scar	skewer
skit	scatter	Scot	sketch
schedule	school	skull	sceptic
scale	schooner	skunk	squire

Medial [sk]

risking	discount	Alaska	Ruskin
discuss	ensconce	basket	landscape
asking	Muskogee	escape	musket

Final [sk]

brisk	whisk	bask	task
disk	desk	flask	tusk
frisk	musk	mask	rusk

Initial [st]

steam	stay	sterile	stark
steel	stain	stirrup	start
steep	station	stew	starve
steer	stealth	stole	style
stiff	step	stone	store
still	stem	stove	stork
stick	stigma	stack	stock
sting	stool	stamp	stop
stint	stout	stub	storm
steady	stoop	stunt	story

Medial [st]

Easter	roster	wasteful	basting
feasting	mastiff	coaster	toasted
blister	tasty	costly	castor
master	blasted	frosted	castaway
monster	aster	musty	punster

Final [st]

beast	mist	past	host
east	best	roast	cost
least	rest	post	frost
priest	pest	roost	lost
yeast	guest	just	first
fist	cast	rust	nursed
list	last	toast	oust
kissed	mast	most	Faust

Initial [skr]

scream	script	scrap	scrawl
screech	scrutiny	scramble	scrub
screen	scribble	scroll	scribe
scrivener	scrape	scruple	scrabble

Medial [skr]

discredit	miscreant	descry	unscrew
discreet	proscribe	describe	prescribe
discriminate	discretion	enscribe	inscrutable

Initial [str]

streak	strain	straw	strut
stream	strength	strong	stripe
strip	strap	strop	strive
stricken	strew	struck	strident
string	stroke	struggle	striate
stray	stroll	strike	structure

Medial [str]

restrict	instruct	upstream	distrust
construe	restraint	district	distress
constrain	unstrung	destroy	dystrophy
constrict	hamstring	distraught	frustrate
construct	restrengthen	distract	prostrate

Initial [sm]

smear	smack	smart	smug
smithy	smooth	smolder	smudge

smitten	smote	smother	smile
smell	small	smirk	smite
smelter	smock	Smyrna	smirch

Initial [sw]

Sweden	swing	swoon	swan
sweep	sway	swoop	swamp
sweet	sweat	swollen	swallow
swig	swelter	swarm	swine
swim	swear	swirl	swipe
swivel	swag	swap	swindle

Initial [sn]

sneak	snap	snare	snatch
sneer	snoop	snort	snipe
sniff	snow	snub	snicker
snip	snob	snuff	snug
snail	snarl	snake	snore

Final [ns]

wince	fence	glance	romance
pence	quince	lance	prance
hence	mince	manse	enhance

Medial [ns]

answer	balancing	instead	punster
dancer	instant	install	bouncing
Frances	instill	ensnare	winsome

Initial [sp]

speed	span	spore	spun
speak	sparrow	sparse	spunk
spill	spat	spark	spy
spin	spew	spare	spike
speck	spool	Sparta	spine
spell	spook	spirit	spout
spade	spoof	spur	spoke
Spain	Spode	spurt	spoil
spent	spawn	sponge	spider

Final and Medial [sp]

lisp	crisp	despondent	despoil
asp	grasp	despair	despot
hasp	rasp	desperate	respect
clasp	cusp	aspire	respond
wasp	grasping	despise	respite
wisp	resplendent	bicuspid	perspire

[spl]

split	splendid	splurge	splotch
spleen	splice	splutter	splendor
splay	splint	splash	splat

[spr]

sprain	sprinkle	sprout	sprung
sprig	sprint	spruce	sprocket
spread	sprite	spry	spring

PRACTICE MATERIALS FOR BLENDS

Sentences

1. The sponge is the internal skeleton of a marine animal.
2. A scallop is a bivalve mollusk.
3. Scones are thin cakes made skillfully by the Scots.
4. Skelton swung his ax skillfully to split the stack of logs.
5. The squid is a species of cuttlefish.
6. The northwest coastal area of the United States is warmed by steady moist winds called chinooks.
7. Stewart and six hunters set out to obtain scarce elephant tusks.
8. The swift schooner brought in a catch of sea horses and starfish.
9. Prescott always felt like strutting when he squired his sweet Stella.
10. Scribbled and scrawled manuscripts are likely to receive scanty attention from schoolmasters.
11. The old scow was covered with scale.
12. The sudden squall upset the skiff.
13. Spring rains may come in sprinkles.
14. The sprite was a spry spirit.
15. Smith was smitten by a small girl in a smock.
16. Sperry was smart but not smug.
17. Stacy's voice demonstrated frequent strident tones.

18. Snead was famous, or perhaps infamous, for his stentorious snoring.
19. Struggle, if it is not fruitless, helps to make the struggler strong.
20. The scribe scrutinized his efforts on his manuscript.
21. Swenson was fond of his wife's quince jelly.
22. The boa constrictor was ensnared in a skillfully constructed trap.
23. Lance and Frances aspired to perform in the circus with an expert balancing act.

[sts] and [sks]

The combinations [sts] and [sks] are somewhat difficult because of the quick and precise tongue action needed in their production.

PRACTICE MATERIALS

The following word lists and sentences should be useful as practice materials.

beasts	pests	boasts	toasts
feasts	rests	coasts	bursts
fists	casts	posts	firsts
lists	lasts	roasts	jousts
pastes	boosts	ghosts	musts
waists	roosts	hosts	rusts
discs	asks	tasks	whisks
risks	basks	husks	flasks
frisks	masks	tusks	casks

Sentences

1. The insect pests spoiled the outdoor feasts for the guests.
2. Two blasts signaled that the jousts were about to begin as tests for the knights.
3. Ghosts do not bother with boasts.
4. Six gun blasts were fired at the animal pests.
5. Good hosts demonstrate an air of unconcern about costs.
6. Risks must be assumed in many tasks.
7. Large oaken casks were used as tops for desks.

Initial and Final [s]

sauce	source	slips	smacks
sense	seats	slants	streets

since	souse	spots	sinks
saints	sites	spurts	stunts
sweets	saps	speaks	squeaks
swaps	surfs	spouts	scuffs
sass	stoops	smokes	skirts

ADDITIONAL PRACTICE MATERIALS FOR /s/
IN VARIOUS CONTEXTS

Sentences

1. Genius without a striving for work may be a waste of superior intelligence.
2. Signs on the highways offer sage advice to passing motorists.
3. Simonson's satire was frequently indistinguishable from his attempts at farce.
4. Charles Dickens opens his *Tale of Two Cities* with the words: "It was the best of times. It was the worst of times."
5. Susan was pleasant and almost always easy to please. Sam was unpleasant and almost impossible to please.
6. Unseasonal scarcity of rains as well as inconsistent distributions have resulted in producing America's dust bowls.
7. Stanley observed that disease frequently attracts more attention than a healthy state of affairs, whether it be in persons or in nations.
8. Sooner's sullen silences spoke eloquently for his negativistic notions.
9. Jurists are supposed to listen to all aspects of arguments and issues presented to them.
10. The rising moon cast a silvery light over the serene sea.

Selections

1. Ah, how unjust to Nature and himself
   Is thoughtless, thankless, inconsistent man!
   —EDWARD YOUNG, *Night*
2. On top of Old Smoky
   All covered with snow,
   I lost my true lover
   By courtin' too slow.
   —*On Top of Old Smoky*, American folk song
3. The love of praise, howe'er conceal'd by art,
   Reigns more or less, and glows in ev'ry heart.
   —EDWARD YOUNG, *Love of Fame*
4. H. L. Mencken, the so-called sage of Baltimore, enjoyed having people think of him as an acidic and outrageous per-

son. He sometimes earned this right by sentences such as:
"Philosophy consists very largely of one philosopher arguing
that all others are jackasses."

5. How Homo sapiens arrived at speech is lost in prehistory.
    Speaking man speculates about the onset of speech and
    through speech conjectures and rationalizes, each according
    to his needs, present interests, prejudices, and inclinations.
    The mystery and beginning of speech may be repeated in
    the cycle of infant development, but the infant forgets how he
    acquired speech as soon as he becomes a speaking child. Once
    again, adults speculate about the onset of speech in the child,
    and about his prelingual stages of development. This is
    history, fascinating speculative history, with testimony ab-
    stracted from those who speak without telling us how or why.
    The task of learning to speak is immense. The immensity of the
    task, fortunately, is unconsciously and unwittingly assumed
    by the child. Before he knows the size or significance of his
    responsibilities he has assumed, the normal child has ac-
    cepted and practiced the verbal habits—the ways of speaking
    —of his special culture and thus himself becomes a trans-
    mitter of the verbal habits of those with whom he lives.
    Speech is considered by most linguists to be a human species-
    specific function.

6. Life's a pudding full of plums,
    Care's a canker that benumbs,
    Wherefore waste our elocution
    On impossible solution?
    Life's a pleasant institution,
    Let us take it as it comes!

                              —W. S. GILBERT, *The Gondoliers*

7. The silent colossal National Lie that is the support and the
    confederate of all the tyrannies and shams and inequalities
    and unfairnesses that afflict the peoples—that is the one to
    throw bricks and sermons at.

                    —MARK TWAIN, *My First Lie, and How I Got Out of It*

/z/ As in *Zoo, Cousin, Azalea,* and *Buzz*

Except for accompanying vocalization for the /z/, the sound is produced like the /s/. /z/ may be described as a lingua-alveolar voiced
fricative. Generally it is produced with somewhat less tongue muscle
tension than is necessary for the /s/.

The spellings for /z/ are varied and include *z* as in *zero*, *s* as in *rose*
and *nasal*, and *zz* as in *buzz*.

Persons who have difficulty with the articulation of the /s/ are also likely to find the /z/ troublesome. Vocalization, however, may conceal some of the acoustic faults that become apparent when an /s/ is defectively produced. If your best /s/ is articulated with the tongue tip behind the lower teeth rather than behind the upper gum ridge, the same adjustment should be made for the production of /z/.

PRACTICE MATERIALS

Initial

zebra	zest	zircon	zeal
zee	zephyr	Zouave	Zeno
Zeeland	Zachary	Zurich	zone
zinc	zoo	zither	zip
zinnia	Zeus	zyme	zoology
zany	zoom	zealous	zounds
zenith	zodiac	Zion	Zoe

Medial

teasing	spasm	designate	design
pleasing	plasma	nozzle	desire
blizzard	music	cousin	enzyme
lazy	using	dozen	raising
daisy	dozing	used	noisy
pleasant	causing	desert	reason
resin	buzzer	deserve	appeasing
hazard	poser	preserve	resign

Final

ease	whose	because	toys
please	choose	repose	annoys
tease	doze	crows	boys
his	woes	yearns	ties
fizz	hose	spurns	replies
raise	grows	burns	dyes
maize	goads	buzz	rhymes
days	claws	eaves	wise
has	flaws	cows	surmise
lads	calls	browse	symbols

Morphemic /z/

The list for the final /z/ included several examples in which the sound had morphemic significance as a plural marker and/or an indicator of grammatical tense. These examples include the words *claws, calls,* and *toys.* The following list is for words in which the final *s,* pronounced /z/, is part of a separate, final syllable. Many of the words may serve either as nouns or verbs.

aces	doses	exposures	lunches
bunches	dozes	hunches	plunges
buzzes	eases	hunters	raises
chooses	entices	inducers	reposes

Sentences

1. Zebras are animals found in most zoos.
2. The museum was open eight hours a day in all seasons.
3. Zoe wisely dozed off when others fell victim to their desires and yearnings.
4. Symbols are man's and only man's way of preserving and communicating his ideas.
5. Zachary was not able to afford diamonds and so presented zircons to his best girls.
6. Snows make the mountains near Zurich ever-pleasant views.
7. The Mormons converted the desert into green pastures.
8. Girls and boys soon learn that some words can tease and others can please.
9. Zinnias bloom late in the summer season, but daisies are early flowers.
10. The blizzard caused the travelers hours of delay in their journeys.
11. Plasma can be preserved for many days.
12. Maize grows in many farms and fields.

[dz]

Persons who have difficulty with the articulatory position for /z/ might find it helpful to begin with /d/ and to "move" from /d/ to /z/. Be sure that you start with a tongue tip to gum ridge contact for the /d/ and then retract the tongue tip slightly for the /z/. Practice with the following:

weeds	cads	chords	cards
beads	lads	fords	rods
lids	moods	hoards	brides
bids	foods	birds	chides
maids	toads	herds	tides
raids	loads	builds	grounds

/z/ Blends

Many of the words of the practice lists for medial and final /z/ contain blends of /z/ preceded by an /m/, /b/, /v/, /n/, /l/, or /d/. The word lists and materials that follow feature these combinations.

PRACTICE MATERIALS

Final [mz]

beams	gems	brooms	alms
creams	frames	combs	calms
reams	names	domes	charms
teams	crams	homes	harms
rims	lambs	storms	qualms
whims	booms	forms	alarms
hems	tombs	norms	farms
stems	chums	climbs	germs
clams	crumbs	chimes	firms
hams	numbs	dimes	terms

Final [bz]

Thebes	webs	dabs	tubes
cribs	ebbs	stabs	absorbs
fibs	jabs	tabs	cobs
nibs	cabs	cubes	nobs
robs	lobes	hubs	disturbs
swabs	jobs	nubs	herbs
squabs	robes	stubs	verbs

Final [vz]

believes	delves	wharves	shoves
deceives	shelves	carves	drives
eaves	elves	starves	hives
thieves	calves	curves	knives
gives	halves	nerves	strives
lives	grooves	serves	thrives
braves	moves	swerves	wives
knaves	proves	doves	leaves
staves	roves	gloves	weaves
waves	stoves	loves	saves

Final [nz]

beans	stains	ruins	darns
screens	remains	fawns	burns
bins	dens	mourns	turns
fins	glens	dawns	spurns
grins	bans	groans	guns
brains	clans	owns	runs
trains	loons	stones	tons
lanes	boons	barns	gowns
refrains	tunes	earns	clowns
mines	signs	coins	joins

Final [lz]

deals	gales	coals	boils
keels	jails	doles	coils
wheels	nails	foals	spoils
hills	bales	moles	tiles
tills	duels	goals	miles
frills	fools	falls	wiles
mills	spools	appalls	jowls
stills	tools	stalls	cowls
gills	pulls	lolls	towels
wills	bulls	hobbles	owls

Final [dz]

beads	heads	goads	birds
bleeds	weds	loads	herds
creeds	cads	frauds	curds
deeds	lads	swords	words
weeds	goods	towards	abides
bids	hoods	hods	hides
rids	foods	nods	chides
aids	moods	pods	abounds
fades	broods	floods	hounds
wades	intrudes	buds	rounds

Sentences

1. Jones had qualms about touching coins because they might be covered with germs.

2. Ben's wife believed that homes are kept clean by new brooms and frequent sweepings.

3. The ornate picture frames were encrusted wtih semiprecious gems.

4. Grimes had whims that resulted in his telling many fibs.

5. Hundreds of corncobs were stored in cribs on farms.

6. The thieves wore gloves when they stole the wares from the wharves.

7. Human brains are able to deal with symbols and signs.

8. The young of horses and asses are called foals.

9. Trains still carry goods to and from farms as do planes.

10. The storm's fury left many of the town's homes in ruins.

11. Ned's dreams were to write the country's refrains.

12. Ted's moods led him to take long walks down country lanes.

/z/ and /s/

Some persons with foreign language backgrounds have difficulty in distinguishing between /z/ and the /s/. If the element of voice is not distinctive, then both phonetic and semantic differences may be broken down in word pairs such as *price* and *prize; race* and *raise;* and *zoo* and *sue.*

PRACTICE MATERIALS

Practice with the word pairs and the sentences that follow to make certain that the /z/ is clearly voiced and that the /s/ is voiceless.

zee	see	lose	loose
zeal	seal	prize	price
zip	sip	doze	dose
zinc	sink	pads	pats
zoo	sue	sends	cents
zone	sown	bids	bits
peas	peace	codes	coats
rays	race	kids	kits
maize	mace	beds	bets
his	hiss	knees	niece

Sentences

1. A seal eats fish with considerable zeal.

2. The bids ran high for the bits of gems.

3. The prize was won at a large price.

4. Selma and Zelda went to see the Zuyder Zee.

5. Zinc was used to line the sink.

6. Cousin Sue enjoyed her trip to the zoo.

7. The lost codes were found in the pockets of the coats.

8. The maize was pounded with a mace.

9. Grace disliked to see her cattle graze in rented fields.

10. The racer was given a razor as a prize.

11. Simpson, although not a psychologist, astutely observed that the things persons say to themselves constitute the basis for deciding what they will say to those who supposedly are listening to them.

12. When Susan sighed there was little need to explain her sighs by spoken words.

13. Sylvia was statuesque and stately, and yet blissfully unconscious of these signal attributes.

14. The twins insisted that all the tales to which they listened be twice-told tales.

15. The American Psychological Association includes a division called the Society for the Psychological Study of Social Issues.

Selections

1. In his *An Unsocial Socialist,* George Bernard Shaw argues that "a day's work is a day's work, neither more nor less, and the man who does it needs a day's sustenance, a night's repose, and due leisure whether he be a painter or plough-man."

2. Speaking of himself in his *Sixteen Self Sketches,* Shaw said, "I always astonish strangers by my amiability, because, as no human being could possibly be so disagreeable as they expect me to be, I have only to be commonly civil to seem quite charming."

3. In his summary statement of an essay entitled "Symptom Substitution?" the author, a psychologist and speech patholo-gist, says: "An analytic theory holds, as has been shown, that if a symptom is taken away from an individual without re-duction of causal factors, strong possibility exists that an-other symptom will replace it. This process is known as *symptom substitution.* Some authorities, of course, deny that symptom substitution can take place. For example, some behaviorists deny the existence of a symptom and insist that we are dealing with behavior *per se.* Other individuals feel that a symptom is best defined not necessarily as evidence of an internal conflict but rather as nonadaptive behavior and that nonadaptive behavior is subject to the same learning and maintenance laws as are other behaviors."
   —JOHN V. IRWIN, *Acta Symbolica,* Vol. II (1971)

4. There is some soul of goodness in things evil,
   Would men observingly distil it out;

For our bad neighbor makes us early stirrers,
Which is both healthful and good husbandry.
Besides, they are our outward consciences,
And preachers to us all, admonishing
That we should dress us fairly for our end.
Thus may we gather honey from the weed,
And make a moral of the devil himself.
                              —WILLIAM SHAKESPEARE, *Henry V*

5.   There is a silence where hath been no sound,
        There is a silence where no sound may be,
          In the cold grave—under the deep, deep sea,
     Or in wide desert where no life is found,
     Which hath been mute, and still must sleep profound.
                              —THOMAS HOOD, *Silence*

6.   Terms ill defined, and forms misunderstood,
     And customs, where their reasons are unknown,
     Have stirred up many zealous souls
     To fight against imaginary giants.
                              —MARTIN F. TUPPER, *Of Tolerance*

7.   Good laws lead to the making of better ones; bad ones bring
     about worse. As soon as any man says of the affairs of the
     State, "What does it matter to me?" the State may be given
     up for lost.
                              —JEAN JACQUES ROUSSEAU, *The Social Contract*

8.   In this best of all possible worlds, the Baron's castle was the
     most magnificent of castles, and his lady the best of all pos-
     sible Baronesses.
                              —VOLTAIRE, *Candide*

9.   It is indeed a desirable thing to be well descended, but the
     glory belongs to our ancestors.
                              —PLUTARCH, *Of the Training of Children*

10. Of all the causes which conspire to blind
     Man's erring judgment, and misguide the mind,
     What the weak head with strongest bias rules,
     Is pride, the never-failing vice of fools.
                              —ALEXANDER POPE, *An Essay on Criticism*

THE POSTALVEOLAR SOUNDS /ʃ/ AND /ʒ/

/ʃ/ (sh) As in *She*, *Ashore*, and *Ash*

With the consonant /s/ as a basis for comparison, the /ʃ/ (sh) should
be easy to master. The sound is produced with the entire tongue drawn

Figure 17–3 Articulatory adjustments for /ʃ/ and /ʒ/.

a little farther back than for the /s/. The tongue surface is broadened and flat so that there is no groove or channel as is required for /s/. The stream of breath is forced over the flat tongue surface and emitted between the rows of teeth. /ʃ/ is usually produced with slight lip rounding. Acoustically, the principal concentration of acoustic energy is in a lower frequency band than that of /s/. Phonetically, /ʃ/ may be described as a voiceless, orally emitted, blade-tongue, postalveolar fricative sound.

/ʃ/ has several spellings. The most frequent is the combination *sh* as in *she.* Other frequent spellings include *ti* as in *nation, si* as in *tension, ci* as in *precious, ch* as in *machine,* and *s* as in *sure.*

For some speakers with foreign language backgrounds and for some who may have high-frequency hearing losses, the similarities in spelling and in manner of articulation may cause confusion between the /ʃ/ and the /s/. Emphasis on lip rounding and on the more retracted and flattened tongue for the /ʃ/ should help to contrast it with and distinguish it from the /s/.

PRACTICE MATERIALS

Practice before a mirror with the word pairs that follow should be helpful.

she	sea	shoe	sue
sheik	seek	shoot	suit

sheep	seep	show	sew
shield	sealed	shawl	Saul
ship	sip	shore	sore
shin	sin	shop	sop
shay	say	shot	sot
shake	sake	shock	sock
shad	sad	shy	sigh
shall	sal	shed	said
brash	brass	gash	gas
clash	class	plush	plus
mesh	mess	rushed	rust
leash	lease	fashion	fasten
mash	mass	crash	crass

Maintain the difference between the /ʃ/ and /s/ in the following phrases and sentences:

Shad looked sad	clash in class
a sealed shield	she went to see
shipped to be sipped	no shoe for Sue

1. Sue held that it was no longer in fashion to use buttons to fasten shoes or shirts.

2. The brass instruments clashed with a sound that was brash.

3. The mess of mash was shipped by sea.

4. Sam enjoyed steamed shad that he bought in a shop along the seashore.

ADDITIONAL PRACTICE MATERIALS FOR /ʃ/

she	shoe	shirt	shriek
sheen	shoot	shirk	shrimp
ship	should	shut	shred
shin	shook	shun	shrewd
shay	shone	shout	shrub
shame	show	shower	shrine
shell	shawl	shine	shroud
shed	shore	shy	shrank
shall	shop	sugar	shrink
shaggy	shock	shark	shrug
leashing	lashes	pressure	fission
wishing	passion	quashed	hushing
ashamed	fashion	machine	Flushing
glacier	pushing	pension	national
nation	cushion	delicious	fractious

patient	lotion	conscience	crashed
precious	ocean	anxious	rushing
dashes	caution	mission	washed
leash	hash	hush	Danish
wish	crash	harsh	blemish
fish	bush	marsh	English
dish	push	rush	garnish
mesh	burnish	tarnish	Flemish
flesh	furnish	varnish	brandish
flash	punish	Amish	gnash
cash	blush	vanish	lush

Sentences

1. Ocean fishing furnishes a livelihood for many British fishermen.
2. The shaggy Prussian brandished his tarnished sword.
3. Hamlet had an anxious and disturbed conscience.
4. Shaw was not ashamed to be fractious.
5. The chef earned a pension for his well-garnished dishes.
6. Sheila shrugged her shoulders as she added sugar to her milk shake.
7. The motion of the ship on the ocean made a patient of the man from Flushing.
8. A flash flood transformed the shrubless field into a marsh.
9. Some nations have a passion for peace; others seem to have a passion for aggression.
10. Ship-to-shore communication is available for most of our nation.
11. Do you anticipate a clash among the boys in the class?
12. Sam Sherman shunned the sun.

Selections

1. I think that, as life is action and passion, it is required of a man that he should share the passion and action of his time at peril of being judged not to have lived.

   —JUSTICE OLIVER WENDELL HOLMES,
   Memorial Day Address, 1884

2. For he might have been a Roosian,
   A French, or Turk, or Proosian,
   Or perhaps Itali-an!
   But in spite of all temptations
   To belong to other nations,
   He remains an Englishman!

   —W. S. GILBERT, *H. M. S. Pinafore*

3. Friendship is a sheltering tree;
    Oh the joys that came down shower-like,
    Of friendship, love, and liberty,
    Ere I was old!

    —SAMUEL TAYLOR COLERIDGE, *Youth and Age*

4. Daniel Shays was a captain of the militia during our Revolu-
    tion against the British. Later, during the period of the Con-
    federation and in a time of financial depresssion, Shays led
    an armed insurrection against the Massachusetts government.
    The insurrectionists were made up substantially of farmers.
    They protested that the salaries of public officials were too
    high. In addition they petitioned against the imposition of
    high taxes. Shays' petitions, protestations, general dissensions,
    and finally his insurrection are believed to have hastened the
    ratification of the Federal Constitution by Massachusetts.

/ʒ/ (zh) As in *Azure, Treasure, Rouge,* and *Decision*

The sound /ʒ/ is a voiced, postalveolar fricative. It is produced like
the /ʃ/ with accompanying vocal fold vibration.

/ʒ/ occurs medially or finally in English words. The most frequent
spellings for this sound are the z as in *seizure,* s as in *treasure,* si as in
vision and ge as in *rouge.*

PRACTICE MATERIALS

azure	intrusion	vision	persuasion
casual	measure	regime	incision
confusion	pleasure	glazier	derision
contusion	seizure	delusion	precision
decision	treasure	implosion	exposure
explosion	usual	erosion	illusion
conclusion	version	lesion	occasion
beige	corsage	garage	persiflage
camouflage	entourage	ménage	rouge

Sentences

1. The Eurasian found nothing more pleasurable than an azure sky.
2. The collision was a result of one driver's poor vision and another's
    poor decision.
3. The physician had to make an incision to cut through the
    adhesion.

4.   A mirage is a visual delusion causing mental confusion.

5.   Because he was given to persiflage, his decisions always seemed casual.

6.   The invasion by an infantry division was preceded by an explosion of the camouflaged airfield.

7.   The glazier won prestige by the precision of his work.

8.   Confusion resulted in numerous contusions among members of the treasure-hunting entourage.

9.   The intrusion of the police prevented the seizure of the gold.

10.   Persuasion brought about legislation to prevent soil erosion.

Selections

1.   He weaves, and is clothed with derision;
    Sows, and he shall not reap;
His life is a watch or a vision
    Between a sleep and a sleep.
        —ALGERNON CHARLES SWINBURNE, *Atalanta in Calydon*

2.   Rich the treasure,
Sweet the pleasure,
Sweet is pleasure after pain.
        —JOHN DRYDEN, *Alexander's Feast*

3.   Frazier, an expert glazier, was given to visual illusions and to occasional delusions. Unfortunately, he also acted in the light of these visionary aberrations. Frazier's demise was a result of this inclination. On the final and fatal occasion, Frazier was confronted with an escaped tiger which had hidden in his garage. Because of a visual illusion, Frazier insisted that the tiger was a house cat. In the light of this decision, he began to pat the animal. The beast, not sharing the illusion and having no delusions about himself as a domestic treasure, attacked and devoured Frazier. The job was done with dispatch and precision. Thus poor Frazier was consumed, a victim of a visual illusion and of delusionary behavior. Frazier was no measure for a real tiger.

4.   When a man's busy, why, leisure
Strikes him as wonderful pleasure:
'Faith, and at leisure once is he?
Straightway he wants to be busy.
        —ROBERT BROWNING, *The Glove*

5.   Coleridge, a visionary poet, on frequent occasions welcomed illusions. He wrote of pleasure-domes and of rivers that casually wound their way "through caverns measureless to man."

/tʃ/ (ch) As in *Chest, Orchard,* and *Match*

The sound /tʃ/ (ch) is a blend of /t/ followed immediately by /ʃ/. It may occur initially, medially, or finally. The blend, a combination of a stop and a voiceless fricative sound, is classified phonetically as an *affricate*. This voiceless affricate is regularly represented by the letters *ch* in spelling.

The sound may be troublesome for speakers for whom English is not a first language and in whose native language the /tʃ/ does not occur. For example, it may be troublesome to native French speakers because it does not occur in French. For such persons, the most frequent tendency is to substitute the second element [ʃ] for the blend /tʃ/.

PRACTICE MATERIALS

The exercises that follow should be of help in differentiating between /tʃ/ and /ʃ/.

cheer	sheer	hatch	hash
cheat	sheet	latch	lash
choose	shoes	march	marsh
chairs	shares	match	mash
chin	shin	much	mush
catch	cash	witch	wish
crutch	crush	watching	washing
ditch	dish	catching	cashing
leech	leash	hutch	hush

Sentences

1. The sailors had to chip the charred paint from the ship.
2. Fido, a shaggy dog, liked to chew on an old shoe.
3. The sheik had a scar on his cheek.
4. On chosen occasions it may be pleasant to share a chair.
5. Cheryl bruised her chin and her shin.
6. Charles insisted that one spoonful of mush is much too much.
7. The cheerless marines went on a march through the marsh.
8. Macbeth hoped that the witch would help him realize his cherished wish.
9. After a tennis match, Tom enjoyed a dish of hash.
10. The fishermen had a good fish catch that they sold for spot cash.

ADDITIONAL PRACTICE MATERIALS FOR /tʃ/

cheese	chance	churn	chore
chief	chant	chug	change

chill	chewed	chum	Charles
chimp	choose	chunk	chirp
chain	choke	chowder	choice
chafe	chose	chide	chat
check	chalk	China	chicken
chess	chuck	chive	chin
channel	chop	chime	Chester
champ	char	child	chap

reaching	brooches	marching	bachelor
beeches	broaching	urchin	batches
pitcher	coached	birches	paunches
kitchen	encroaching	lurching	parched
exchange	orchard	searching	righteous
hatchet	launched	bunched	preaching

each	match	staunch	couch
teach	dispatch	porch	slouch
speech	blotch	scorch	pouch
ditch	watch	torch	touch
witch	pooch	lurch	clutch
fetch	encroach	birch	such
wrench	coach	bunch	research
detach	reproach	hunch	squelch

Sentences

1. Charles was taught by those he coached to observe the difference between teaching and preaching.
2. After searching in the orchard, Chester found the chart under the beech tree.
3. Chuck liked cheese and chives.
4. The church supper featured chicken and chowder.
5. The child was chided for chewing his chalk.
6. The farmer had a hunch that the peaches in his orchard needed watching.
7. In a close match, the Chilean champion won the chess contest.
8. Some choose to eat their steak charred.
9. Birches are a climbing challenge for many children.
10. Chilton was partial to chowder.

Selections

1. When I was a child, I spake as a child, I understood as a child, I thought as a child; but when I became a man, I put away childish things.

—I Corinthians 13:11

2. Choice word and measured phrase, above the reach of ordinary men.

—WILLIAM WORDSWORTH, *Resolution and Independence*

3. I'm not a chicken, I have seen
Full many a chill September.

—OLIVER WENDELL HOLMES, *The September Gale*

4. Said Chester to Chase,
You chew as you race,
Though chewing's a chore
A choice chop's not a bore

Said Chase to friend Chester
As a child it was best, sir,
To chomp as I'm able
Or I'd have no choice at table.

—J. E., *The Race Is to the Quick*

/dʒ/ (dzh) As in *Age, Adjust,* and *Budge*

/dʒ/ is the voiced cognate of /tʃ/. This voiced sound blend may occur
either initially, medially, or finally. In *judge* and *George* it occurs both
initially and *finally*. In *agent* and *engine* the affricate /dʒ/ occurs medially.
The most frequent spellings for /dʒ/ are *g, j,* and *dg* as in *wage, jam*
and *ridge*.

Many American and English speakers tend to unvoice /dʒ/ when the
blend occurs in final positions. French, Spanish, and German speakers
may have difficulty with the voiced affricate because the sound does not
occur in their native languages.

Speakers who have difficulty in deciding whether a given word calls
for /dʒ/ or /tʃ/ should be helped by the relative frequency of the *ch*
spelling for the unvoiced sound and the inclusion of the letter *j* or *g* for
the voiced affricate.

PRACTICE MATERIALS

The first set of exercise materials is for the purpose of establishing the
distinction between the two affricates.

gin	chin	jigger	chigger
jar	char	jug	chug
jeer	cheer	bridges	breeches
jest	chest	badge	batch
jump	chump	ridge	rich
jeep	cheap	surge	search
joke	choke	liege	leech

But Hudibras gave him a twitch
As quick as lightning in the breech
Just in the place where honour's lodg'd
As wise philosophers have judg'd;
Because a kick in that part more
Hurts honour than deep wounds before.
                    —SAMUEL BUTLER, *Hudibras, Part II*

ADDITIONAL PRACTICE MATERIALS

jeans	jewel	germ	junior
jib	June	jar	jury
giraffe	judicial	journey	just
gipsy	joke	jowl	jute
jig	jovial	jug	jade
jail	Jonah	jump	jilt
jay	jaunt	giant	general
jet	jaw	jibe	germane
gem	job	joint	genius
jack	jog	join	gentle
besieged	agent	adjust	larger
regent	changed	adjourn	margin
imagine	ranging	surgeon	region
regenerate	major	urgent	disjoint
hedging	stranger	merger	enjoin
wedged	ajar	legion	lounging
ledger	rajah	soldier	gouging
badger	plunged	budget	rejoin
liege	huge	nudge	sponge
siege	sledge	grudge	bilge
ridge	forge	oblige	discharge
bridge	engorge	gouge	dirge
rage	barge	singe	grange
stage	large	fringe	strange
edge	urge	surge	derange
wedge	merge	emerge	average
carriage	bulge	orange	peerage
marriage	fudge	revenge	steerage

Sentences

1. Jones, an imaginative lawyer, begged the judge and urged the jury to be judicious.

2. A legion of soldiers was landed by giant jet planes.

3. Dr. James, a surgeon, adjusted Joe's disarranged jaw.
4. Jonah had a strange journey in a giant whale.
5. Gerald, a gentleman of the peerage, once traveled by steerage.
6. Justice cannot always be determined by jurists.
7. Jargon is a strange form of language usage enjoyed by children.
8. June was in a rage because she was rudely nudged by Julian, who generally was considered near genius.
9. Jim was gentle in making germane judgments.
10. Sturgeon is a major Russian item exported in jars and jugs.
11. The hedge under the bridge was edged with geraniums.
12. Jade is a semiprecious gem.
13. Julie thought it a joke for James to adhere rigidly to his budget.
14. Sponges were found along rock ledges under the huge bridge.
15. Marge and Jane joined a jaunty group for a trip on a barge.

The sentences that follow should be practiced with a view toward maintaining vocalization for the final /dʒ/. Make certain that vocalization continues so that there is no substitution of /tʃ/ for the voiced affricate.

Sentences

1. The judge enjoined George and Marge from marriage.
2. Madge would not budge from her strange position.
3. John stood at the edge of the ridge but did not jump.
4. Jones yielded to his urge and ate a large orange.
5. At two years of age the average child can speak his language.
6. A large suspension bridge was built over the huge gorge.
7. The grange was the scene of a battle of revenge.
8. The stage was set for a strange play.

In the following sentences make certain that you distinguish between the /dʒ/ and the /ʒ/. The first italicized word will include the blend /dʒ/; the second will have the voiced fricative /ʒ/.

Sentences

1. A *general* commands a *division*.
2. Charles *pledged* himself to a life of *pleasure*.
3. A *jury* found Wilson guilty of *usury*.
4. *Agile* Peter climbed a hill to admire the *azure* sky.
5. *Drudgery,* in *measure,* is part of living.
6. Ben *rejected* attempts at *collusion*.
7. *Judge Johnson* carefully announced his *decision*.
8. Charles liked to *imagine* finding rich *treasure*.

Selections for /dʒ/

1. Casey Jones was a railroad engineer and a figure legendary for his courage. Casey had a predecessor, an engineer named Jimmie Jones, for whom the following verses were written:

   On a Sunday mornin' it began to rain,
   'Round the curve sped a passenger train,
   On the pilot lay poor Jimmie Jones,
   He's a good old porter, but he's dead and gone.

   This verse for Casey Jones varies somewhat:

   On a Sunday morning it begins to rain,
   'Round the curve sped a passenger train,
   Under the cab lay poor Casey Jones,
   He's a good engineer, but he's dead and gone—

   Casey, born John Luther Jones, for all the legend built about him, was a real engineer who worked for the Illinois Central Railroad. When he had his fatal collision, Jones headed engine Number 638 out of the Memphis yards. The switchmen "knew by the engine's moans that the man at the throttle was Casey Jones." Casey, cannonballing through the rain, knew that he was about to pile up into a freight train on the siding. He ordered his fireman to jump, and Casey himself died an engineer's death, one hand on the brakes and the other on the whistle cord.
   —JOHN A. and ALAN LOMAX, eds. Adapted from "The Legend of Casey Jones," *American Ballads and Folk Songs*

2. And what's a life?—a weary pilgrimage,
   Whose glory in one day doth fill the stage
   With childhood, manhood, and decrepit age.
   —FRANCES QUARLES, *What Is Life?*

3. George Jenson generalized that judgments are generally made most judiciously when the judger does not jump too hastily to conclusions. This generalization, Jenson acknowledged, was a subjective judgment, but one about which he could feel objective because it germinated slowly after genuine and judicious study.

4. Although psychology had its genesis in philosophy, many psychologists as well as sociologists are urging that psychology emerge as a genuine science. Through technology and research, the general public may be the large gainers from the marriage of technology with scientific psychology.

THE LINGUA–ALVEOLAR NASAL

/n/ As in *No, Any,* and *Again*

/n/ is a voiced, nasal, tongue tip to upper gum ridge sound. In common with the other nasal consonants, /n/ requires nasal reinforcement and is emitted nasally. /n/ is a continuant sound.

To produce the /n/, the tongue should be elevated and the entire tongue tip should be in contact with the upper gum or alveolar ridge. The soft palate is relaxed (see Figure 17–4).

In spelling, /n/ is represented by the letter *n*. In some words a silent letter precedes the *n* as in *know, gnat,* and *pneumatic*.

The sound /n/ presents little difficulty except that it may be slurred or replaced by a nasalized vowel in medial positions, especially in unstressed syllables as in *contact, infer,* and *inform*. The /n/ is likely to be treated with greater articulatory respect in initial and final positions. Because of the high frequency of occurrence of the sound in American-English speech, careful articulation of the /n/ is strongly recommended.

PRACTICE MATERIALS

/m/, we recall, is produced with the lips in gentle contact and, like [n], with the soft palate lowered. For /m/ the tongue usually lies relaxed

Figure 17–4 Articulatory adjustments for /n/. Note relaxed (lowered) soft palate.

at the floor of the mouth. You may increase your awareness of the difference between the /n/ and /m/ by practice with the word pairs that follow.

knit	mitt	knock	mock
knee	me	knob	mob
need	mead	note	mote
nude	mood	neat	meat
nail	mail	night	might
net	met	nice	mice
name	main	Norse	Morse

Initial

knee	natal	node	nut
niece	knell	notary	knuckle
neat	neck	gnome	number
kneel	nebula	gnaw	knife
near	knack	naughty	nice
knit	gnash	nautical	noise
nip	narrow	knob	now
nimble	natural	nocturn	notch
nape	nasty	nurse	pneumonia
name	nook	nerve	knew
nail	noose	nurture	knoll
nasal	nose	nub	knowledge

noise in the night · near the nook
gnawing note · now or never
nice number · narrow notch
nimble gnome · nape of the neck

Make certain that an articulatory contact is made between your tongue tip and upper gum ridge for the medial and final /n/. Failure to make this contact will result in the substitution of a nasalized vowel for the nasal consonant. Prolong the contact with the words of the lists and phrases that follow.

Medial /n/

anneal	grinning	plaintive	fender
menial	spinet	fainting	rented
screening	sinful	feigned	banded
dinner	hinted	fence	handed
sinner	tainted	fend	landing
thinner	saintly	defense	standing
blandish	demanded	intoned	spondee

vanish	cannibal	morning	respond
candy	stoned	dawning	despondent
dandy	telephoned	bonfire	fonder
bundle	bind	joining	pinch
trundle	kindly	connect	bench
cunning	miner	intact	branch
hunted	finer	instead	launch
gunner	ground	confer	munch
burning	hound	consume	lynch
turned	pound	confess	binge
furnace	frowning	definite	strange
burnish	lounge	inflect	lounge
furnish	coined	infest	sponge

Andy Dandy   fender bender
ineffective defense   feigned a faint
plaintive sound   intoned the lines
pounded the ground   turned around

Final

bean	amen	cone	spurns
lean	main	hone	stern
scene	lane	drone	burn
dean	grain	moan	run
mean	can	roan	done
sin	fan	brawn	stun
win	plan	faun	fine
tin	began	scorn	dine
hen	span	barn	down
ten	spoon	darn	frown
again	loon	gone	crown
when	dune	turn	brown

The consonant /n/, like /m/, can sometimes have syllable value without the "help" of a vowel. /n/ is or may be pronounced as a syllabic sound when it occurs in a final unstressed position. This is the case in the words that follow.

button	kitten	mutton	seven
cotton	leaden	open	sudden
deaden	maiden	oven	token
heaven	mitten	rotten	leaven

ADDITIONAL PRACTICE MATERIALS

main avenue   mutton dinner
strange scene   cunning hunter

dine at seven	fine and dandy
eleven turns	morning news
again and again	tin horn
barn dance	change of plan
munch lunch	cotton mittens
ground sirloin	pound of beans

Sentences

1. Diana and Dan were fond of meandering in the garden.
2. Nathaniel wondered why his friend Ron, the owner of a ninety-foot launch, could ever find reason to frown.
3. The missionary endeavored to teach the cannibal the difference between having a friend for dinner and having dinner with a friend.
4. Nona, as a sign of affection for her husband, began baking in her oven at seven in the morning.
5. Frances looked stunning in her ten-pointed crown.
6. Minton confessed that he was inclined to strange hunches.
7. Nine sloops were anchored at Blanding's Landing.
8. Nettleton insisted that today's apparently insane notions may be the next day's brilliant insights.
9. Spencer and his son used a bundle of branches for their bonfire.
10. Every morning Ben intoned nine plaintive tunes.
11. A neologism is a new, or invented, word.
12. The new highway connected nine old towns.
13. The maiden was smitten by the antics of the kitten.
14. Cotton was inserted between the partitions to deaden the sound.
15. Nell knitted mittens for her friend Newton.

Selections

1. The true test of civilization is not the census, nor the size of cities, nor the crops—no, but the kind of man the country turns out.

   —RALPH WALDO EMERSON, *Society and Solitude*
2. John Henry, Cardinal Newman, in his *Idea of a University* considered that "it is almost a definition of a gentleman to say he is one who never inflicts pain."
3. There were gentlemen and there were seamen in the navy of Charles II. But the seamen were not gentlemen, and the gentlemen were not seamen.

   —THOMAS BABINGTON MACAULAY, *History of England*
4. Experience informs us that the first defence of weak minds is to recriminate.

   —SAMUEL TAYLOR COLERIDGE, *Biography Literaria*

5. Know then thyself, presume not God to scan;
   The proper study of mankind is man.
   —ALEXANDER POPE, Essay on Man

6. A nap, my friend, is a brief period of sleep which overtakes superannuated persons when they endeavor to entertain unwelcome visitors or to listen to scientific lectures.
   —GEORGE BERNARD SHAW, Back to Methuselah

7. I have met with women who I really think would like to be married to a Poem and to be given away by a Novel.
   —JOHN KEATS, Letters to Fanny Braun

8. Yet half the beast is the great god Pan,
      To laugh as he sits by the river,
   Making a poet out of a man:
   The true gods sigh for the cost and pain—
   For the reed which grows nevermore again
      As a reed with the reeds of the river.
   —ELIZABETH BARRETT BROWNING, A Musical Instrument

9. When Nan was young and had no sense
   She bought a horn for eighteen pence,
   But the only tune that Nan could learn
   Was "High on a Hill and Around a Turn."
   —Adapted from an old English ballad

10. Sicilian tyrants never invented a greater torment than envy.
    —HORACE, Epistles, Book I

THE LINGUA–ALVEOLAR LATERAL

/l/ As in *Late, Alone,* and *Bell* [1]

/l/ is a lingua-alveolar, voiced, lateral sound. This vowel-like consonant may occur initially, medially, or finally. As may be noted from the spellings of several of the words in the first two sentences of this paragraph, /l/ is represented in spelling by the letter *l* or the letters *ll*.

/l/, like /t/ and /d/, is produced with the tongue tip in contact with the upper gum ridge. Unlike the stops /t/ and /d/, the /l/ has a continuant and vowel-like quality. To achieve this quality, the blade of the tongue (the portion just behind the tongue tip) is lowered to permit vocalized breath to escape over the sides. The soft palate is raised to prevent nasal emission of sound. Vocal-fold vibration regularly accompanies the articulatory action for the /l/.

Figure 17–5   Articulatory adjustments for /l/.

PRACTICE MATERIALS

In producing the sound /l/ make certain that the *tip* and *not the blade* of your tongue is in contact with the gum ridge. Avoid contact between the tongue tip and teeth.

[1] The /l/ is designated by some phoneticians as a liquid sound.

Initial

lean	loose	lock	lace
leap	lute	learn	lake
lip	loom	lug	lower
late	load	lie	lapse
let	lawn	like	lane
lack	lot	low	linger
laugh	lost	lout	loin

In some contexts, before consonants and in final positions, a variant of the /l/ sound may be produced with a quality referred to as "dark." This results from a slight elevation of the back of the tongue. It may be heard in many of the words that follow.

Medial

heels	pooled	alike	allow
hills	pulse	align	pallid
hailed	cold	sleep	palace
held	stalled	ballad	tailor
gals	gold	elope	tilt
bells	enfold	alter	build

Final

deal	zeal	jail	kale
keel	tool	earl	gale
till	full	gull	ball
pale	foal	foil	guile
fell	hall	tile	eel
pal	doll	cowl	pearl
dale	roll	broil	hurl

Initial and Medial

lability	lollipop	literally
lively	listless	lifelong
lonely	lullaby	likely
lowly	Lillian	leaflet
lately	lilting	liability

Initial and Final

legal	lawful	Lionel
labile	lentil	loll

Phrases

likely tale	lordly labor
light laughter	tile floor
lie low	cold lair
learn a lot	clanging bells
linger longer	build a wall
let live	gold and pearls
lovely lullaby	hill and dale
sleep well	mail a letter
dull tool	lower the load
held Hal	dill pickles
languish alone	pallid lady

/l/ Preceded by [p] or [b]

Some persons produce an "infantile" sound in contexts in which the /l/ is immediately preceded by a /p/ or /b/. This effect is frequently a result of failure to make the tongue tip to gum ridge contact for /l/. A /w/-like sound is produced as a carry-over of the lip movement of the /p/ or /b/.

PRACTICE MATERIALS

For the following practice materials, avoid lip movement for the [l]. Make certain that there is a definite tongue tip to gum ridge contact for the sound.

please	plume	bleed	blue
Pliocene	pluck	blame	blood
pleasant	plausible	blink	bloat
play	plot	blend	bluff
plan	plunder	bland	blot
pledge	plight	black	blind

The following word pairs should help to establish a clear distinction between /l/ and /w/.

weep	leap	wade	laid
wack	lack	wit	lit
wag	lag	way	lay
wax	lacks	wear	lair
went	lent	wet	let
wick	lick	wane	lane

ADDITIONAL PRACTICE MATERIALS

lean	loom	glide	claw
lip	law	glaze	clue
lace	lock	glower	club
left	log	glimpse	cloy
lance	learn	glue	clan
glance	lunch	glutton	climb
loot	lion	clean	clutter
lose	glow	class	cluster

Sentences

1. Lola rarely listened to her lover's lilting lyrics.
2. The melodramatic play had an implausible plot.
3. Lila dreamed of a knight with a plume and a lance.
4. Lyman hoped to lead Linda to the altar.
5. William built a pool in the middle of his lawn.
6. The gulls flew over Great Salt Lake.
7. Hal and Lou were childhood pals.
8. The politician was long on verbiage but short of lucid explanations.
9. Light laughter may be eloquent if well timed.
10. Gold was found in the hills of California.
11. Dale planned to pilot his own plane.
12. The ballad related an unlikely tale.
13. Lillian was scolded for falling asleep in her Latin class.
14. A gold locket was lost on the lawn near the lodge.
15. Wilson was slow at leaping—especially to misleading conclusions.

Selections

1. In his *Popular Fallacies*, Charles Lamb held, "A pun is a pistol let off at the ear; not a feather to tickle the intellect."
2. The cruellest lies are often told in silence.
   —ROBERT LOUIS STEVENSON, *Virginibus Puerisque*
3. Old and young, we are all on our last journey.
   —ROBERT LOUIS STEVENSON, *Crabbed Age and Youth*
4. Glory be to God for dappled things—
   For skies as couple-colored as a brindled cow;
   For rose-moles all in stipple upon trout that swim.
   —GERARD MANLEY HOPKINS, *Pied Beauty*
5. I do not love thee, Doctor Fell,
   The reason why I cannot tell,

But this alone I know full well;
I do not love thee, Doctor Fell.

—THOMAS BROWN (Paraphrase of Martial)

6. Political democracy, as it exists and practically works in America, with all its threatening evils, supplies a training school for making first class men. It is life's gymnasium, not of good only, but of all.

—WALT WHITMAN, *Democratic Vistas*

7. Charles Lamb, prolific letter writer and essayist, was versatile and eclectic in his interests. In his *Essays of Elia* he lamented, "The red-letter days, now become, to all intents and purposes, dead-letter days." In a letter to poet-laureate Southey, Lamb acknowledged: "Anything awful makes me laugh. I misbehaved once at a funeral."

   Lamb had a low opinion of people who borrowed books. He held them to be "mutilators of collections, spoilers of the symmetry of shelves, and creators of odd volumes."

   Recalling his childhood days, Lamb wrote sentimentally:
   I have had playmates, I have had companions,
   In my days of childhood, in my joyful school days.
   All, all are gone, the old familiar faces.

8. James Russell Lowell in his *Rousseau and the Sentimentalists* wrote: "Every man feels instinctively that all the beautiful sentiments in the world weigh less than a single lovely action."

   In his verses on *International Copyright*, Lowell wrote lines that became the motto of The American Copyright League:

   In vain we call old notions fudge,
   And bend our conscience to our dealing;
   The Ten Commandments will not budge,
   And stealing will continue stealing.

9. The world is a difficult world, indeed,
   And people are hard to suit,
   And the man who plays on the violin
   Is a bore to the man with the flute.

—WALTER LEARNED, *Consolation*

10. When the lion fawns upon the lamb,
    The lamb will never cease to follow him.

—WILLIAM SHAKESPEARE, *King Henry, VI*

CHAPTER 18

The Vowel-like Sound /r/[1]

There is considerable variation in the production and pronunciation of /r/ according to context and regional practice. In regard to the latter, as we indicated earlier, some persons in the areas of eastern New England, eastern Canada, New York City, and the southern coastal states pronounce an /r/ only when it is immediately followed by a vowel as in *reach, rise, grows, boring,* and *Marion* and omit /r/ in other contexts. Most Americans, however, pronounce an /r/ sound whenever the letter *r* appears in the spelling of a word regardless of whether the immediate next sound is a vowel or a consonant. The general tendency for most Americans is to produce an /r/ in words such as *cart, bargain,* and *turn* as well as for contexts such as *around, through,* and *pour it.*

We consider three varieties of /r/. Two of these call for the production of the *r* as a semivowel or vowel-like consonant. The third is a fricative, more characteristically consonant sound.

[r] As in *Rise, Rose,* and *Around*

There are two ways of producing an [r] when the sound is immediately followed by a vowel in a stressed syllable. The first method is to raise the tongue tip toward the roof of the mouth. The tongue tip may

[1] Allophones of /r/ will be presented in brackets [ ].

be brought close to the gum ridge, but actual contact with the gum ridge should be avoided. The tongue tip may also be flexed slightly toward the back of the mouth. Compare Figure 18–1 demonstrating production of this type of [r] with Figure 14–1 illustrating the /t/, /d/, and /l/ sounds.

The second method of articulating an [r] before a vowel in a stressed syllable more nearly approximates the production of a vowel sound. The tip of the tongue is lowered and the central portion of the tongue is raised toward the roof of the mouth about where the hard palate ends and the soft palate begins. This is illustrated in Figure 18–2. For both of these varieties of [r], the sound is produced with accompanying vocal-fold vibration.

If you have no difficulty with either variety of [r], there is no need for concern or consistency as to manner of production. If you have difficulty with the sound, however, and tend to produce this [r] so that the effect is much like /w/, then you should analyze your efforts for tongue-tip and central [r] and try to produce consistently your best [r] sound. Experience suggests that persons who tend to confuse /w/ and /r/ usually improve by establishing and regularly using a tongue-tip [r]. Persons who tend to confuse /l/ and /r/ may do better by establishing and consistently producing a central position [r], a variety usual for combinations or blends when the preceding sound is /k/ or /g/ as in *crease* or *great*. Whichever variety you produce, do not prolong the sound excessively and do not convert the [r] into a distorted vowel.

Figure 18–1   Articulatory adjustments for retroflex [r].

Figure 18–2   Articulatory adjustments for central [r].

PRACTICE MATERIALS

Initial

read	rail	room	roll
reach	rage	rude	rope
ream	red	rule	raw
rid	rest	rook	wrought
rim	rack	roof	rock
rate	rap	rote	rod
rug	rice	royal	wren
rough	rise	roam	wreck
run	rhyme	roost	roast
rout	ripe	raucous	wrangle
round	real	road	wrestle

Medial (Followed by a Vowel)

dream	street	three	trait
drip	stream	threat	try
drench	stress	thrash	trail
drank	strain	through	trump
dry	strip	thrust	trust
drug	stride	thrush	treasure

draw	straight	treat	truth
drown	street	trip	marry
freeze	straw	tryst	peril
freedom	struggle	tramp	arrange
merit	stirrup	trigger	erode
morose	syrup	tripe	awry

Phrases

green grass	orange drink
grim bride	merry marriage
grinning bridegroom	gross grub
red rose	grubby drag
riffraff and rubble	brandy grog
raw rope	enraged parent
royal road	rhythmic run
raucous wrangle	rain rinse
rough rider	rudely raging
rote memory	really rugged
wrought iron	rim of brine
roam forests	run around
rice bread	wretched aroma
rise proudly	wrecked lorry
ripe berries	arose in peril

For the medial [r] followed by a consonant check your practice and pronunciation with what is current in your community. Do you include or omit this [r]?

Medial (Followed by a Consonant)

pierce	art	smart	mourn
fierce	part	dart	dormitory
beard	warm	swarm	wired
seared	warn	forlorn	tired
chart	farm	orphan	hired
charm	unharmed	scarf	Martha
storm	absorb	dwarf	Marvin
alarm	fork	north	York
harm	pork	forth	inform
ark	hard	ward	torn

Phrases

northern storm	target for darts
partly warm	pierce the pork

tired and forlorn	inform the partner
orphan of the storm	harmful warts
absorbing art	charming in parts
bearded dwarf	chart the course
fierce farmer	alarmed York

For the final [r], is your practice for the omission or inclusion of the final [r] consistent with that for medial [r] followed by a consonant? It is, for most speakers.

Final

dear	are	four	bother
hear	bar	more	mother
fear	car	lore	ignore
near	far	core	father
care	mar	soar	sister
dare	star	ire	tower
fair	boor	dire	shower
mare	moor	sire	paper
their	cure	sour	plumber
lair	tour	flower	summer

Phrases

pare the pear	winter shower
hear sister	ignore brother
near the bar	tour the moor
their paper	lair for the bear
dire cure	summer flower
dear mother	four to a car

For special medial [r] words review the discussion of the /ɜ/ and /ɝ/ vowels (see pages 188–190).

Special Medial Words

birth	burn	turf	curl
mirth	stern	shirt	curtain
terse	girl	girth	certain
first	whirl	nerve	lurch
nurse	heard	serve	churl
purse	hurl	spurn	yearn

Phrases

first thirst	churned and hurled
terse girl	burned earth

earn the purse	heard in church
lurch and whirl	burst with mirth
serve the nurse	uncertain person
first spurned	hurled to the turf

Distinction Between /r/ and /w/

Persons who tend to produce /r/ so that it resembles /w/ should work to establish a clear acoustic difference between these sounds. The /r/ should be produced without lip activity and, preferably, with the tongue-tip raised toward the gum ridge. The /w/ should be produced with lip movement and without front of the tongue activity.

PRACTICE MATERIALS

The following materials should help to establish the distinction. Use a mirror to see what you do, and listen carefully to hear what happens with and without lip movement.

Distinguish between /r/ and /w/:

rack	wack	rill	will
reap	weep	roof	woof
read	weed	run	won
reek	week	ring	wing
red	wed	rue	woo
wren	wen	room	womb
rest	west	row	woe
rag	wag	ride	wide
rage	wage	rise	wise
rate	wait	rare	wear
rain	wane	rile	wile

Difficult [r] Combinations

Words beginning with [p] and [b] followed by [r], as in *prize* and *breeze,* may be troublesome because of the lip activity required for the first sounds. The fault is similar to the one in our previous discussion of the [l] preceded by [p] or [b].

PRACTICE MATERIALS

Avoid lip movement for the [r] as you practice with the materials that follow.

preach	praise	prude	sprawl
preen	press	prove	proud
prince	precious	probe	prow

print	prank	prone	pride
pray	prattle	prawn	price
pretty	prudent	spry	spring

breech	braise	brood	brought
breeze	breast	brew	broad
brick	break	broke	brow
bring	brain	broth	bride
bray	brash	brawn	brine
brass	abrasion	brief	upbringing

Sentences

1. Brooks declared that it is easier to preach than to practice, but more productive to practice than to preach.

2. Kurt Lewin presented psychologists with the provocative assertion that there is nothing as practical as a really good theory.

3. It was frequently difficult to determine whether Brown was erudite or broadly abstruse.

4. Preston's behavior seemed to be crisp and abrupt, but his friends protested that it was probably pretense.

5. Pritchard's manners made it apparent that his abruptness was nurtured by underlying rudeness.

6. Frequently cries of outrage may be avoided when competitors are made aware of the ground rules.

7. Many laboratories for testing hearing have specially treated rooms for audiometric evaluations.

8. Brenda's bright laughter brought warmth to mornings that would otherwise have been gray and dreary.

9. The bridge crumbled under the burden of the overloaded truck.

10. The soprano virtuoso performed brilliantly in a program of original lyrics.

Some persons find the combinations [gr] and [kr], as in *green* and *cream,* somewhat difficult. If you are one of those, we suggest that you establish a central tongue [r], the second of the [r] sounds described, for the [gr] and [kr] combinations (see Figure 18–2).

PRACTICE MATERIALS

The following materials should be of help.

cream	crest	crew	crock
creek	crept	crude	crowd
crib	cram	crow	crown
crayon	crash	croak	crime
cradle	craft	crawl	scribe

green	grew	grind	grist
greet	group	grape	grief
grin	grope	grime	grace
grit	grow	groom	grade
grate	gross	gruel	grant
grain	groan	groove	graze
grenadine	grog	grand	growl
grass	grotto	grunt	grudge
grapple	grub	grasp	gruff

Phrases

green grass	grand grin
grind grain	prone to prattle
grunt and groan	pride in upbringing
greet Grace	crash the craft
ground grain	Cripple Creek
craved a crumb	grew grapes
green grub	greasy crock

Sentences

1. Grace ground the organically grown grain for bread.
2. Great pride may bring greater grief.
3. The gray horse was well groomed.
4. The green car crashed into the gray cart.
5. Grayson, a practical man, came to grips with his problem.
6. More than grain may be grist for a mill.
7. Brian poured the grog out of the cracked crock.
8. The wrestlers grunted and groaned as if they carried a mutual grudge.
9. The proud groom grinned at his prudent bride.
10. Graceful Greta pruned the blue green grape vine.

Another combination that causes some difficulty is [r] preceded by [f]. Practice with the following words.

free	freckle	fruit	from
freeze	fresh	frugal	frock
frigid	friend	fro	front
frail	fragile	froze	fry
freight	frank	frog	fraught

Sentences

1. Freya enjoyed fresh fruit .
2. Fred and his French friend François enjoyed frogs' legs.

3. The fragile frame was shipped by air freight.

4. Freedom will survive only if it is nurtured and shared by those who are free.

5. The frantic general avoided the dangers of exposure at the front.

[r] As in *True, Through,* and *Dry*

A third variety of [r] approximates a fricative sound in manner of production. It is articulated by placing the tip of the tongue close to but not quite touching the gum ridge. When air is forced over the tongue tip, a fricative [r] is produced (see Figure 18–3). When this variety of [r] occurs in the initial position, the sound is vocalized. When it occurs after a voiceless sound, as in *three* and *tree,* the [r] may be completely or partly unvoiced. The [r] is not as frequently produced by American speakers as the other varieties considered earlier.

This variety of [r] is described as a postdental fricative. It is most likely to be produced after tongue-tip consonants such as [t], [d] and [θ] (th).

PRACTICE MATERIALS

Practice with the material that follows:

| treat | tread | true | trot |
| tree | track | troop | trouble |

Figure 18–3   **Tongue position for fricative [r].**

trip	trap	truce	trunk
trigger	trash	trout	tripe
train	tram	trophy	try
trade	transit	tropic	trowel
three	thrash	throttle	throng
thrift	through	thrush	Thrace
thrill	throne	thrall	threaten
thresh	throw	thrive	throat
thread	throb	thrombus	thrust

Sentences

1. The weary troops arranged a morning truce.
2. Trenton enjoyed his train trips.
3. The fast-running stream was noted for its trout.
4. The triple-threat athlete won several trophies.
5. Dumas observed that truth is great because fire cannot burn nor can water drown it.
6. For many persons tripe is a nourishing if not a thrilling food.
7. The throng cheered as the trotters raced around the track.
8. Throttle in hand, the engineer sped the train through the night.
9. A thrush built a nest in the branch of the tree.
10. Trash should not be thrown from moving trams.

Linking [r] and Intrusive [r]

Earlier, we discussed the regional tendencies in producing and pronouncing words in which the letter *r* is final in the spelling. The [r] in contexts such as *far away, near us, for it, for old,* and *bear it* is usually heard as a linking sound between vowels. If you listen closely to the production of the linking [r], you will note that it is produced with less vigor and is of shorter duration than the initial [r] or the medial [r] in stressed positions. Acoustically, the sound is much like the [r] in unstressed syllables, as in the words *berry, marry, carry,* and *ferry.*

Occasionally, an [r] sound is intruded where the spelling of the word does not include the letter *r.* It is most likely to be intruded in combinations such as *law and order, idea of, America is,* and *vanilla ice.* It is apparently easier to maintain speech fluency by inserting an [r] between words when one ends and the next begins with a vowel than to produce two vowels in succession. The intrusive [r] is generally considered substandard and its use is therefore not recommended.

PRACTICE MATERIALS

Practice the following sentences. Read each slowly and avoid the intrusive [r].

Sentences

1. North America and South America are in the Western Hemisphere.
2. I saw Edna order a vanilla ice cream soda.
3. Peterson liked his job as a law officer.
4. Barbara is fond of sliced banana in her breakfast cereal.
5. The idea of an essay should be apparent to an intelligent reader.
6. Grandma almost always enjoyed reading stories to her grand-children.
7. We saw a three-act drama at the Astor Theater.
8. Nora enjoyed resting on the sofa at noon.

/l/ and /r/ Contrast

Some speakers for whom English is a second language seem to have difficulty in making clear distinctions betweeen /l/ and /r/. The phoneme /l/ is not present in some Asiatic languages and the phoneme /r/ is absent in others. The following pairs of contrast words and the phrases should help to establish the distinction between the phonemes.

leap	reap	look	rook
leaf	reef	law	raw
lend	rend	load	road
lid	rid	lock	rock
lip	rip	lot	rot
laid	raid	low	row
lap	rap	lie	rye
lack	rack	lies	rise
lug	rug	light	right

Phrases

lacked a rack	late for the rate
lot of rot	look for the rook
right sheds light	a load on the road
lie in the rye	a lack of a rack
a leaf of the reef	a wrap for the lap

The material following should provide practice for /r/ in various positions.

Sentences

1. Brown showed no gratitude for the state's providing him with free room and board for four years and broke out of the brig.

2. O'Brien took every possible opportunity to proclaim his Irish breeding and his proud name.

3. Random thoughts are the products of free reveries.

4. The mixture contained approximately four parts of nitrogen to one part of oxygen.

5. The timorous groom was afraid to carry his bride across the threshold into their new and very own three-room apartment.

6. Crisp and crackly leaves inform us of summer's end.

7. Contemporary weather forecasters are much more accurate than were their predecessors a generation ago.

8. Rabies are transmitted by animals that have contracted hydrophobia.

9. Vandenburg Air Force Base has rocket-firing apparatus.

10. Thoreau for long periods lived as a recluse.

11. The crafty real estate broker appropriated the poor widow's property when she could not meet the mortgage requirements.

12. Theories should be supported by relevant data and proven by experience.

13. In *Prue and I*, George Curtis remarks: "The pride of ancestry increases in the ratio of distance."

14. Three officers of the law arrested the disturbers of the peace.

15. The right to freedom of expression is part of the American heritage.

Selections

1. How was the Devil dressed?
   O, he was in his Sunday's best;
   His coat was red, and his breeches were blue,
   And there was a hole where his tail
   Came through.

   —ROBERT SOUTHEY, *The Devil's Walk*

2. Dear mother, how pretty
   The moon looks tonight!
   She was never so cunning before:
   Her two little horns
   Are so sharp and so bright,
   I hope she'll not grow any more.

   —ELIZA FOLLER, *The New Moon*

3. Before the beginning of years
   There came to the making of man
   Time with a gift of tears,
   Grief with a glass that ran.

   —ALGERNON CHARLES SWINBURNE, *The Year of the Rose*

4. Richard Rumbold's last words, according to the historian
   Macaulay, were "I never could believe that Providence had
   sent a few men into the world, ready booted and spurred to
   ride, and millions ready saddled and bridled to be ridden."
   —THOMAS BABINGTON MACAULAY, *History of England*

5. Come all you fair and tender ladies,
   Be careful how you court young men,
   They're like a star of summer's morning,
   They'll first appear and then they're gone.

   They'll tell to you some loving story,
   They'll declare to you their love is true;
   Straightway they'll go and court some other,
   And that's the love they have for you.

   I wish I was some little sparrow,
   That I had wings, could fly so high;
   I'd fly away to my false lover,
   And when he's talkin' I'd be by.

   But I am not a little sparrow,
   And neither have I wings to fly!
   I'll sit down here in grief and sorrow
   To weep and pass my troubles by.

   If I'd a-known before I courted,
   I never would have courted none;
   I'd have locked my heart in a box of golden,
   And pinned it up with a silver pin.
   —*Come All You Fair and Tender Ladies,*
   American Ballad

6. To most English-speaking persons who know of Richard III,
   this king who reigned briefly from 1483 to 1485 is reputed to
   be a villain. Shakespeare is probably responsible for Richard's
   characterization. In his melodramatic historical play about
   the allegedly arch-Machiavellian monarch, Shakespeare has
   Richard utter the following:

   I, that am curtail'd of this fair proportion,
   Cheated of feature by dissembling nature,
   Deform'd, unfinish'd, sent before my time
   Into this breathing world, scarce half made up,
   And that so lamely and unfashionable
   That dogs bark at me as I halt by them . . .

   A more kindly and generous characterization of this English
   king is presented by Paul Murray Kendall in his biography
   Richard the Third. Kendall holds that Richard tried to en-

force laws that were proper and just; that his brief reign is remarkable for enlightened legislation that safeguarded the rights of individuals against abuse. Richard tried to be a just and humane sovereign. Unfortunately, he alienated some of the nobility by curtailing their rights to abuse others, and in doing so, lost their military support.

7. I go for all sharing the privileges of the government who assist in bearing its burdens.

—ABRAHAM LINCOLN, Letter to an Editor

8. And down in fathoms many went the
captain and the crew;
Down went the owners—greedy men
whom hope of gain allured:
Oh, dry the starting tear, for they
were heavily insured.

—W. S. GILBERT, *Etiquette*

CHAPTER 19

The Velar and Palatal Sounds and the Laryngeal Fricative

THE VELAR PALATAL SOUNDS /k/ AND /g/

/k/ As in *Key, Because,* and *Luck*

/k/ is a voiceless, velar, stop sound. It is produced by raising the back of the tongue to the elevated soft palate so that a firm contact is made between these articulators (see Figure 19–1). In contexts in which the [k] is followed immediately by a vowel, air is impounded at the place of contact and suddenly and completely released when the contact is broken. The sound is then said to be aspirated.

The sound of /k/ has several representations in spelling. The most frequent include *k* as in *key, c* as in *cat, ch* as in *chasm, qu* as in *quick,* and one element of the sound blend of *x* as in *fix* and *six.*

The /k/ sound must be produced with energetic action of the articulators. Persons with normal control of their articulatory organs should find the /k/ sound an easy one to make, regardless of contextual position.[1]

---

[1] Persons with weak palates and those with cleft palates, often even after repair, tend to nasalize the /k/.

Figure 19–1   Articulatory adjustments for /k/ and /g/.

PRACTICE MATERIALS

cape	kale	come	coat
keep	could	came	cough
key	coach	cap	cod
queen	cope	calf	chord
chemical	chorus	character	quash
ken	caught	cool	curb
kit	call	coop	curt
bacon	became	token	minks
beacon	because	blacken	Manx
weaken	recourse	reckon	thanks
bicker	require	booked	attacking
wicked	requite	looking	blocked
checker	enquire	turkey	boxed
ache	stake	rake	fork
beak	stork	lake	forsook
meek	talk	take	mistook
sick	Turk	back	stock
tick	spike	rack	dike
fake	amuck	hook	like

cake	cock	chaotic	kapok
kick	quack	kirk	coke
kink	cook	quirk	comic
quick	cosmic	konk	cork

Phrases

keep calm	honking turkey
keen kitten	basket of biscuits
camp cook	murky liquid
calm cow	mocked uncle
queer cat	quick kick
quaint chorus	cock crow
quiz kid	sick calf
call Kate	cook book
sick knocks	thank Carl

Blends: [kl] and [kr]

clean	class	clot	climb
cleat	clue	clergy	cloud
click	close	clerk	clown
clip	claw	club	cloister
cleanse	clod	clump	Klondike
clash	clog	clutch	clause

cream	credit	crew	crust
crease	credulous	crude	crouch
creed	crest	crow	crowd
creek	crane	crawl	crown
crib	crag	crop	crime
crisp	crack	cross	cry

critical crowd	clean cloth
crusty crown	clumsy clown
crude crystal	clatter and clash
crossed crop	cloistered clergy
Kris Kringle	clever clue
crackle and crunch	clippety clop
creep and crawl	cluttered closet

Sentences

1. Kent kept his collie in a kennel.
2. Kate was calmed by the ticktock of the clock.
3. The drunkard was lachrymose because his crock contained no alcohol.

4.   Quartz is a common mineral that occurs in crystals and is a frequent component of many rocks.

5.   Carl found it calming to bask in the sun.

6.   The schooner carried a cargo of crackers, cookies, and kindred cakes for tykes.

7.   Connie liked percolated coffee and scones for breakfast.

8.   The choir sang quaint songs in the Scottish kirk.

9.   Kitson was the captain of the cruiser that carried a cargo of Turkish goods to the Congo.

10.   The blackhearted crook was caught in the crowd.

Selections

1.   Themistocles, being asked whether he would rather be Achilles or Homer, said, "Which would you rather be—a conqueror in the Olympic Games, or the crier that proclaims who are conquerors?"

    —PLUTARCH, *Themistocles*

2.   Nor all that heralds rake from coffin'd clay,
    Nor florid prose, nor honied lies of rhyme,
    Can blazon evil deeds, or consecrate a crime.

    —GEORGE GORDON, LORD BYRON, *Childe Harold's Pilgrimage*

3.   By the pricking of my thumbs,
    Something wicked this way comes.

    Open, locks,
    Whoever knocks!

    —WILLIAM SHAKESPEARE, *Macbeth*

4.   Harlequin without his mask is known to present a very sober countenance, and was himself, the story goes, the melancholy patient whom the Doctor advised to go and see Harlequin.

    —WILLIAM MAKEPEACE THACKERAY, *The English Humorists*

5.   I know the Kings of England, and I quote the fights historical,
    From Marathon to Waterloo, in order categorical.

    —W. S. GILBERT, *The Pirates of Penzance*

6.   Nice customs curtsy to great kings.

    —WILLIAM SHAKESPEARE, *Henry V*

/g/ As in *Go, Forget, Aghast, Egg,* and *Rogue*

/g/, the voiced cognate of /k/, is a velar, stop sound. It is produced like the /k/, except that a less vigorous contact is required for the /g/.

/g/ is usually represented by the letter *g* in spelling; less frequently it is represented by *gh*. The sound is also part of the consonant blend represented by the letter *x* in words such as *examine* and *exact*. The sound may occur initially, medially, or finally.

PRACTICE MATERIALS

gear	gale	gherkin	gird
geese	gape	goat	girth
gift	gaff	gall	gull
give	gap	gauze	goiter
guilt	ghoul	got	gown
guest	ghetto	guard	guide
meager	vaguely	embargo	beguile
begin	began	regard	disguise
digging	aghast	engulf	misguided
signal	again	laggard	tiger
forget	lagoon	beggar	bogus
regale	regulate	haggard	dugout
league	Hague	rogue	bug
fatigue	plague	morgue	snug
intrigue	vague	hog	shrug
dig	hag	log	dug
rig	snag	iceberg	flog
egg	fugue	erg	vogue

[g] *Blends:* [gl] *and* [gr]

glean	glad	glob	mingle
glib	gland	glum	single
glisten	glass	glut	haggle
glitter	gloom	glide	tingle
glaze	gloat	glower	tangle
glen	globe	eagle	struggle
greed	grand	grope	grind
green	grass	groan	gripe
grid	grew	grow	egress
grip	groom	gross	angry
grade	group	growl	engrave
grain	groove	ground	ingrate

Phrases

grape grower	great engraving
grin grimly	growl and gripe
glitter and glisten	grind grain
angry ingrate	glum glower
glad groom	global struggle
green grass	engrossed group
grim greeting	graph diagram

Contrasting /k/ and /g/

There are two elements of contrast for the /k/ and /g/. The first is the readily apparent element of voice that is present for the /g/ and absent for the /k/. The second is the less obvious aspect of vigor of articulation that characterizes the /k/ more than the /g/.

PRACTICE MATERIALS

cam	gam	pick	pig
cat	gat	rack	rag
kill	gill	hack	hag
cap	gap	peck	peg
coat	goal	tack	tag
coast	ghost	sack	sag
cool	ghoul	buck	bug
cull	gull	tuck	tug
cut	gut	chuck	chug

Sentences

1. Chuck liked to hear the chug-chug of locomotives.
2. The half-empty sack was inclined to sag.
3. An old ghost haunted the Gold Coast.
4. Goatskin makes a crude but warm coat.
5. A tack was used to hang the rag tag on the rack.
6. A gull can cull food along a seacoast.
7. When Buck was tucked into his sleeping bag, he felt as snug as the proverbial bug in the rug.

ADDITIONAL PRACTICE MATERIALS

Sentences

1. Margo, a good cook, gained a reputation for her baked goose.
2. Morgan, a gourmand, was glad to be married to Margo.
3. An embargo was placed on the cargo of sugar.
4. Greta was aghast when, in an unguarded moment, she forgot to stop for a traffic signal.
5. Gordon's luggage had an engraved name tag.
6. Despite his name, Goodfellow was a rogue whose beguiling smile ensnared the misguided.
7. Despite his hunger, the beggar would eat nothing but frogs' legs.
8. The fog lingered on and grounded the planes in Gander.
9. Peg, like most girls, was eager for a bargain.
10. The gargoyle appeared to have a vague grin.

Selections

1. "All that glitters (glisters) is not gold" is a line that most English speaking boys and girls regard as Shakespeare's. Yet, a bit of digging reveals that the "gold glitter or glisten or glister" theme is repeated in English as well as non-English literature. Cervantes wrote "All is not gold that glisters." From Chaucer, in his *Canterbury Tales*, we gather that "But al thyng which that shineth as the gold, Nis not gold. . . ." Spenser in his *Faerie Queen* also regretfully recalls that "Gold all is not that doth golden seem."

   —Based on notes from JOHN BARTLETT, *Familiar Quotations*,
   13th ed., p. 77

2.   The Gods
   Grow angry with your patience, 'tis their care,
   And must be yours, that guilty men escape not:
   As crimes do grow, justice should rouse itself.

   —BEN JONSON, *Catiline*

3. The gift, to be true, must be the flowing of the giver unto me, correspondent to my flowing unto him.

   —RALPH WALDO EMERSON, *Of Gifts*

4. Great is the art of beginning, but greater the art is of ending.

   —HENRY WADSWORTH LONGFELLOW, *Elegiac Verse*

5. Oh, Brignall banks are wild and fair,
       And Greta woods are green,
   And you may gather garlands there
       Would grace a summer's queen.

   —SIR WALTER SCOTT, *The Bridal of Triermain*

THE VELAR NASAL /ŋ/

/ŋ/ (ng) As in *Wing* and *Singer*

/ŋ/ is a velar nasal sound. It is produced, as indicated in Figure 19–2, by raising the back of the tongue so that it is in contact with the lowered soft palate while the vocal folds are in vibration. /ŋ/ is a continuant sound that is reinforced and emitted nasally. In American-English speech the /ŋ/ occurs either medially or finally, but never initially.

The /ŋ/ is represented by the letter *n* or the letters *ng*. The sound occurs usually in words in which the letter *n* is followed by either a *k* or a *g* in the same syllable. /ŋ/ is generally not heard in standard speech in combinations where the *n* and the *g* that follows are in different syllables, as in *ingrate*, *congratulate*, and *engross*.

Except for possible confusion between the /n/ and the /ŋ/, there is seldom any difficulty in the actual articulation of the velar nasal sound. There is some tendency, however, for some speakers to add either a /g/ or a /k/ following the /ŋ/ so that all words containing the velar nasal sound are pronounced either [ŋg] or [ŋk]. This tendency may frequently be traced to the influence of a foreign dialect. A second influence may be attributed to the speaker's failure to remember the pronunciation of the particular word relative to the omission or inclusion of the /g/ or /k/. A third influence is a direct result of the manner of articulating the /ŋ/. If the soft palate is raised before the contact between the tongue and

Figure 19–2 Articulatory adjustments for /ŋ/. Note relaxed (lowered) soft palate.

palate is broken, a /k/ or /g/ sound is produced. To avoid adding either of these sounds when only the velar nasal is required, the speaker must watch his articulatory timing. Specifically, he must make certain that the back of his tongue is moved away from his soft palate before he raises his soft palate to block off the entrance to the nasal passage.

To know how to produce an /ŋ/ is not enough. We must also know whether the velar nasal is to be followed by a velar stop /k/ or /g/, or by some other sound. There is, of course, only one reliable way to learn the pronunciation of a word with velar nasal consonants. The reliable way is to study each word individually, using an up-to-date large dictionary as a pronunciation guide. A second approach of general help is to learn the so-called rules for the use of the velar consonants in English speech.

1.   When a word ends with the letters *ng* or *ngue*, the pronunciation calls for the /ŋ/. Examples include *wing, rang, tongue,* and *meringue.*

2.   Usually, when a suffix is added to a root word that is pronounced with the /ŋ/, the pronunciation calls for the /ŋ/. Examples include *swings, rings, singer, longing,* and *stinging.* The exceptions to this general tendency include the comparative and superlative forms of the adjectives *long, young,* and *strong*—e.g., *longer, longest; younger, youngest; stronger, strongest.* These are pronounced with [ŋg].

3.   Where the letters *ng* are medial in a root word, as in *finger, tingle, hunger, angle, extinguish,* and *single,* standard pronunciation calls for the use of [ŋg]. An exception is the pronunciation of *gingham* as [giŋəm].

4.   In combinations in which the letter *n* is immediately followed by *k, c,* or *x* in the same syllable, the [ŋk] is used. Examples include *link, hank, distinct, anxious,* and *larynx.*

Note that not all words that include the letters *ng* in their spelling call for /ŋ/ in their pronunciation. For example, words such as *range, singe,* and *longevity* are pronounced with the combination [ndʒ] rather than with either the /ŋ/ or the [ŋg].

Apply these rules to the list of words that follow.

[ŋ]	[ŋg]	[ŋk]
wing	single	link
rang	spangle	anchor
young	younger	wink
harangue	elongate	sank
evening	anger	bunk
ringing	bungalow	trinket
longing	longest	sphynx
swings	tingle	length [1]
strong	stronger	strength [1]
singing	longest	larynx

---

[1] The words *strength* and *length* are acceptably pronounced with or without a [k] before the final sound.

Practice to Establish a Final /ŋ/

Speakers who tend to add a /g/ or /k/ to words that should properly end with the /ŋ/ should be helped by contrasting the stops /g/ and /k/ with the nasal continuant /ŋ/. The stop sounds call for an abrupt stopping of the breath and frequently by the emission of a puff of air. The /ŋ/ should be produced so that the nasally emitted sound dies away gradually. At the outset, exaggerate the length of the sound so that it is prolonged to two or three times what it might be in normal conversational speech.

PRACTICE MATERIALS

In your practice with the material that follows, establish your timing and control. Prolong the /ŋ/ and continue, without stopping, to complete the phrase.

hang on	reaching it
young once	during an evening
giving up	baking apples
swing it	exciting acts
going on	being able
teaching all	altering everything
cooking oil	telling a truth
trying on	tongue exercise
staying away	exciting events
running on	cutting up
standing up	cruising around
doing all	taking a break

Sentences

1. Browning occasionally failed to see the distinction between teaching and preaching.
2. Cumming's affable wife was fond of baking animal cookies.
3. Blanding explained his behavior by reminding all who observed his fooling that one can be young only once.
4. Maturing is often more painful than growing up.
5. During his childhood young Albert learned that telling a truth may solve as many problems as running away.
6. Boring always longed for things that past hoping did not give him.
7. A throng assembled at the Long Island train station.
8. Long ago is a fond and indefinite time for recalling old dreams.
9. Young Arthur, the future king, did not know the source of his strength for pulling out the sword from the stone.
10. Baring unfortunately learned that to be smiling and beguiling is not easy for one lacking in aptitude for acting.

11. Exciting events are not always as edifying as they might be for those who have a yearning for action.

12. Bingham was ever insisting on knowing all that was going on about him.

Final /ŋ/

Practice the following final /ŋ/ words and then incorporate them into phrases in which each word is followed by one beginning with a vowel—e.g., *among us.*

among	morning	asking	rang
bang	owning	boring	swing
bring	pacing	chanting	tong
doing	putting	fading	yearning
everything	sing	gasping	zooming
fling	sting	handing	daring
hang	throng	humming	darling
king	wrong	landing	fang
long	young	moaning	amazing
mining	looming	nothing	being

Medial /ŋ/

The words that follow conform to rule 2; a suffix is added to a word ending in the letters *ng.*

bearings	longs	borings	clanged
beings	mornings	fangs	endings
bringing	paintings	gaspings	firings
darlings	pronged	hanged	gangster
evenings	questionings	longing	drawings
flinging	songbird	throngs	strongly
hangmen	tracings	twangy	tongueless
kingly	wrongly	youngster	winged

Sentences for Medial and Final /ŋ/

1. "Shooting the stars" enables navigators to get their bearings at sea.

2. Young Loring banged on the door because there was no response to his shouting and ringing.

3. Many Swiss youngsters belong to bellringer societies.

4. The mockingbird can imitate the songs of other songbirds, but has no identifying song of his own.

5. The king's minstrel sang a song portending exciting events.

6. Billings, in a complaining voice, asked his wife to stop rearranging the furniture without first warning him of what she was intending.

7. As a youngster, Sterling learned that telling the truth was more than a tongue exercise.

8. Topping specialized in raising longhorn cattle.

9. Corning enjoyed teaching all he knew to his young students.

10. Mrs. Channing thought her children to be darlings whenever they listened to her singing.

[ŋg]

When the letters *ng* occur within the root of a word, the pronunciation includes [ŋg] as in *angle*.

PRACTICE MATERIALS

anger	fungus	languish	tangle
Anglican	ganglion	languor	tingle
anguish	gangly	mangle	wrangle
Bangor	hunger	mingle	distinguish
bungle	ingot	Mongol	Rangoon
Congo	jangle	mongrel	sanguine
dangle	jingle	penguin	singular
dungaree	jungle	shingle	triangle
England	kangaroo	single	linger
finger	language	spangle	elongate

The following suffix words are pronounced [ŋg] and are exceptions to the *ng* rule.

longer	stronger	younger	prolongate
longest	strongest	youngest	diphthongal

[ŋk]

The following words are pronounced with [ŋ] followed by [k]:

anchor	dank	Manx	slink
ankle	drink	mink	spunk
banker	dunk	monk	tank
bankrupt	flunk	monkey	trunk
blank	frank	pink	twinkle
brink	hanker	plank	uncle
Bronx	ink	rank	lynx
bunker	jinx	rink	larynx
clink	junk	sank	pharynx
crank	lanky	sink	conquer

PRACTICE MATERIALS FOR [ŋg] AND [ŋk]

English language	Uncle Frank
singular Anglican	trunk of junk
anger and anguish	ranking banker
elongated wrangle	dunk in tank
hungry mongrel	blink and wink
single spangle	Bronx conqueror
Congo jungle	pink mink
linger longer	larynx and pharynx
dangling dungarees	lanky Yank
mangled ganglion	slinking lynx

Although rules have been suggested for determining the pronunciation of words spelled with *ng* and *nk*, there are many words that do not conform to the rules and have current pronunciations that are a result of assimilative influences or of the influences of analogy. Thus, a word such as *hangar* is now likely to be pronounced no differently from the word *hanger* (influence of analogy); *income* is likely to be pronounced with a velar adjustment /ŋ/ rather than the alveolar /n/ (influence of assimilation). In the final analysis, if the speaker is not certain of the pronunciation of an *ng* or *nk* word, he must check the pronunciations either by listening to other respected speakers or by consulting an "authoritative" current dictionary. It is suggested that the student check the following words if he is at all uncertain about the pronunciations.

banquet	fishmonger	rancor
Binghamton	gingham	tranquil
congress	inquest	wrangler

Sentences for [ŋg] *and* [ŋk]

1. Although Waring was the youngest sibling, he was more daring than Hank, the oldest and strongest brother.
2. Franklin irritated his larynx and pharynx by making throaty, angry noises.
3. Despite their natural carrying cases it seems unlikely that kangaroos will replace donkeys for bearing our burdens.
4. Fielding wanted to become a distinguished linguist.
5. If vowels are elongated, they tend to become diphthongized.
6. The New York Yankees have their ball park in The Bronx.
7. Uncle Sam's nephews speak with some distinctive differences from their English cousins.
8. Corning's wife could not decide whether lynx or mink was her favorite fur.

9. Waring enjoyed eating languidly at banquets.
10. The bronchi divide into bronchioles in the lungs.

ADDITIONAL PRACTICE MATERIALS FOR [ŋ]

1. The youngsters enjoyed singing "The Daring Young Man on the Flying Trapeze."
2. Movements of the tongue modify breath from the lungs in creating articulate speech.
3. Wilding learned that listening for longer periods than speaking was earning him a reputation for conversing.
4. After long years of waiting and striving, Browning's yearnings were rewarded.
5. Planes flying at ever-increasing speeds are making small ponds of our oceans.
6. The angry waves pounded the New England shore.
7. The word *wrangler* has distinctly different meanings in England and in the United States.
8. Loring was no stranger to angling in swift-running waters.
9. Although she was dressed in gingham, the maid from Birmingham caught the eye of the young king.
10. The bellringer needed all his strength to keep the bells clanging.
11. Many banquets are spoiled by long harangues.
12. Bob enjoyed filling his lungs with the fresh morning air before undertaking the day's chores.

Selections

1. The cataract strong
    Then plunges along,
    Striking and raging
    As if a war waging
    Its caverns and rocks among;
    Rising and leaping,
    Sinking and creeping,
    Swelling and sweeping,
    Showering and springing,
    Flying and flinging.
    Writhing and ringing,
    Eddying and whisking,
    Spouting and frisking,
    Turning and twisting,
    Around and around
    With endless rebound;
    Smiting and fighting,

A sight to delight in,
Confounding, astounding,
Dizzying and deafening the ear with its sound;
                    —ROBERT SOUTHEY, *The Cataract of Lodore*
2.   O strong winged soul with prophetic
         Lips hot with the bloodbeats of song,
     With tremor of heartstrings magnetic,
         With thoughts as thunders in throng.
                         —ALGERNON CHARLES SWINBURNE,
                              To Walt Whitman in America
3.   On deck beneath the awning,
     I dozing lay and yawning;
     It was the grey of dawning,
         Ere yet the sun arose;
     And above the funnel's roaring,
     And the fitful wind's deploring,
     I heard the cabin snoring
         With universal noise.
                    —WILLIAM MAKEPEACE THACKERAY, *The White Squall*
4.   Deep in that darkness peering, long
         I stood there, wondering, fearing,
     Doubting, dreaming dreams no mortal
         Ever dared to dream before.
                         —EDGAR ALLAN POE, *The Raven*
5.   As I went out one morning to breathe the morning air
     I heard a dear old mother saying, "O my daughter fair,
     You better go wash them dishes and hush that flattering
         tongue,
     You know you want to marry and that you are too young."
                    —Adapted from *Lolly-Too-Dum*, American Ballad
6.   A little learning is a dangerous thing;
     Drink deep, or taste not the Pierian spring.
                         —ALEXANDER POPE, *An Essay on Criticism*
7.   A very merry, dancing, drinking,
     Laughing, quaffing, and unthinking time.
                         —JOHN DRYDEN, *Alexander's Feast*
8.   Day in the melting purple dying,
     Blossoms all around me sighing,
     Fragrance from the lilies straying,
     Zephyr with my ringlets playing,
     Ye but waken my distress:
     I am sick of loneliness.
                         —MARIA G. BROOKS, *Song of Egla*
9.   From grief, that is but passion;
     From mirth, that is but feigning;

From tears, that bring no healing;
From wild and weak complaining;
Thine old strength revealing;
    Save, oh, save.

                                —MATTHEW ARNOLD, *Stagirius*

10.   A man—I let the truth out—
Who's had almost every tooth out,
Cannot sing as once he sung,
When he was young as you are young,
When he was young and lutes were strung,
And love-lamps in the casement hung.

  —WILLIAM MAKEPEACE THACKERAY, *Mrs. Katherine's Lantern*

THE PALATAL GLIDE

/j/ (y) As in *Year, Unite, Humid,* and *Argue*

/j/ is a vocalized, palatal glide sound. In acoustic effect, because it is an unobstructed and continuant sound, it is vowel-like in quality. /j/ glides or moves from the initial position of the vowel /i/ to a final position determined by the sound that immediately follows it. The initial articulatory position calls for the tongue to be arched toward the front of the hard palate and for the lips to be parted and retracted as though for a smile. The soft palate is raised and the vocal folds are in vibration throughout the production of the sound.

When the /j/ sound is represented by a single letter in spelling it is by the letter *y.* In medial positions /j/ may be represented in spelling by the letters *io, ie,* and *ia.* Frequently, however, in both initial and medial positions, there is no spelling representation for the /j/. The sound often becomes part of vowel blends as in *unite* and *unify.*

PRACTICE MATERIALS

yield	yak	yoho	Europe
yeast	Yankee	yacht	young
yearly	you	yonder	yowl
yes	youth	yard	yucca
yen	York	yule	yesterday
yet	yawn	yearn	usual [2]
yellow	yawl	use [2]	usurp [2]
yank	yoke	unit [2]	eulogy [2]

[hj] Check your pronunciation for the following words:

huge	humid	humility	Hugo
human	humidor	humor	humus

Medial [j]

Daniel	companion	accuse	volume
genial	familiar	refuse	collier
genius	billiard	confuse	review
senior	canyon	amuse	stallion
vineyard	million	onion	beauty
lanyard	abuse	bunion	opinion

[2] In these words the /j/ may be considered part of the diphthong /ju/. Other words of this type include *unite, union, Ural,* and *euphony.*

[j] Preceded by an Initial Consonant

The inclusion of a /j/ after an initial consonant varies according to context and regional practice. It is optional in words such as *Tuesday, tune,* and *new* and in many other words that begin with the sounds /t/, /d/, or /n/. If there are no special influences to direct your choice, regional usage should be followed.

PRACTICE MATERIALS

/j/ is regularly included after the first consonant in the word list that immediately follows. It is optional for the second word list.

pure	fuel	cute	music
pupil	few	future	futile
beauty	feud	huge	fusion
muse	humane	view	mule
mute	humorous	cupid	puny
Tuesday	due	knew	nuisance
new	tube	nuclear	nude
tune	numerous	duke	Nubian
tuba	duty	tumult	newt
constitute	reduce	institute	gratuity
destitute	annuity	plume	restitute
induce	platitude	acumen	enduring

Sentences

1. The feud began on Tuesday over a puny gratuity.
2. Daniel's attitude indicated that he had no use for platitudes.
3. The dude took a dim view of his own future.
4. A united Europe has not yet been achieved.
5. The youth yearned for baked yams.
6. Cupid sometimes seems amused by those he seems to confuse.
7. The pack mule carried a huge load through the canyon.
8. William, a Yale student, enjoyed yesteryear's music.
9. Newton, a Yankee, enjoyed sailing his yawl.
10. Eugene, a Yorkshire millionaire, was fond of playing billiards.

Selections

1. Bad language or abuse,
   I never, never use,
   Whatever the emergency;

Though "Bother it" I may
Occasionally say,
I never use a big, big D—

—w. s. GILBERT, *H. M. S. Pinafore*

2.   Millions of spiritual creatures walk the earth . . .

—JOHN MILTON, *Paradise Lost*

THE LARYNGEAL FRICATIVE

/h/ As in *He* and *Who*

The sound /h/ lacks fixed or distinctive articulatory position. The sound that immediately follows the /h/ determines the position assumed by the lips and tongue for this usually voiceless fricative.

/h/ consists of a stream of breath made discernible by the degree of contraction and vocal-fold vibration in the larynx.

Few persons are likely to have difficulty in the actual production of the /h/. The most likely basis for difficulty is that of determining whether, despite or because of the spelling of the word, an /h/ is to be produced or omitted in the pronunciation. It may be of help to know that in American-English speech the /h/ is appropriately included chiefly before vowels in stressed syllables as *he, hot,* and *hate.* Some speakers also include the sound in words that begin with a *wh* as in *which* and *whale.* /h/ is usually not pronounced in medial, unstressed syllables.

PRACTICE MATERIALS

Initial

he	help	hoof	harm
heed	ham	home	harsh
hit	hatch	hope	her
hilt	hoot	haughty	hurl
haste	who	halt	hurt
hate	whom	hog	heard
head	hood	hot	heart
hull	height	house	humid [3]
hump	hide	howl	huge [3]
hungry	hoyden	human [3]	humor [3]

Medial (Note Its Position in Stressed Syllables Before Vowels)

unheeded	behind [4]	unharmed	coherent [4]
reheat [4]	behold [4]	unheard	dehydrate

[3] In words such as *human, humid, huge,* and *humor,* some speakers blend or merge the initial [h] with the immediately following [j] so that a "new" and distinctive voiceless palatal fricative sound is produced that may be represented by the symbol [ç]. If the blending is not complete, the result may be represented by the symbols [hj] as in [hjudʒ] for *huge.* We shall accept C. K. Thomas' suggestion that "Since . . . no change in meaning is effected by the shift from [hj] to [ç], most students will prefer not to bother with the extra symbol /ç/." See his *An Introduction to the Phonetics of American English,* 2nd ed. (New York: The Ronald Press Company, 1958), p. 138.

[4] In words in which the [h] occurs between vowels, as in *reheat, behave,* and *behead,* the [h] may be produced with voice. The IPA symbol is [ɦ].

inhabit	inhuman	rehearse [4]	inherit
inhale	overhaul	uphold	upheaval
behave [4]	rehash [4]	rehouse [4]	prehistoric [4]
behead [4]	cohort [4]	somehow	enhance

Sentences

1. Henry paid little heed to heights.
2. Harry was so hungry that he enjoyed Hazel's reheated ham.
3. Horton enjoyed living in high mountain areas that had low humidity.
4. The hen was heard to cackle after she hatched her egg.
5. Hate can be inherited if it is not inhibited.
6. The hog who had a habit of entering the new house was cured as a ham.
7. Hiram's heart and his sense of humor were humane.
8. The hyena held up his head and howled to the heavens.
9. Harriet's uninhibited behavior won her a reputation as a hoyden.
10. The rehearsals for *Hamlet* were held in a house held to be haunted.
11. Schopenhauer held that hatred comes from the heart and contempt from the head.
12. Hildred happily announced that Hope found a home in her new house.

Voice Improvement Check List

Breathing

1. Is amount of air intake adequate for speech effort? _____
2. Is breathing controlled and synchronized with speech effort? _____
3. Is flow of breath sustained for proper phrasing? _____
4. Is breath expelled between phrases? _____
5. Is muscular action basically abdominal-thoracic? _____ Clavicular? _____
6. Is there any evidence of excessive tension in the larynx or throat? _____

Pitch

1. Is range narrow ? _____ Wide? _____ Patterned (monotonous)? _____
2. Are changes consonant with meanings? _____ Feelings? _____
3. Is habitual pitch the same or close to your optimum pitch? _____
4. Does the major part of the speech effort occur within the optimal range? _____
5. Are individual inflectional changes appropriate to the meanings and feelings you intended to communicate? _____
6. Is the overall intonation suggestive of a foreign pattern? _____

Loudness

1. Is the loudness of your voice adequate for the size of your group of listeners? _____

2. Do any of your listeners have to strain to hear you? _____

3. May your voice be characterized as full? _____ Thin or weak? _____ Overloud? _____ Sufficiently varied and appropriate for meanings? _____

4. Are changes independent of variations in pitch? _____

Quality

1. Is your voice hypernasal? _____ Denasal? _____ Breathy? _____ Husky? _____ Guttural? _____ Hard or metallic? _____

2. Is your voice reinforced only within part of the pitch range? _____

3. Is your voice varied according to the nature of the content? _____

Pronunciation and Articulation Check List

Pronunciation

1. In your overall pronunciation are you aware of any individual variations of vowels or diphthongs from those current in your community? _____

2. Are these variations ones you wish to maintain or modify? _____
3. Do you follow regional practices with regard to /r/? _____
4. Are you aware of any dialectical pronunciations? _____ Do you wish to maintain them? _____

Articulation

1. What sounds or sound blends need improvement:
   a. Consonants? _____
   b. Vowels? _____
   c. Diphthongs? _____
2. Is there any tendency to slur or to overassimilate? _____
3. Are medial nasal consonants given full value? _____
4. Do you tend to give excessive nasal "coloring" to vowels or diphthongs that are in close proximity to nasal consonants? _____
5. Do you tend to unvoice final sounds such as /z/, /ʒ/, and /dʒ/?

Glossary of Terms

Abdominal breathing—Breathing characterized by controlled action of the abdominal muscles.

Affricate—The blend of a stop and fricative sound; the phonemes /tʃ/ (ch) and /dʒ/ (dzh) are affricates.

Allophones—Members or varieties of sounds within a phoneme. The sounds that are classified as belonging to a phoneme in a given linguistic system (see *Phoneme*).

Articulation—The modification of the breath stream by the organs of the mouth (the lips, tongue, and palate) and the laryngeal mechanism to produce identifiable speech sounds (phonemes).

Arytenoid cartilage—A pyramidal-shaped cartilage situated in the posterior portion of the larynx. There are two arytenoid cartilages in the larynx to which the vocal bands are attached. The movements of the arytenoids influence the position and state of tension of the vocal bands.

Aspirate quality—Breathiness that accompanies vocalization or articulation.

Assimilation—The phonetic changes that take place in connected speech when one speech sound is modified as the result of a neighboring sound or sounds.

Back vowels—The vowel sounds produced as a result of the action (position) of the back of the tongue.

Bilabial consonants—The consonants that are produced as a result of lip-closing action that stops or diverts the flow of breath.

Breathiness—An excess of breath that may accompany vocalization.

Buccal cavity—The oral or mouth cavity.

Cavity reinforcement—The building up of selected vocal tones resulting from the size and shape of the individual cavity. Cavity resonance.

Central Nervous System (CNS)—The parts of the nervous mechanism that include the cerebrum, cerebellum, medulla, and spinal cord. The CNS is responsible for the coordination, control, and regulation of responses to stimuli and so for the establishment of patterns of behavior.

Central vowels—Vowel sounds produced as a result of the action (position) of the central or mid-portion of the tongue.

Cerebellum—The "little brain," a part of the Central Nervous System, situated posteriorly and under the cerebrum. The cerebellum is importantly involved in the coordination of motor activity needed for speech production.

Cerebral cortex—The gray outer covering of the cerebrum. The cortex contains billions of nerve cells. Some portions of the cortex have special functions that are significant for the understanding and production of speech.

Clavicular breathing—Breathing characterized by action of the upper part of the rib cage and the shoulders.

Consonants—Speech sounds produced as a result of either a partial or complete (temporary) obstruction or modification of the breath stream by the organs of articulation.

Continuant consonant—A consonant sound having duration and produced with the articulator in a fixed position, such as /s/ and /l/, in contrast to stop consonants that are short and result from the interruption of the breath, such as /p/ and /g/.

Cricoid cartilage—The ring-shaped cartilage in the lower and back portion of the larynx. The posterior part of the cricoid serves as a base for the arytenoid cartilages.

Diacritical symbols (marks)—A system of alphabet letters and a number of markings used by dictionaries to indicate phonetic values.

Diaphragm—The double, dome-shaped muscle of respiration situated between the chest and abdominal cavities.

Diction—The production of speech sounds for a given linguistic code; also the selection of words within a linguistic system.

Diphthongs—Vocalic glides of two vowels uttered in a single breath impulse within one syllable. The phonetic symbols of the diphthong represent the approximate initial and final sounds of the glide.

Front vowels—The vowels produced as a result of the action (position) of the front, or blade, of the tongue.

Fundamental pitch—The pitch resulting from the frequency of vibration of the body as a whole; the lowest tone in a complex tone.

Glide sounds—Sounds produced as a result of the continuous movement of the articulators. The initial position of the articulators in the production of a glide is stable. The final position of the articulators is determined by the sound that immediately follows.

Glottal—Referring to sounds produced as a result of laryngeal tension and action, as by a sudden stoppage and release of breath by the vocal bands.

Glottis—The opening between the vocal bands.

Habitual pitch—The pitch level at which an individual most frequently initiates vocalization.

Inflection—Pitch changes that occur without interruption of phonation during the production of a syllable or word. Inflectional changes may be *downward, upward,* or *circumflex* (downward and upward or upward and downward).

International Phonetic Alphabet (IPA)—A system of representing the distinctive sounds (phonemes) of a linguistic code through special visual symbols.

Labiodental sounds—Consonants produced as a result of activity of the lip (lower) and teeth (upper); lip-teeth sounds.

Laryngeal fricative—The sound /h/ made discernible as a result of laryngeal tension and vocal-fold activity.

Laryngopharynx—The portion of the pharynx nearest to the larynx.

Larynx—The uppermost part of the trachea; the structure that includes the vocal bands; the voice box.

Lateral consonant—The sound /l/ produced as a result of the emission of vocalized breath at both sides of the tongue with the tongue tip at the gum ridge.

Lingua-alveolar consonants—The consonants produced as a result of contact between the tongue tip and the gum (alveolar) ridge.

Midvowels—See Central vowels.

Nasality—The quality of voice resulting from reinforcement in the nasal cavities.

Nasal cavities—The cavities in the head directly above the roof of the mouth.

Nasal consonants—The speech sounds produced with nasal reinforcement. In American English these are /m/, /n/, and /ŋ/.

Nasopharynx—The portion of the pharynx nearest the entrance to the nasal cavities; the uppermost portion of the pharynx.

Optimum pitch—The pitch level at which one can usually achieve the best vocal quality and the necessary loudness with the least expenditure of energy; the pitch level at which one can initiate voice with greatest ease and effectiveness.

Oral cavity—The cavity of the mouth; the buccal cavity.

Oral resonance—The reinforcement of vocal tones by the oral cavity.

Oropharynx—That portion of the pharynx nearest the oral cavity; the middle portion of the pharynx.

Palatal sounds—The sounds produced as a result of activity of the mid-tongue or back of the tongue and the palate.

Pharynx—The cavity between the esophagus and the entrance to the nasal cavity; the throat.

Phoneme—The basic unit or sound family within a linguistic system; a group or family of closely related sounds that share distinctive acoustic characteristics; the distinctive phonetic or sound "elements" of a word. Phonemic differences permit us to distinguish between spoken words.

Phonetic alphabet—See International Phonetic Alphabet.

Pitch—The attribute of sound resulting from the frequency of vibration of the vibrating body; the attribute of auditory sensation in terms of which sounds may be ordered on a scale from high to low; our subjective reaction to frequency changes or differences.

Plosive sounds—The consonants produced by a stoppage and release of the breath stream.

Postdental sounds—The consonants produced as a result of contact between an anterior portion of the tongue and the area of the mouth behind the dental ridge.

Pronunciation—The articulation of meaningful units of speech; the combining of phonemes in meaningful contextual utterance; the utterance of appropriate sounds and the placement of stress in the production of contextual speech.

Resonance—The strengthening or building up of sound either through cavity reinforcement or through sympathetic vibration of a body in close proximity to the source of sound (the vibrating body); the vibratory response of a body or a cavity to a sound frequency imposed on it.

Resonators—Structures so shaped that they can reinforce selected pitch ranges of sound; the principal human resonators are the cavities of the mouth, throat, nose, and larynx.

Stop sounds—Those produced by a complete closing of the breath channel.

Thoracic cavity—The chest or thorax.

Thyroid cartilage—The large, shieldlike fused cartilage of the larynx.

Trachea—The cartilaginous tubelike structure between the pharynx and the bronchi; the windpipe.

Velar sounds—Sounds produced as a result of articulatory activity between the soft palate and the back of the tongue.

Vocal attributes—The characteristics by which we distinguish vocal efforts—pitch, loudness, duration, and quality.

Vocal bands—Two small, tough bands, or folds, of connective, or ligamentous, tissue situated in the larynx. The vocal bands are continuous with folds of muscle tissue and are connected to cartilages in the larynx. Pulsations of the vocal bands give rise to *voice.*

Vocal cords—See Vocal bands.

Vocal folds—See Vocal bands.

Voice box—See Larynx.

Vowels—Sounds produced as a result of articulatory action without obstruction or interference of breath; unobstructed sounds produced by changes in the size and shape of the oral cavity and by differences in the elevation of portions of the tongue.

Windpipe—See Trachea.

L·149